Messages, Meanings, and Culture

The Rhetoric and Society Series
Bruce G. Gronbeck, Series Editor,
University of Iowa

MODERN RHETORICAL CRITICISM
Roderick P. Hart

MESSAGES, MEANINGS, AND CULTURE:
Approaches to Communication Criticism
Malcolm O. Sillars

MESSAGES, MEANINGS, AND CULTURE:

APPROACHES TO COMMUNICATION CRITICISM

MALCOLM O. SILLARS

University of Utah

HarperCollins*Publishers*

To Charlane

Sponsoring Editor: Melissa A. Rosati
Project Editor: Shuli Traub
Cover Coordinator: Dorothy Bungert
Cover Design: Nadia Furlan-Lorbek
Production: Willie Lane/Sunaina Sehwani
Compositor: David E. Seham Associates, Inc.
Printer/Binder: R. R. Donnelley & Sons Company
Cover Printer: New England Book Components, Inc.

Messages, Meanings, and Culture: Approaches to Communication Criticism

Library of Congress Cataloging-in-Publication Data

Sillars, Malcolm O. (Malcolm Osgood), 1928–
    Messages, meanings, and culture : approaches to communication
criticism / Malcolm O. Sillars.
        p.   cm.—(The Rhetoric and society series)
    Includes bibliographical references and index.
    ISBN 0–673–46030–4
    1. Rhetorical criticism.   I. Title.   II. Series.
PN4096.S55   1991
808—dc20   90–46352
                                                        CIP

90 91 92 93 9 8 7 6 5 4 3 2 1

Contents

Preface

The historical, rhetorical, and poetic orientations of communication criticism before 1960 were rich. They constituted a set of traditions traceable to ancient times that must be admired for their clarity, intellectual integrity, and usefulness, and are still with us, albeit in somewhat modified forms. NeoAristotelian rhetorical criticism and literary New Criticism, for example, are still powerful forces. But the very fact that we must acknowledge modifications of the traditional approaches indicates that something has happened to alter the study of communication criticism significantly.

Indeed, the past three decades have seen a dramatic alteration of American communication critical theory. Thirty years ago, American critics worked in virtual isolation; today there is a growing awareness of the rich traditions of European critical scholarship. Each field oriented to the examination of texts—English, history, speech, and journalism, for example—had its own set of critical procedures and its own canon of acceptable texts. Today, scholars in each field are more open to insights from other fields and exhibit greater willingness to examine outside texts; this is most evident in the fields of English, history, political science, and even economics. Today there is great diversity in critical theories and practices, which enables the critic to choose from many alternatives.

Diversity has been a mixed blessing, however. While it has introduced into communication criticism a more varied system of perspectives, it has, at times, encouraged disciplinary chauvinism, as each school of critics defends what it consider its own turf. This has meant that critics with essentially the same objectives do not always interact with, or even read, one another because disciplinary walls have grown up. These walls should be scaled, though, because an examination of communication criticism reveals significant similarities across disciplinary boundaries.

Messages, Meanings, and Culture is intended to cross these boundaries by showing how eight approaches (see below for a description) characterize contemporary communication criticism. Crossing boundaries does not mean sameness. The branch of communication criticism from which I come, rhetorical criticism within the public address tradition, is still heavily oriented to understanding persuasion. Literary criticism is still heavily influenced by poetic theory, and journalistic criticism is still greatly influenced by the desire to judge accuracy and fairness. In short, fields have their individual orientations, but many critics are willing to use approaches from other fields or to incorporate elements of other approaches into their more traditional ones.

The first chapter of this book defines communication criticism and the contexts in which it is found. A second chapter deals with the methods of analyzing messages. The eight chapters that follow are summaries of the available approaches to communication criticism. The first three are the traditional approaches that follow what Catherine Belsey calls "common sense": accurate interpretation (Chapter 3), which lives by the standards of traditional journalistic and historical scholarship; formal criticism (Chapter 4), which pursues the aesthetic worth of messages with the tools of traditional literary criticism; and neoclassical criticism (Chapter 5), which works from the rhetorical tradition typical of critics oriented to persuasion. These three are identified as common sense approaches because, for the most part, they view a world that can be known and criticism as a reasonable means of assessing messages within or against that world.

The second half of the book deals with critical approaches that fall under the broad definition of deconstruction. That is, critics who use them are not looking for ways that messages (texts) reflect the natural condition. Rather, they see the world as constructed by symbolism and thus attempt to "deconstruct" messages to discover how culture is defined within them.

Chapter 6 is the swing chapter. It identifies semiotics as "the turn to deconstruction." Semiotics develops from assumptions that humans are symbol-using animals and that the meanings people find are not natural but produced by their own signifying practices. Semiotic critics attempt to understand meaning and culture by examining how words, images, and actions are used.

The next four chapters derive from semiotic assumptions, but each presents a distinctive way of deconstructing a message. Critics using value analysis (Chapter 7) look for cultural meaning in the value systems embedded in messages and their contexts, while narrative analysis critics (Chapter 8) look for cultural meaning in the stories people tell one another. Psychoanalytic critics (Chapter 9) apply psychoanalytic theory to explain the human, personal, and social condition found in such messages. Ideological critics (Chapter 10) seek to see how symbols are used to empower certain social classes and to place others in subservient position.

I have deliberately chosen the word "approaches" rather than methods because each critical approach combines several more specific methods of criticism. For instance, the critical theory of Kenneth Burke is included as a phase of the narrative approach, and feminist criticism is featured in both the psychoanalytic and ideological approaches. Some readers may feel that critical theories that I have treated as subcategories (feminism and Burke are prime examples) deserve recognition as separate approaches. However, rather than emphasize separation, I have chosen to look for unifying characteristics. What unites these theories are common assumptions about messages, meanings, and culture.

Each of the eight chapters begins with an examination of the assumptions underlying the approach being discussed, followed by a description of the particular procedures typical of the approach. Finally, some of the potential weaknesses of the approach are identified.

My focus on eight distinct approaches with differing assumptions should not exhaust the potential for the individual critic. Even though approaches differ in their assumptions, critics frequently appropriate insights from one approach to clarify another. Neoclassical, persuasion-oriented, critics frequently use the categories of formal criticism or incorporate values in their analysis. Similarly, narrative critics are strongly influenced by values and the categories of formal criticism. Ideological critics often link their criticism to value, narrative, and psychoanalytic insights. Thus, although each of the chapters defines and shows the workings of a particular approach, critics should also recognize the potential for borrowing from one approach to strengthen another.

This book is, therefore, based on the conviction that pluralism is desirable in contemporary communication criticism. Pluralism means both combining useful insights from different approaches and choosing different approaches in different situations.

I have chosen not to provide exercises or study texts for instructors to assign their students. Most teachers of communication criticism have individual preferences for texts they wish studied. A course may focus on specialized forms of communication, such as television, public speeches, literary, and filmic literature, or popular culture icons. Or it may focus on the individual student's interests.

I have taught courses in communication criticism to students who were primarily interested in studying speeches. I have also taught courses to a mix of students oriented to print journalism, radio and television, speeches, and *belles lettres*. Different courses in communication criticism will be geared to different combinations of these groups. Therefore, because criticism is more open than any one of these approaches implies and, because different courses will have different emphases, this book is intended for combination with specific texts of the instructor's and the student's choosing.

I wish to credit those friends who have helped me along the way and without whom this book could not have happened. My indebtedness goes back a long time to A. Craig Baird and Orville Hitchcock, who put me in touch with the strong traditions of American public address and rhetorical criticism at the University of Iowa.

In more recent times I mention only those from whom I directly sought assistance with the content of the book. There are many more colleagues and students who asked questions or made arguments that forced my reexamination of particular ideas. In this regard I am indebted to the open interactive atmosphere of the Department of Communication at the University of Utah.

Those I must specifically acknowledge here are Charles Mudd of California State University, Northridge; Michael Salvador of Washington State University; Robert Tiemens of the University of New Mexico; David Werling of California State University, Chico; Dennis Alexander, James Anderson, Douglas Birkhead, DeAnn Evans, Milton Hollstein, David Jabusch, Christine Oravec, and Richard Rieke of the University of Utah; and Michael McGee and Dana Cloud of the University of Iowa. The University of Utah and its College of Humanities provided me with leaves of absence to work on the book. Norman Council, Dean of the College, was particularly helpful in providing time, travel, and advice.

Three individuals had a major influence on the book. Mary Strine, my colleague at the University of Utah, showed me how to make sense of the many critical voices on the contemporary scene. She directed me toward the organization and title of the book and critiqued some particularly difficult chapters. Bruce Gronbeck, of the University of Iowa, helped me to obtain the A. Craig Baird Visiting Professorship during the 1989–1990 academic year. This experience permitted me to learn from the Iowa faculty and graduate students and gave me almost constant access to his advice in the final stages of preparation. He read every chapter and made line-by-line improvements in style and substance that saved me from serious errors. Charlane Sillars was my editorial associate throughout the project. She caught innumerable errors and stopped me when my academic jargon and tortured syntax interfered with my communication.

A final thanks to Richard Welna for launching the Advanced/Scholarly Books Division of (then) Scott, Foresman and Company, with books on rhetorical criticism, and to Melissa Rosati and Anne Smith of HarperCollins for continuing the Rhetoric and Society Series and encouraging this book. My further thanks to Shuli Traub of HarperCollins for the careful and competent editorial work of bringing this book to print.

Malcolm O. Sillars

CHAPTER ONE

Defining Communication Criticism

The president addresses the Congress on the state of the union. Spike Lee, as Morris Blackman, tells viewers about "my main man" Michael Jordan. Stephen King's novel *The Drawing of the Three* is on the best-seller list. Alex Trebek gives the clue, "the only president who also served as ambassador to the United Nations," and Gail Painer responds, "Who is George Bush?" The billboard just west of Davenport, Iowa, reads "There Is No California: Stay In Iowa." Dave and Kathy Jensen discuss whether to send Lynn to public or Lutheran school. *Driving Miss Daisy* is admired as a play and as a movie. Thousands of people march in South Africa calling for an end to apartheid. These situations, representative of millions of others, illustrate how vital communication is to our personal and social well-being.

Communication is expressive of what a person is and essential to the establishment of social relationships among people. Since communication is an essential process in defining what we are, it is inevitably subject to criticism. We want to know "What did she mean when she said . . . ?" "Why did he say that?" "What does that statement mean to our society?" "Isn't that statement inaccurate?" "Does the speech damage or enlighten people?"

With communication so vital to our personal and social lives, it is important that our criticism results from thorough and rigorous thinking. We have many questions we want answered about communication. But how good are our answers? The quality of those responses is the subject of this book. Subsequent chapters will look at various approaches to communication criticism. You will learn that there is no one way to critique messages, that competent critics who follow different approaches have disagreements over assumptions and procedures. But all critics have a common objective of carefully examining communication situations and making useful observations about them. This chapter will define communication criticism and preview later chapters.

WHAT IS COMMUNICATION CRITICISM?

A communication critic seeks to make an argument that interprets or evaluates the messages to which the individual or society is exposed. This definition of criticism begins with the critic because critics differ in assumptions and procedures. Criticism is not an activity that can be described once for all times and persons. It has two purposes, to interpret and to evaluate, which may appear together or separately. It is centered on messages that relate to the individual or society. The product, the communication criticism, is an argument. Let us look at that definition more closely.

Critics Can Approach Criticism in a Variety of Ways

There are many different kinds of criticism. One critic may be interested in whether a message is accurate, another will ask if it is persuasive, still another will ask what it reveals about the nature of society. Some critics follow one approach. Others choose different approaches in different situations. Still others use a combination of approaches. Each of the last eight chapters of this book will discuss a different approach to criticism.

Michael C. McGee (1984b), in his analysis of how a fundamentalist Christian, the Reverend Jerry Falwell, could read Judges 19–21 as an argument against contemporary secular humanism, exemplifies this last type of critic. Briefly, Judges 19–21 is the story of a man who, with a servant and his runaway wife whom he has reclaimed from her father, visits Gibeah, a town of the tribe of Benjamin. When a mob wants his host to send out the man and his servant so that they "may know him," the man sends out his wife, who is gang raped and dies. The man takes her body home and cuts it into 12 pieces, sending one each to the 12 tribes of Israel who, as a result, declare war on the perpetrators—the Benjamites. Thousands of people are killed and only 600 Benjamite men survive. To preserve this twelfth tribe the Israelites attack the town of Jabesh-Gilead, which did not participate in the war with the Benjamites, and kill everyone except a group of virgins who can be wives to the Benjamites. Because there were not enough virgins in Jabesh-Gilead, the Israelites held a celebration of their victory and looked "the other way when a Benjamite man kidnapped a woman."

Following Falwell's lead in arguing from the message in Judges which ends, "In those days, there was no king in Israel," McGee examines the passage first for an essentially objective interpretation of what the biblical story says. But Jerry Falwell, McGee knows, has used this story "as a parallel to the fundamentalist Christian's view of America's present political and social condition" (1984b, 6). How does one translate an ancient story of sodomy, rape, murder, and genocide into a critique of contemporary conditions?

McGee looks past the pattern of events and the characters. Instead, he looks "for the voices of the narrator, assuming that he or she is construct-ing a tale built upon a contradiction between patterned and ruptured hu-man experience" (1984b, 14). He describes three different narrators: The first sees injustice, indifference, and inhumanity; the second sees laws bro-ken, social order lacking, and irrational collective action; and the third nar-rator sees a synthesis of the first two, a world without an authoritative voice. In this analysis, McGee is not interested in raw accuracy or even in the story's order. He is interested in the ideas implied by the changing storytellers.

Finally, McGee looks at the story as a persuasive document addressed to fundamentalist Christians about contemporary conditions. Falwell sees "secular humanism" as responsible for today's evils: women running away from home, homosexuality, drugs, pornography, criminals released on technicalities. All these are in the experience of the audience and they re-late to the events in the story. According to McGee, they prove to Fallwell's audience that "there is no king in Israel" (1987b).

Here then is a critical analysis, albeit richer than my summary, that involves, at least, three of the approaches discussed in this book: accurate interpretation, narrative analysis, and neoclassical analysis. Even in evalu-ating a single text, a variety of approaches is available to the communica-tion critic.

Critics Seek to Interpret or Evaluate

The communication critic has two functions: to interpret and to evalu-ate. Some critics claim that they are interested only in understanding how a particular communication event took place, to understand its form, or to understand how an audience found meaning in it. Such a critic might be interested in how Franklin D. Roosevelt worked with his speech writers to produce his Fourth Inaugural Address (Ryan 1975). Or such a critic might be interested in defining the forms of political cartoons (Medhurst and De Sousa 1981). Such a critic also might be interested in how audiences re-sponded to Archie Bunker's racism and sexism in *All in the Family* (Vidmar and Rokeach 1974).

Most interpretive critics seek to explain the meaning of messages to individuals and society. They examine the text of a message and the con-text in which it is found to discover its significant meanings. Such was the case when Robert L. Ivie (1986) explained how President Truman, during the Korean War, enveloped "the metaphor of Soviet savagery in his sim-ple, straightforward language [to enhance] its capacity for constructing re-ality" and, thus, played an important "role in institutionalizing the cold war" (105).

Not all criticism is interpretive alone; much of it goes beyond interpre-tation to evaluation. Some critics would say that there is no criticism with-

out evaluation (Campbell 1979, 10). Such critics find that criticism "is always partially persuasive" and that every decision made involves a
judgment (Campbell 1972b, 1). "Why," they would ask, "did you choose
to study FDR's ghostwriters if you did not have some judgment to make
about FDR or about ghostwriters?" Or, "Why concern yourself with racism
or sexism in Archie Bunker if that subject is unimportant to you?" Some
critics argue that even those who claim to use an "objective" interpretive
approach do so, perhaps, without realizing that objectivity is itself an evaluative judgment (Eagleton 1983, 195). "Even the purely technical objective
of understanding how a discourse works," says Edwin Black (1965a), "carries the assumption that it *does* work, and that assumption is an assessment" (2). In addition, many critics and historians have argued that, in the
words of Stephen Lucas (1981), "Perception itself is evaluative: . . . facts
are never neutral and have no objective existence apart from the frame of
reference of the person who apprehends them" (12).

Even if arguments against a purely interpretive criticism are correct,
important differences in the final product will still depend on the critic's
purpose. Some critics will seek openly to argue a claim about the worth of
a piece of communication. Other critics will not openly evaluate a work.
This difference in intention can make for significant differences in the writing strategies embodied in the criticism.

Critics Center on the Message

The message communicated may be verbal, visual, written, oral, picto-
rial, or some combination of these, but it will always occupy the center
of any critical analysis. In this sense, a study of a television production
organization unrelated to the program produced may make a critical judgment about a particular management style's effect on the organization's
fiscal stability. But this study will not be communication criticism. A study
of how a particular writer was educated, unless it provides insight into the
poems or novels the writer produced, is not communication criticism either. These are management studies, biographies, or histories, but not
communication criticism.

Nonetheless, problems do arise when ruling out certain items as communication criticism. In general, all criticism is historical. One can imagine
a criticism of a potential act. For instance, you tell a friend, "Don't use
masculine pronouns to refer to all people or you will be thought sexist by
some." But, in practice, most criticism takes place after the communication
act has occurred. Even the commentary of Rowland Evans and Robert No-
vak on CNN television following George Bush's acceptance address at the
1988 Republican National Convention in New Orleans is historical because
the event it criticizes had already taken place. And one historian, Dominick

LaCapra, has argued that intellectual history, at least, is textually based and is, therefore, a critical activity. However, there is considerable disagreement over the position that all history is criticism (Lucas 1981).

Likewise, one could argue that all management studies are critical because they seek to understand and evaluate a management process. So a study of how ABC's national news is produced could be communication criticism. However, the methods discussed in this book—those used by most communication critics—are based on an assumption that messages are central to communication criticism. The more a criticism relates to a message the more viable it is.

In this book, criticism will be applied to public messages. Of course, private messages, for example, those taking place privately between two people, could be the subject of critical study. But this book will discuss only public messages.

Traditionally, criticism of public communication has focused on single texts: a novel, a speech, a magazine, a film, or, at times, the works of a particular person. Of late, there has been increased interest in the communication practices of large groups, campaigns, or movements. This extension has broadened the definition of message to include a combination of mediated and nonmediated print and oral and visual codes as parts of a single overarching message.

Many public communication situations are made more complex by media. Talking about "the author" of a television show becomes difficult because of all the persons who have roles in its development. Examining a single production becomes difficult when we consider how characters change over time on shows such as *M*A*S*H*, *Cheers*, or *Family Ties*. James A. Anderson and Timothy Meyer (1988) have argued that the text in television is particularly difficult to define because each program is enmeshed in the daily viewing program, a matrix of other competing programs, and the commercials which, while not defined as part of a particular show, are part of the viewer's experience (32–35). While there is still a place for examining a single message, for a variety of reasons, critics increasingly are moved to examine wider ranges of messages in broader contexts.

Critics Relate Messages to Someone Other Than the Author

Saying "the messages to which the individual or society is exposed" signals that diverse concepts of receivers are possible. Receivers could include almost anyone from the solitary newspaper reader to the millions who viewed the 1988 Olympic games through worldwide media coverage. But there must be a receiver if a message is to be communicated.

Critics Make an Argument

When a critic claims that a particular interpretation is best, that critic must argue the point. To just say "I like it" is poor criticism. One reason there is so much dissatisfaction with contemporary television criticism is that it lives up to the Latin dictum *de gustibus non disputandum est*—there is no argument about taste. Saying that a critic likes or does not like something is not criticism. The critic must have some reason for the critical claim and this reason must be made clear.

Wayne Brockriede (1974) explains what it means to make a critical argument:

> By "argument" I mean the process whereby a person reasons his way from one idea to the choice of another idea. This concept of argument implies five generic characteristics: (1) an inferential leap from existing beliefs to the adoption of a new belief or the reinforcement of an old one; (2) a perceived rationale to justify that leap; (3) a choice among two or more competing claims; (4) a regulation of uncertainty in relation to the selected claim—since someone has made an inferential leap, certainty can be neither zero nor total; and (5) a willingness to risk a confrontation of that claim with one's peers. . . .
>
> These characteristics are not usefully applied one-by-one as a kind of checklist to help one see if something "adds up" to an argument. Rather, they are interrelated dimensions of the concept of argument and may, each of them, serve usefully as an entry point or as a mode of emphasis in criticizing a rhetorical experience (166).

Thus, there is created a kind of continuum along which a piece of criticism may be placed between argument and nonargument. Some criticisms will be more argumentative than others. The degree of argumentativeness is determined by the extent to which the criticism meets all of these characteristics as a whole. For instance, one could make an inferential leap, take a controversial position, risk a confrontation, and regulate uncertainty by claiming that Stephen Spielberg is an unimaginative movie producer. But, without a rationale to justify the claim, there would be no real argument. It would be a nonargument: an assertion of taste, not a complete criticism. Similarly, to claim that Shakespeare was a great playwright is not very argumentative because there really are no competing claims. That is what is meant when Brockriede says the characteristics need to be taken holistically. They work together to define argument.

It stands to reason, therefore, that the stronger the argumentative quality of each of these characteristics the richer the critical argument will be. More important, a criticism must have at least a basis in each characteristic to be viable.

APPROACHES TO CRITICISM

The eight approaches to criticism discussed in this book generally define the practice of critics. These approaches (Chapters 3–10) are organized by the assumptions critics follow and the procedures they use. To understand each approach and its assumptions and procedures, it is useful to understand three characteristics in the critical situation. These are the variables of the approach, its reliance on common sense or deconstruction, and its objectives.

Variables of Criticism

By examining a multitude of communication criticisms, Lawrence W. Rosenfield (1968) developed "the anatomy of critical discourse." That anatomy identifies four gross variables: "the source(s) or creator(s) of the message, the message itself, the context or environment in which the message is received (including both the receivers and the social 'landscape' which spawns the message), and the critic. . . ." "For the sake of convenience," says Rosenfield, "let us label the variables 'S' (source), 'M' (message), 'E' (environment), and 'C' (critic)" (58).

You will see immediately why this is called "the anatomy of critical discourse" and why these are "gross variables." They represent large, rather unsophisticated parts of the body of criticism as head, torso, arms, and legs represent the human body in gross terms. Nonetheless, the way they are combined into *foci* of criticism helps to explain differences among approaches.

Source.   With modern media, the source of a message can be complex and difficult to determine. We know Abraham Lincoln had help with the Gettysburg Address, but we are inclined to see him as a source. We are less likely to see Michael Dukakis or George Bush as the source of a speech because we are more aware of modern ghostwriting practices. But even this pales before the task of defining what the source is for a single 30-second commercial on TV: the writers, the producer, the director, etc.

Message.   Earlier, we observed that message is central to all criticism. Message in the tradition of literary and rhetorical studies is made of verbal language. The message is what the writer wrote, what the speaker said. But modern communication has made the concept of message more complex. What about the visual elements? Or music? The music video is a perfect example of how the increasing complexity of communication and its means of transmission have been followed by more complex forms of more traditional messages such as advertisements or even situation comedies or speeches.

Can anyone doubt that radio and television as entertainment and information media have changed political speaking? Before radio and television, speeches served as an important source of entertainment. The "oratorical style" and talks of two or three hours' duration attest to that. With radio there came a change. Franklin Roosevelt pioneered the "fireside chat" where plain style and the conversational delivery of one sitting in the living room became his hallmark. Every president since has used this technique on radio and television. Traditional oratory is still heard and appreciated but not as often, and it is surely not as lengthy as in the nineteenth century. And now, political speeches may be interspersed with clips of film or graphics, thus adding to the complexity of the message.

Environment.   Twenty years ago, when Rosenfield described these variables, most critics would have said "audience" or "reader," not "environment." And some criticism is still oriented to seeing how a specific reader or audience might respond to a novel, speech, film, or newspaper article. Much of the research in communication is audience centered. What is the readership of the *New York Times?* Who reads *Cosmopolitan,* or *Family Circle?* How do the readers relate them to their lives? What is the magazine's effect on them? Janice A. Radway's (1984) *Reading the Romance* is a study of how women who read romance novels relate them to their traditionally middle-class lives.

But the advent of mass media and a more complex society have caused critics to become interested in something socially broader than reader or audience: environment. This means that instead of looking at how specific audiences respond to messages, the critic frequently takes an expanded look at how messages reflect or shape the environment.

Robert Sklar's (1982) "The Fonz, Laverne, Shirley, and the Great American Class Struggle" exemplifies this focus. Sklar notes how Fonzie, "a working class figure in a blatantly middle class setting," (78) serves as a symbol of morality compared to the upper-class persons who wander into *Happy Days*'s middle-class world. And in this brief selection of the spin-off from *Happy Days, Laverne and Shirley*, which depicts two young women living in a basement apartment and working at a Milwaukee brewery putting caps on bottles, class conflict in society is clearly reflected. The episode concerns Laverne and Shirley, the two working-class women who go looking for clothes in a "stylish boutique":

The shop's officious manager bustles over to discourage the declasse intruders. "We cater to the well-to-do, the creme de la creme," he says haughtily. Laverne and Shirley don't shrink at his aggressiveness, they give it back with both barrels. "Us two girls wouldn't buy dresses here if we were rich and naked," says Laverne. And Shirley makes it personal:

"We two girls wouldn't want to buy something from a man who smells like the inside of my grandma's purse" (1982, 80).

With this and other examples from television sitcoms, Sklar builds an argument that, exaggerated as they are, these programs reflect the thinking of the class culture they portray and thus describe not only their audience, but also the environment in which the audience lives.

Environment, therefore, is a broader variable. It includes within it the reader of a short story, the listeners to President Bush's Inaugural Address, or the viewers who watch *L. A. Law*. It also includes the general culture of a society that shapes, and is shaped by, messages. Some situations fit the traditional term *audience*. But, like the broader culture, they (the audience) are part of the communication environment.

Critic.   Some critics see themselves as objective observers by way of an approach termed *accurate interpretation* (Chapter 3). A critic using that approach assumes that facts exist independent of observers and looks to see if the message (e.g., a television news story) reports the facts accurately. Because such critics are outside observers who pass judgment based on facts outside themselves, they are outside the criticism, or so they claim.

There are others, of course, who argue that critics cannot escape their own aesthetic, political, or theological biases. But, if critics realize their biases and account for them in their analyses, such critics can claim to be essentially objective and, therefore, also outside the criticism.

Either of these notions of objective analysis tends to be held by critics who follow the approaches of accurate interpretation (Chapter 3), formal (Chapter 4), or neoclassical criticism (Chapter 5). Others will argue that the critic is always in the judgment (see Chapters 6–10) and must be in the formula.

Foci.   From these four variables a series of foci develops. All criticism, as noted earlier, involves a variable: the message. Thus, a criticism can be defined by the array of other variables brought to bear on the message, which are seven: Source-Message, Message-Environment, Message-Critic, Source-Message-Environment, Source-Message-Critic, Message-Environment-Critic, and Source-Message-Environment-Critic. Each identifies what will be covered in a particular approach to criticism. A critical focus that involves source, for instance (as four of these foci do), indicates an orientation quite different than does one without it. Attention to source usually implies some concern with intent. For example, here is an interpretation based on intent: When George Bush (Source) spoke at the Iwo Jima Memorial in favor of a constitutional amendment against desecrating the flag (Message), he was trying to maintain his patriotic image from the 1988 presidential campaign (Intent). On the other hand, message-environment criticism excludes intent because the source and its motives are not important, but society is. For example, the enthusiasm for a constitutional amendment against desecrating the flag demonstrated by all the statements of support by public officials including President Bush's speech at the Iwo Jima Memorial (Message) is a reflection of the attractiveness of that patriotic symbol to the American people (Environment). Even though George Bush is a part of the message in both statements, in the first he and his intention are central. In the second he is only a part of the message and the nature of the society is central.

These foci will become clearer as they help to differentiate among the eight approaches discussed in this book.

Common Sense Versus Deconstruction

A sense of pluralism guides the organization of this book. Following Chapter 2, which deals with methods of analysis (the essential data-gathering part of any critical act), we will examine two perspectives on criticism: the objectivist and the deconstructive. Broadly defined, three approaches result from the objectivist perspective: accurate interpretation, formal criticism, and neoclassical criticism; five perspectives result from the deconstructionist perspective: semiotics, value analysis, narrative criticism, psychoanalytic criticism, and ideological criticism. Critics who work from the first three tend to see communication events from a common sense point of view, although they are individually quite different from one another.

The term *common sense* comes from Catherine Belsey (1984, 2). It suggests a type of judicial criticism where critics assume explicit features of messages that can be assessed against reality-based standards. It is called *common sense* because common standards of accuracy, beauty, or effectiveness are used to assess the manifest features of messages. Therefore, common sense critics evaluate the accuracy of factual statements, the beauty of linguistic expressions, or the rhetorical skills of orators against ideal standards, each of which has its own complexity. Consider, for a moment, the many interacting or conflicting aesthetic standards used for evaluating a poem. However, once such standards are known, anyone can use them to understand or to judge a poem.

Deconstructive critics assume that the world as humans know it is defined by the language they use to explain it. So, a critic deconstructs a message (takes it apart) to discover what the message says about the human condition. Although there are social conventions that tell us what statements mean, there are no natural meanings to language. Therefore, any message is open to different interpretations, depending upon the receiver and the critic of the message.

Deconstructive criticism is a type of legislative or interpretive criticism where critics attempt to probe implicit features of messages and understand the ways in which those features govern humans' communicative experiences. It is called deconstructive because messages are constructed and the critic's goal is to breach the superficial constructions of the text to reveal its operative powers. To take messages apart and examine their implicit or hidden constructive principles are the twin goals of deconstructive critics as discussed in this book.

Deconstructive critics probe such matters as the values or ideologies that lie beneath the surface of political talk, the sexist conceptions that govern advertisements for laundry soap, or the ways we use stories or narratives to sell ethical systems.

Although deconstruction rejects the assumptions of common sense criticism, the two frequently overlap. Each deconstructive approach is a reaction to one or more common sense approaches and draws upon them. Formal criticism is concerned with the literary form of narrative, and neoclassical criticism uses values to explain what makes an argument effective, for instance. Thus, narrative analysis bears some resemblance to formal criticism and value analysis draws some of its procedures from neoclassical criticism. There is, therefore, some possibility of confusion.

Two critics might look at the TV sitcom *Roseanne* by examining how the character of Roseanne is developed. A formal critic would test Roseanne's believability as a lower-middle-class working wife and mother, find a significant theme, and judge Roseanne by established artistic standards. A critic interested in narrative analysis would be interested in Roseanne as a character but not in judging the character by artistic standards; rather, such a critic would deconstruct Roseanne's character to see what definition of society it provides. You can avoid confusion if you keep in mind that it is not *what* message a critic looks at that distinguishes common sense from deconstruction but *how* the critic looks at it.

Objectives of Criticism

In addition to defining an approach to criticism by what combination of Source (S), Message (M), Environment (E), and Critic (C) is used and whether the approach follows a common sense or deconstructive orientation, a criticism may also be defined by its objective: accuracy, quality, effect, or social role, respectively.

Accuracy.   Obviously, a critic who is interested in the accuracy of the text is concerned with knowing how well the text reflects the known world. Frequently, a critic who finds a text to be inaccurate makes an ethical judgment about it. In the 1988 presidential campaign, Republican speakers, printed material, and commercials portrayed Democratic candidate Michael Dukakis as soft on crime. The Commonwealth of Massachusetts, with Dukakis as governor, gave a furlough to convicted murderer Willie Horton, who then raped a Maryland woman and beat and terrorized her and her husband. George Bush and the Republicans were criticized because of what they left out of the story: that Dukakis had inherited the furlough program from his Republican predecessor, that he had restricted the program after the incident, that Ronald Reagan had instituted a similar program as governor of California and had a similar program in effect in the federal government. Thus, critics said, the Republican campaign was inaccurate and unethical.

David Paul Nord (1984) analyzed the business values that were revealed in the editorials of the Chicago *Daily News, Times,* and *Tribune* in the late nineteenth century. Although they had "sharply opposing views on business-labor questions [they] tended to share certain fundamental values: a commitment to public interest consumerism, an obsession with commercial order and social harmony, and a growing faith in organizational modes of conflict resolution" (272). This criticism might have only explained the content of the editorials to assess the accuracy of interpretations. But it also illustrates a second level of accurate interpretation. It linked the texts to the growing progressive movement. Nord's explanation clarifies for the reader what he considers an accurate picture of the editorials and their relation to the society.

Quality.   The artistic quality of a fictive work is separate from its accuracy. Concern for artistic quality is an objective arising from the strong tradition of formal criticism among literary critics, but it is not limited to literary critics. Jane Feuer (1987) was interested in questions of quality when she compared two sitcoms, Tandem Production's *Maude,* a spin-off of Norman Lear's *All in the Family,* and MTM's *Rhoda,* a spin-off of *The Mary Tyler Moore Show:*

> Maude is far more politically astute than Rhoda; she deals with controversial issues such as alcoholism and abortion; she is far more the "liberated woman" than Rhoda aspires to be. Yet the show *Maude* is structurally simplistic: there is one important dilemma per week which is usually resolved at Maude's expense, the main comedy technique is the insult, and the characters are unidimensional and static. Even those episodes of *Maude* which announce their experimental quality—Maude's monologue to her therapist, Walter's bout with alcoholism—seem to thrust themselves upon the viewer. *Rhoda,* whose most controversial moment occurred when Rhoda divorced her husband, nevertheless took the sitcom in new directions, employing a variety of comic techniques, and evolving central character and, arguably, moving toward the comedy-drama blend that would become the MTM formula of the late 1970s. The MTM sitcoms inflected the form in the direction of "quality TV," of complex characters, sophisticated dialogue, and identification. "Character comedy" in the hands of MTM became synonymous with "quality comedy" (56).

Effect.   Neoclassical criticism defines its objective principally as the identification of communicative effects. Neoclassical critics, therefore, judge whether or not a message is persuasive to an audience. Drawing their authority from Aristotle's *Rhetoric,* the neoclassical critics focused initially on public speaking. Although neoclassical critics no longer limit themselves to determining the effect of a speech on an audience, the public-speaking situation remains their prototype for criticism. Even when considering types of communication other than speeches, neoclassical critics usually choose texts that are consciously persuasive, for example, editorials, essays, brochures, and television commercials.

This orientation to the persuasive effect of a speech on an audience brought neoclassical criticism into direct conflict with the dictates of aesthetic quality, which took its assumptions from poetic theory. Its most often quoted dictum, Herbert Wichelns's 1925 statement, separated it from literary theory on exactly the grounds being discussed here. "Its [rhetorical criticism's] point of view is patently single. It is not concerned with permanence, nor yet with beauty. It is concerned with effect" (35). Although the severity of Wichelns's statement has been modified by neoclassical critics, it still stands as the central statement differentiating a goal of quality from one of effect.

Social Role.   A fourth objective of criticism has been identified as social role (Andrews 1983, 10–12). With this objective in mind, a critic wants to know if, and to what extent, the message defines, influences, or reflects the society in which it originated. Such a purpose is found in a wide variety of approaches. Sometimes it will be reflected in a concern for effects, where judgments are made by the critic about the effects that a particular message or set of messages had on the society. It also can be reflected in judgments about the accuracy of a particular message. For example, one may argue that inaccurate messages have an inappropriate social role because they violate an ethical standard of not misleading people.

Social-role objectives will also be found in those kinds of criticisms that seek deeper social meanings of messages. Elaine Showalter notes that one form of feminist criticism directs our attention to "the way in which the hypothesis of a female reader changes our apprehension of a given text, awakening us to the significance of its sexual codes" (Culler 1988, 18). Thus, social criticism has a wide variety of applications from the most traditional desires to judge messages by accepted standards of social ethics (e.g., one should not lie) to a complex effort to use messages to define the society they represent (e.g., sexist codes).

PLURALISM IN CRITICAL ARGUMENT

When accepting the idea that there are many ways to engage in criticism, it is easy to suppose that such pluralism leads to relativism or to accepting individual tastes as a basis for judgment. Be that as it may, advocates of pluralism would deny such an interpretation. Although critics may differ over which approach is best, regardless of text, circumstance, or approach, a good argument is still an obligation. The interpretation of what a good argument is, however, may differ from one approach to another.

For example, compare the common sense with the psychoanalytic approach. Because psychoanalytic critics assume that human action is produced by an interaction between conscious and unconscious impulses, they accept inferences most other critics would refuse. A television commercial for the 1989 Mitsubishi Galant shows a rain-covered, winding, rural road with a car, driven by a man, easily negotiating turns, splashing water as it moves down the road. The voice-over with printed captions corresponding to it reads:

> In Japan 60 automotive journalists named the 1989 Mitsubishi Galant "Car of the Year." Now the Americans report "a refined, impressively built sports sedan." "Everything about the Galant GS works well." "Galant will blow away the higher priced competition." "Pure heaven to drive." "Perhaps *Car and Driver* sums up the Galant best when it writes 'Watch out Honda'" [Symbol of Mitsubishi Motors comes on the screen with the printed caption "Suddenly the obvious choice"].

The common sense interpretation of this advertisement is that it is aimed at small-car owners (compared to Honda). It is easy to handle, less expensive, sporty. It is "the obvious choice" of the knowledgeable driver. But psychoanalytically it is a mix of conscious and an unconscious meaning. The male driver is shown full face with a pleasurable expression as the words "Pure heaven to drive" are heard. Immediately a latent suggestion of sexual relations is supposed. He is in control of this automobile as perhaps he is not in control on the slippery road of male/female relations. Here he can be sure. He has made "the obvious choice." There, with women, perhaps he is not so sure nor are his choices so obvious.

Of course, differing critical arguments would differ somewhat with each approach used. We must remember that although there are general understandings about what an argument should do to gain adherence, there are also special rules that apply in specific fields. For instance, a fundamental form of argument in religion is the appeal to sacred texts to support a position: the Bible, Torah, or Koran. Such sources, even such a way of arguing, are not acceptable in the physical sciences where a good argument is marked by observational and mathematical verification. Likewise, an attempt to apply statistical methods to faith is inappropriate. Neither one is right or wrong but subject to the conventions of those who engage in a particular field of argumentation (Rieke and Sillars 1984, 214). Similarly, formal criticism seeks to make arguments about the aesthetic worth of a text by judging the extent to which it meets established standards, and accurate interpretation criticism seeks to judge it by outside authoritative historical sources. A good argument in both cases will follow Brockriede's definition discussed earlier, but each will differ from the other based on their objectives.

There are, however, general principles that apply to all critical arguments. Critical claims must be useful and the argument carefully made. These principles apply to all communication research, critical or not (Smith 1972; Gronbeck 1975, 318).

The critic must say to the reader of the criticism something that is worth knowing. Note that three of the five generic characteristics of an argument identified by Brockriede (1974) are particularly oriented to usefulness: "an inferential leap from existing beliefs to the adoption of a new belief or the reinforcement of an old one," "a choice among two or more competing claims," and "a regulation of uncertainty." Therefore, a useful critical claim must provide some insight that was not available before or reinforce some significant belief that people already hold.

Former president Ronald Reagan is called the "Great Communicator." A critic might reasonably argue that he is not, or that his talent is misunderstood, or that while understood, it is not fully appreciated. Each claim acknowledges that there are other possible competing claims and that arguments must be made to support the critic's claim. Supporting a claim that Ronald Reagan is a great communicator using arguments and evidence that have been used before is useless criticism as well. David Smith (1972) calls usefulness "richness of explanation" (179). Criticisms that provide richer interpretations than have previously been provided by others are generally regarded as more useful.

The critic also must be careful to avoid errors in reasoning, such as attributing cause when there is insufficient evidence, ignoring significant counterevidence, being inconsistent, arguing from one principle at one point in the criticism and rejecting the principle without counterevidence later, or reasoning by false analogy. It also implies being sure that the quality and quantity of evidence used to support a claim are adequate to the task depending, frequently, on the potential skepticism of the reader. Carefulness also requires that the claim not shift from one standard to another. Soap operas are very popular; they also may have artistic merit but the two claims are not the same, and proving one does not prove the other.

This call for carefulness points us to the subject of the next chapter. Communication criticism may be undertaken from a number of different approaches; it will relate to the individual or society outside the message. Most important, perhaps, it will make a useful argument about how a communication situation is to be understood or evaluated. To make a useful critical argument, the critic will center on the message. In Chapter 2, therefore, careful analysis of the message is our subject.

CHAPTER TWO

Analyzing Messages

Competent communication criticism makes an argument to advance a critical claim about a message. To make a better argument for a claim requires that it be grounded in the message and the communication situation.

Therefore, this chapter is not about claims; it is about the grounds for the critical claim. The well-known Toulmin model of argument can be adapted to make this point clear (see figure below).

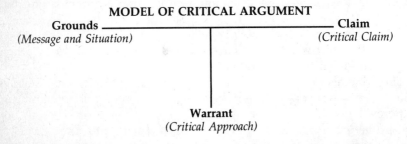

MODEL OF CRITICAL ARGUMENT

Grounds ———————————————————— **Claim**
(Message and Situation)   *(Critical Claim)*

Warrant
(Critical Approach)

After Toulmin (1958, 111).

In order to substantiate a claim, one must have grounds and a warrant. A claim by itself is not an argument. It is an assertion of taste, feeling, or reaction. The grounds make the claim credible if they are warranted by the critical approach used.

A critic claiming that Abraham Lincoln was a master of the use of metaphor must provide grounds to substantiate the claim: "Our fathers brought forth . . . a new nation, conceived in liberty . . ," "a new birth of freedom," "a house divided against itself cannot stand," "the mystic chords of memory," are only some of the examples that might be used to show how metaphors explicated important themes in Lincoln's speeches.

Another critic might observe that Mikhail Gorbachev was quite specific about his plans to reduce Soviet armament in his December 7, 1988, speech to the United Nations. One section could serve to establish the grounds for the claim:

> Today I am able to inform you of the fact that the Soviet Union has decided to reduce its armed forces.
>
> Over the next two years their strength will be reduced by 500,000 men, and substantial cuts will be made in conventional armaments. These cuts will be made unilaterally, regardless of the talks on the mandate of the Vienna meeting.
>
> By agreement with our Warsaw Treaty allies, we have decided to withdraw six tank divisions from the German Democratic Republic, Czechoslovakia and Hungary by 1991, and to disband them. In addition, assault-landing formations and units and some others, including assault-crossing support units with their armaments and combat equipment, will be withdrawn from the Soviet forces stationed in these countries. The Soviet forces stationed in these countries will be reduced by 50,000 men and 5,000 tanks. The Soviet divisions which still remain on the territory of our allies will be reorganized. Their structure will be changed: a large number of tanks will be withdrawn, and they will become strictly defensive. At the same time we shall cut troops and armaments in the European part of the U.S.S.R.
>
> The total reductions of Soviet armed forces in the European regions of the U.S.S.R and on the territory of our European allies will amount to 10,000 tanks, 8,500 artillery systems and 800 combat aircraft (235).

No matter what critical approach is taken, grounds are necessary. Again, finding and developing grounds from messages, texts, and contexts are the subject of this chapter. Consequently, the process of analyzing messages begins with an examination of the nature of messages and texts. Methods of textual analysis then are examined and applied to interpretation and judgment.

WHAT IS A MESSAGE?

At the core of a message is the text that has interested the critic: a newspaper story about arms negotiations, an episode of *Cheers*, a novel by Steinbeck. But a "second persona," a reader, listener, or viewer, is implied by the text (Black 1970). Furthermore, the text is in a rhetorical situation. Thus, the significance of a text is defined by, or perhaps determined by, the events and persons to which it responds (Bitzer 1968). A message then is more than the raw verbal and visual text which exists in the book, speech, videocassette, or record.

Certain traditional approaches to formal criticism examine the text for a meaning exclusive to itself. Thus, E. D. Hirsch, Jr. (1960) argues that the critic must find the stable meaning in the text before a text is evaluated. The critic's main problem is to discover what that meaning is. But even

Hirsch tempers his definition of text by arguing that the meaning is found in the intent of the author. He thus places the meaning not solely in the text but in a source-message relationship.

Other critics claim that the text is given meaning by the receiver. These critics explore the message-environment relationship to find textual meaning. For example, imagine three different interpretations of William Shakespeare's *Hamlet*. One critic looks at the text for its artistic beauty as defined by aesthetic principles. A second tries to determine how persuasive Shakespeare's ideas were for an Elizabethan audience. A third examines the text for a psychoanalytic interpretation of Hamlet's relationship with his mother.

These three interpretations indicate that critics differ widely on the extent to which various other elements influence the meaning of a text. To illustrate how critics may differ in their interpretations of a text, presented below are nine major alternative interpretations:

1. The meaning is in the conventions of language.
2. The meaning is in the author's conscious intent.
3. The meaning is in the author's conscious and unconscious intent.
4. The meaning is what the "best critics" see in the text.
5. The meaning is what the author's contemporaries would have seen in the text.
6. The meaning is what a receiver sees in the text.
7. The meaning is what an "ideal" receiver sees in the text.
8. The meaning is the relationship of the text to the society from which it comes.
9. The meaning is the relationship between contemporary society and the text.

Although such interpretations range through source-message, message-environment, and message-critic criticism, they all involve some outside factor. Even the first alternative, that the text reveals a meaning exclusive to itself, must involve at least an interpretive code and the interpretative critic. So, from a variety of approaches, texts become messages and have, or acquire, meaning. For some critics, meanings are in people (sources and audiences) and are assigned by those people to texts. Nonetheless, critics start with the text however broadly they define the sources of meaning. It is with the verbal or visual text, therefore, that we will begin the process of analysis.

THE NATURE OF CRITICAL TEXTS

No one sets out to be a critic of the first text that comes along—an advertisement for mail order suits, a TV commercial for Lite beer, a press conference by the president, or a short story in *McCall's* magazine. A critic is drawn to a text because of the interest it has for the critic and for the persons that critic wishes to influence. A critic will also choose a particular text because it possesses some degree of authenticity. The text will be unique and hence valued in its rarity, or representative and hence important because of typicality.

Public Texts

For our purposes, a text must be public or capable of being made public. All of the examples given above are of public texts, those that are not for restricted personal use only. However, private correspondence can be made public. Letters, diaries, and journals of ordinary people can be made public if they have public appeal. Perhaps they tell about the times, a way of life, or of important persons and their actions. Several years ago my cousin found a letter my great-grandfather, who was a Union officer in the Civil War, wrote to his sister in Massachusetts. I was struck by how similar his sense of humor was to my father's sense of humor. Although this letter was interesting to me and the few people who knew my father, it did not possess public appeal. On the other hand, had my great-grandfather discussed his reactions to the war, the letter might have thrown light on popular reactions to the Civil War, a much broader and common experience. In that case, the letter could be used as a public document.

Textual Authenticity

The text that is preserved may not be the text originally communicated. This has long been a concern of critics of speeches. Woodrow Wilson had a superb shorthand reporter who took down his speeches but prior to electronic recordings, few other speakers have been so lucky.

Furthermore, written texts from which speeches were delivered have frequently been preserved while variations caused by their extemporaneous delivery were lost. Speakers also have revised a text or written it from memory after the speech was delivered. Even today, speeches in the *Congressional Record* are frequently rewritten before publication, left out of the *Record*, or inserted in the *Record* even though not delivered (Quadro 1977). Even such well-known and recorded speeches as Franklin D. Roosevelt's "Fireside Chats" and Martin Luther King, Jr.'s "I Have a Dream" have slight changes in wording from the recorded to the print sources (Bosmajian 1982), and are distorted further when words are unclear on the recording.

When the text's original form is print, it is easier to authenticate it. But even here, the critic of journalism interested in the work of a particular reporter cannot be sure that the work has not been changed by an editor. Furthermore, critics interested in radical or unusual texts are less likely to find them complete. In the late nineteenth century, for instance, no major library dared to keep radical publications. To study radicalism in that period, for example, the Coxey Army Movement of 1894, the critic often must work with texts pieced together, frequently from hostile sources (Sillars 1980a).

A similar problem applies to film, and particularly to television and radio texts. Only recently has the systematic collection of such materials been undertaken by such institutions as the Museum of Broadcasting in New York City and Chicago, and the Television News Archives at Vanderbilt University (Schatz 1984; Godfrey 1983). Michael Kerbel (1982) describes his difficulty in viewing "The Golden Age of TV Drama," the 1950s:

> I managed to see kinescopes of twenty-four plays (four of them at The Museum of Modern Art)—barely a handful of those grains of sand. *Patterns*, one of the "older" plays viewed, was the 463rd *Kraft* production; *Kraft* alone did 650 plays, and that was just one series. The immensity of the task was daunting—and troubling. The Museum of Broadcasting has concentrated its preservation efforts on the critically acclaimed or award-winning plays, so the one example I'd see from a particular year or series *might* be the best. Still, how can one fully appreciate the "best," when so much of the context is missing? And are these even the best? As I went from one Emmy nominee or winner to another, I couldn't help feeling that I was viewing the TV equivalent of *Around the World in 80 Days* instead of *The Searchers*, *The Defiant Ones* instead of *Touch of Evil*. Are there unknown masterpieces that have already been passed over—and perhaps lost forever? (50).

The problem of finding the most authentic or complete texts does present difficulties. Sometimes, as in the case of Kerbel's project, the critic has to take what is available as better than nothing. In other cases the material is so thin or altered that the critic must abandon the project. But there also exist sensible means for resolving some problems.

First it is necessary to ask the question, what do we mean by "most authentic text"? In many forms of scholarship the answer is simple: the earliest text. To find the earliest text means to find the most accurate text, the one closest to the author. But a critic who is interested in the composing process might, like Halford Ryan (1975) in his study of Franklin D. Roosevelt's speech writing, be interested in many drafts of a text to see how it evolved.

One really has to ask "authentic for what purpose?" Patrick Henry's speech to the Virginia delegates convened in Richmond on the eve of the American revolution is one of the most influential speeches in American history. But in form and structure that speech was not typical of Henry's other speeches. It was, in fact, reconstructed from someone else's notes by

William Wirt some 40 years after Henry delivered it (Oliver 1965, 60; Hample 1977). As a result, little of the speech can be authenticated. What Henry actually said remains problematic. Nonetheless, as an interpretation of the American revolution that has been taught to countless schoolchildren since that time, and as a representation of American patriotic values, it is authentic.

Uniqueness or Representativeness

A critic may choose to examine a text because it is unique, because there is something about the text that distinguishes it. Uniqueness has attracted many critics to texts by persons such as Abraham Lincoln, Ernest Hemingway, or William Faulkner. However, critics also find uniqueness in other, more contemporary forms of communication.

The Wonder Years is not the first situation comedy that features the activities of children in their early teens. *Leave It to Beaver, Growing Pains, The Hogan Family*, and *The Cosby Show* all emphasize some aspect of that age group. But the story of Kevin Arnold, his mother and father, brother Wayne, friend Paul, and sometimes girlfriend Winnie Cooper is unique. Kevin's story is told through the words and actions of the characters. It is also told through Kevin's adult voice-over that explains what is happening or what Kevin is thinking. *The Wonder Years* is part of a genre but in one respect it is unique.

Why would a critic examine a text that was not unique? For one reason only: because it was representative of a general class. If a text is representative of a genre, person, movement, or period, it is useful for explaining what that genre, person, movement, or period is or was like. Movement criticism is a good example of this broad orientation. But, how can critics interpret the civil rights movement, feminist movement, gay and lesbian liberation movement without selecting from a large group of texts those they will examine? They cannot. Selectivity is essential and the primary principle of selection of text from a large body of material is representativeness.

A. Clay Schoenfield examines the environmental movement of the sixties and seventies by looking at its characteristics in American magazines. He shows how environmentalism in the United States changed between 1966 and 1975, with Earth Day 1970 as the turning point, from a minor to a mass movement in America. Says Schoenfield (1983):

> The evidence as shown here is discernible in the appearance of many new specialized environmental periodicals, in the adaptation of antecedent magazines, in the domestic circulation of periodicals from abroad, in the contents of general circulation magazines and in fugitive state newsletters and bulletins (475).

Such a claim can be argued because Schoenfield believes that articles in American magazines are representative of the public opinion.

The prevailing practice of critics is to examine single events, strategies, particular communicators, or specific issues as representative of the movement (Riches and Sillars 1980, 277–281). For Instance, Robert L. Heath (1973), writing on the strategy of black radicalism in the 1970s, finds the strategies of "redefinition," "transcendence," "formalization of counter position," and "scapegoating." He finds these strategies in Malcolm X, Stokely Carmichael, and the Black Panthers whom Heath takes as representative of the movement.

In a similar vein, Ronald H. Carpenter defines the genre of the historical jeremiad by looking at the form and structure of three late nineteenth- and early twentieth-century documents: Frederick Jackson Turner's "The Significance of the Frontier in American History," Alfred Thayer Mahan's *Influences of Sea Power Upon History*, and Sir Halford Mackinder's "The Geographical Pivot of History." These are not the only documents that have the characteristics of the prophet Jeremiah's warnings to Israel but they serve Carpenter as representative.

A critic first must find a claim and then be prepared to argue that the text can ground the interpretation or judgment offered. That argument will be made in the belief that the text is public, authentic, and reveals the uniqueness or representativeness that makes it interesting. To find the grounds that support an interpretive or judgmental critical claim, the text and the communication situation must be carefully dissected.

THE PROCESS OF INTERPRETATION AND JUDGMENT

How does a critic go about analyzing a text and the situation that informs it to make useful and careful interpretations and judgments? Most writers identify three phases in the process: analysis of data, interpretation of data, and judgment. For some critics, these phases occur in distinct steps: analysis being essential to interpretation and interpretation a necessary prelude to judgment. Other critics are more flexible in interpreting the process, with some claiming that judgment comes first (Cathcart 1986, 22; Andrews 1983, 49–63; Hirsch 1960; Fish 1980). Popular is the position taken by Stanley Fish, who argues for an analytical model "in which the facts that one cites are available only because an interpretation (at least in its general and broad outlines) has already been assumed" (32). Nonetheless, this preference does not invalidate the usefulness of the three-part division of the process.

Before proceeding with this discussion, it may be worthwhile to note that no matter how sequential or flexible critics view the analytical process, they do not write the final criticism in this order: analysis, interpretation, judgment. The organization of the critical argument will depend on what is being argued. Unlike scientific and social scientific writing which follows the scientific paradigm, the analytical process is quite different from written criticism. Critics frequently will use a form that reverses the scientific process, for instance, writing a judgment, then proceeding to interpretation, each supported by analysis of data.

Suppose a person views a videotape of a speech such as Martin Luther King, Jr.'s "I Have a Dream" and forms a judgment: "It's a good speech." Thus, the initial examination is judgmental and general. "Why?" one might ask. "Because of the spiritual quality created by the use of metaphor and other stylistic features." Here we have interpretation and we might ask the person what specific textual data support the analysis? The check returned marked "insufficient funds," the repetition of "let freedom ring," and the metaphorical vision in "I have a dream" are evidence that might be used to support the critical claim. The three phases are here but they are in reverse order.

Such a scenario, however, represents only the initial response. To develop a clear and rich claim, and to better ground that claim, the data of the speech situation have to be more carefully analyzed. One is more likely to proceed here by way of analysis, interpretation, and judgment, with the results of careful analysis enriching and modifying, sometimes even changing, the initial judgment and interpretation. The following table will illustrate the connections among these three:

Grounding a Critical Claim

Analysis	Interpretation	Judgment
Data 1 Data 2	Interpretation A	
Data 3 Data 4	Interpretation B	Judicial claim
Data 5 Data 6	Interpretation C	
Data n		
Verbal and visual text influenced by the communication situation	Emphasis Relative significance Overall strategy	Accuracy Quality Effect Social role

Whether the critic arrives at a judgment or interpretation easily and quickly or labors over the data before articulating it, data are necessary to interpretation and judgment. Remember, however, that data are complex in communication situations and may involve, in addition to the verbal or visual text, the communication situation which includes the source of the message and the pertinent environmental conditions.

In "I Have a Dream," it is important to understand Martin Luther King, Jr.'s background as a black Baptist minister, the civil rights movement, the Voting Rights Act before Congress, the location at the Lincoln Memorial, and the composition of the audience. These are but a few of the factors that influenced the verbal and visual text, that become part of the data of the message analyzed.

From a thorough analysis of the data, some interpretation emerges. Interpretations will be about what is emphasized in the text, which parts have the greatest relative significance, or what overall strategy is encased in the text. Thus, the presence of some variety of the word *freedom* 26 times in King's relatively short speech helps to establish the interpretation that freedom is a central value of the speech. The use of repetition establishes a responsive pattern with the audience reminiscent of the call-and-respond communication pattern in many black churches. In addition, the metaphor helps stylistically to lift the speech to a more spiritual stage of argument.

All of these interpretations can lead to a judgment about the worth of the speech as accurate, aesthetic, persuasive, or socially useful. But whether the critic stops with interpretation or proceeds to judgment, both are based on a careful examination of the text and its situation. This careful examination is the subject of the next three sections of this chapter where we will look at some principles of textual analysis, then at interpretation, and finally at judgment.

TEXTUAL ANALYSIS

Any critical claim about a text must be grounded in the text. Frequently, this means that a claim will be supported by a large quantity of evidence in the text, such as the word *freedom* in "I Have a Dream," mentioned above. At other times a single sentence may be representative of the speech. Franklin D. Roosevelt's "So, first of all, let me assert my firm belief that the only thing we have to fear is fear itself," in his First Inaugural Address during the Great Depression of 1932, is the linchpin of the speech. Everything else in the speech relates to it. Yet, the word *fear* is not mentioned again. Instead, Roosevelt's claim is reinforced by his optimistic tone and emphasis on action so that the reasonable response of his audience is not one of fear.

Mindless counting yields mindless interpretations, however. A computer analysis of the 14,283 words in a collection of William Jennings Bryan's 1896 presidential campaign speeches reveals that the most prevalent word is *the* (used 1,089 times or 7 percent). The number of instances should not surprise anyone and surely does not represent Bryan's emphasis on *the*. Remember, counting is only one way to analyze a text. The critic emphasizes *what* to count and supports quantity measures with other means of assessment.

Hawkeye in *M*A*S*H* is a unique character. Are there any others like him? *One Day at a Time* was the first sitcom to feature a divorced mother. How many have there been since? *Murphy Brown* is a story about a recovering alcoholic. Is there even one other serial drama or sitcom character like her? Yes. Frank Furillo of *Hill Street Blues* and Sam Malone on *Cheers* are both recovering alcoholics. But they are male. Is Murphy Brown the first woman recovering alcoholic on a sitcom? No, there is Christine Cagney of *Cagney & Lacey*. How important is that fact to the show? These observations imply something about uniqueness and representativeness and carry some sense of counting but not for its own sake.

The chief advantage of such counting is that it can summarize large segments of texts. For instance, in studying "Television Network News Reporting by Female Correspondents," Loy A. Singleton and Stephanie L. Cook (1982) examined 1,247 network news reports. Very large bodies of data can be accommodated by using a computer-based analysis, as Roderick P. Hart (1984) did in his *Verbal Style and the Presidency: A Computer Based Analysis*. Frequently, modern sampling techniques are used to control the amount of text to be analyzed. Such techniques are beyond the scope of this discussion. Nonetheless, they indicate that means are available for providing a workable base for analyzing large amounts of text.

What to Count

First, critics must examine texts carefully in order to make better interpretations and judgments of the communication situation. However, critics always make interpretations and judgments about the relation of the texts to something else, as well: some standard of accuracy, formal criteria of aesthetic excellence, audience response, or ideological scene. Although critics might attempt to be as objective as possible, the very categories they established as important are influenced by the assumptions that warrant the claim. Therefore, analysis begins with a decision about what to count and why to count it.

A critic will decide what to count based upon his or her particular approach to communication criticism. For example, how do we make a value analysis of a presidential message? First, we must decide what our purpose is. Suppose we want to know how the president's values on a particular issue compare with those of his or her opponent in an election. Here we must find a presidential message by each on the same subject, and then decide what to use as data. Because this is a value analysis, we will want to count values, of course. But how do you know a value when you see one? Certain kinds of words representing "generalized conceptions of the good" are taken as values.

Even though the word *value* is common in our society, it is an abstract concept which is represented by the manifest content of the message. Therefore, words such as *freedom, liberty, work,* and *family* each stand for a value. They are what we count as symbolic of the psychosocial phenomena we call values. We count those words because they are the best indicators we have. We could count other things but a detailed discussion is best left to Chapter 7 on value analysis. Let us stay with this relatively simple measure. These words stand for values and we can, for this message, at this time, on this subject, find the hierarchy of the president's values.

Comparison

And what does a hierarchy tell us? Not much, unless we have some basis of comparison. How does one person, text, or situation compare to another? The answer to that question is essential to a decision about uniqueness or representativeness. One study of the Reagan-Mondale debates in the 1984 election found that the two were remarkably similar in the value clusters they used:

> In the first debate [on domestic policy], for example, nine out of the top 13 numerically superior [value] clusters were expressed by both candidates. The highest cluster for both candidates was one which emphasized the value of "rationality" (86–Reagan, 62–Mondale; ex: "I was openly saying that while we had thought the basis of our plan could have brought a balanced budget; that was no longer possible." Reagan). Another jointly prominent cluster was "people" (Reagan–50, Mondale–46; ex: "I think this is a test of leadership and I think the American people know the difference." Mondale). Other shared clusters which were found include "knowledge" (Reagan–27, Mondale–58; ex: "A president is called the Commander in Chief. And he's called that because he's supposed to be in charge of the facts, and run our government, and strengthen our nation." Mondale), "belief and faith" (Reagan–27, Mondale–35; ex: "But I have . . . the firmest possible belief and faith in God." Reagan), "progressivity" . . . "charity" . . . "leadership" . . . and "unity" (Werling et al. 1987, 231).

This comparison is useful because it tells us that the two opponents were remarkably, perhaps surprisingly, similar. The analysis also notes that "a textual examination of where and how these values were used clearly reveals differences" (Werling et al. 1987, 232). The counting noted above does not get at the "where" and the "how," but it does set the basis for directing the critic elsewhere. The initial assumption was that Reagan and Mondale would differ significantly in values. Not so. Looking elsewhere at where and how did reveal differences, however. Reagan's use of "life" as a value occurred in the first debate on domestic issues and related to his opposition to abortion. Mondale used "life" in the second debate on foreign policy to question Reagan's leadership in the tragic deaths of 241 marines in the Beirut barracks (Werling et al. 1987, 232–233). So, one could conclude that the two presidential candidates argued from essentially the same value warrants but linked them to different issues.

Kinds of Textual Data

Counting cannot provide an analysis of the complete communication situation. It is only a means of organizing, quantifying, and comparing data. The most important function of criticism requires a critic who can "move beyond descriptive analysis (however technologically sophisticated) to reasoned interpretations and evaluations that prove, ultimately, that the facts do not speak for themselves" (Medhurst 1984b, 144). This move is aided by careful decisions about what data are important to the critic's approach.

What are some of the kinds of data a critic might analyze? Here is a list of nine which you may find useful:

1. Themes—statements that indicate a point of view
2. Attributions—characterizations of persons, places, or things
3. Subject matter—characterization of what subject is being discussed or of its contrast with the same or similar sources at another time or place
4. Probable cause—statements that were likely caused by another phenomenon, statements that are likely to cause another phenomenon
5. Stylistic features—distinctive syntax, word choice, figures of speech, one style compared to another
6. Values, attitudes, beliefs; speaker or cultural patterns
7. Argumentative features—argument forms, evidence
8. Intentions, psychological states—statements that reflect a communicator's inner state or intention
9. Political relations—statements that reveal political or power relations (see Krippendorff 1980, 33–35)

This list is not complete. What you look for in a textual analysis depends on what you want to find out, what your claim will be. Stylistic features such as word choice (the number of times a person uses the first person singular, for instance) can be counted directly. Themes (environmental policy) frequently have to be inferred from other content ("We need to do something about cleaning up the air and water") but are not so difficult to do. Intentions ("When George Bush offered his disarmament plan he was trying to put Mikhail Gorbachev on the defensive") require much more sophistication to find.

Determining Thematic Structure

What we have discussed so far will provide information about what is important in a message but it will not reveal the overall structure of a single text very well. Sometimes the way a message is organized is not very important, as when a critic is interested in the value systems developed in a political campaign. Structure also is a very difficult thing to determine in large bodies of texts, for instance, the messages of social movements. However, quite often the critic will find it useful to know the thematic structure of a particular text. The following procedure has been adapted by David Jabusch from the methods used by the Institute of Cultural Affairs to chart, as they call it, the thematic structure of a message. An example, a chart of Malcolm X's speech "The Ballot or the Bullet," made by a group of Jabusch's students is found on page 29:

1. Take a piece of 8 1/2 × 11 paper and turn it sideways. Draw a line across the page about two inches from the bottom. Divide that line into 1/2-inch segments with lines that go to the bottom of the page.
2. Number the paragraphs in the text.
3. Read the text, circle words that seem to be key. Look for structural clues which indicate major and minor breaks ("in the first place," "and," "in addition," "in conclusion," etc.).
4. Find key paragraphs where structure and/or thesis is explained.
5. In your own words write a *brief* statement which summarizes each paragraph. When the theme of two or more adjacent paragraphs is the same, combine them. The themes of paragraphs, or combination of paragraphs, should be written in the numbered boxes at the bottom of the page.
6. Examine these themes for major and minor breaks. On a level above the line identify the larger unifying themes that combine the paragraph themes.
7. Continue this process through subsequent levels until you can state the overall theme of the text.

The chart of "The Ballot or the Bullet" is particularly noteworthy because that speech, at first glance, appears to have no structure. This or a similar analysis of structure frequently will help to place elements of a message into a capsulized picture of what the message is about.

It also points to problematic areas. The bulk of "The Ballot or the Bullet," for instance, seems to speak to white America but right in the center of the chart is the persistent point that Black Nationalism is a worldwide

Idea Chart of the Ballot or the Bullet

We will use violence to ensure our human rights if they are not granted within the establishment

The U.S. is the enemy											Black Muslim philosophy dictates violence if necessary								
U.S. government conspiracy has denied blacks citizenship rights									World-wide solutions preserve human rights		Goal of Black Nationalism is control							Solution of Black Nationalism	
Blacks are not American			Southern Democrats' con game		Voting rights denied		U.S. society has denied blacks human rights		Human rights a world issue		Philosophy of Black Muslims			Practicality of Black Nationalism				Violence as a reaction	
Time has run out	Blacks built Am.	Johnson administration	Dixiecrats	Seniority	South denies voting rights	Northern gerrymandering	New strategy	Grievances	World issue	Guerrilla war	Political	Economic	Social	White gospel Graham	Black Nat party	Work with anyone	Segregation means lack of control	Not aggressive	Violence if necessary
5-6	7-10	11-12	13-14	15-16	17-19	20-21	22-24	25-30	31-38	39-40	41-42	43-44	45-46	47-48	49-50	51-52	53-54	55-57	58-59

solution to the problem of human rights. Is that just a way of increasing the credibility of an American movement? Does it signal a move to a broader stage of argument? Does it mean that the United States will have to fight a worldwide battle if it does not ensure human rights at home?

Such an examination of thematic structure may point to the unity or disunity of a text. It may identify where values, metaphors, personal references, or the like are concentrated. It should reveal the structure and the central theme of the text. This is particularly useful when the stated and the actual themes are quite different.

These then are some of the principles for analyzing a text. They apply to the analysis of single texts and large bodies of data. They will be more informally observed by some critics than by others. A critic must keep in mind that data are not assembled just "because they are there" but in order to make some interpretation or judgment about the communication situation. The critic uses standards outside the text to influence what is counted. The words, phrases, and sentences that are isolated are only indicators of the conditions the critic is after. The data assembled need some further basis of comparison. Determining the thematic structure can assist in cases where the objective of criticism calls for it. In all cases, however, careful data analysis must produce interpretations.

INTERPRETATION

Communication criticism must make an argument that will establish its critical claim as more probable than other possible competing claims. This point implies, of course, that several possible claims could be made about a particular communication event. This does not mean, however, that all claims are equally useful or carefully arrived at. Even the most relativistic critic does not argue that any claim is as good as any other. How, then, do we differentiate those critical claims that are carefully developed from those that amount to little more than personal taste?

We determine the more carefully developed critical claim by the argument that supports it and, specifically, by the grounds of textual and situational data assembled to support the claim. The number of interpretations that can be defended will be limited and their plausibility will be enhanced by the case with which the text is explicated.

Finding an interpretation all parties would accept remains an ideal, if unlikely, obtainable objective—because there are two sets of standards for judging the quality of an interpretation. One set is general standards appropriate to all criticism; the other is a set of more specific standards determined by the particular critical approach taken. Therefore, a single most probable interpretation would be agreed to only among critics who shared both general and specific standards. What we can hope for, however, is an interpretation that can be understood and appreciated for its carefulness by critics of different points of view.

The analysis should permit even a critic who is committed to an alternate approach to appreciate the care with which that other approach was developed. Readers may not accept the assumptions of Marxist ideological criticism but they should see the difference between a simple-minded Marxist analysis and one that is careful and rich in interpretation.

General standards can be used to separate a careful analysis from a sloppy analysis regardless of approach. But to choose a formal analysis over a mythic analysis involves choosing one set of assumptions and procedures over another. Because Chapters 3 through 10 review the specific approaches, at this point we will deal only briefly with specific standards of textual interpretation and then look in more detail at general standards.

Specific Standards of Textual Interpretation

No matter how much critics may be devoted to their particular approach, they must acknowledge that no perspective is assumption free. Ideological critics believe that all criticism reflects a point of view toward the political condition of the society; even some critics who cannot be identified as ideological accept this notion in part. When arguing for historically based norms, E. D. Hirsch, Jr. (1982), who believes in the "objective interpretation" of literature, agrees that the interpretation is governed by the particular "cypher key" with which a critic chooses to associate (239). Thus, each approach has assumptions that serve as organizing principles. Assumptions guide the selection of useful data, and any careful interpretation will be expected to explicate them as grounds for an interpretive critical claim.

Accurate interpretation, for instance, assumes that there is some standard of accuracy against which a message can be assessed. In this case, the critic has a standard of accuracy that is applied to the message. The critic will sometimes see accuracy as the center of an ethical evaluation. The critic may also understand ethical standards as universal, religious, or societal. Nonetheless, there is an organizing principle in the concept of "accuracy." Here, then, the data most often examined are statements of fact. For instance, Jean-Luc Renaud (1985) has documented how Kent Cooper, Associated Press (AP) general manager from 1925 to 1948, used the U.S. Department of State to help the Associated Press expand globally at the same time that AP publicly opposed government intervention in the press. Thus, Renaud had data that showed Cooper acted in ways inconsistent with his stated position.

Neoclassical criticism is, because of its interest in persuasion, message-environment centered. The message must be interpreted as a series of arguments designed to have an effect on an audience. Therefore, neoclassical critics focus primarily on the components of the arguments: evidence, reasoning, values, credibility, style, and delivery.

For example, Rebecca S. Bjork (1988) concentrates on reasoning and values to show how Ronald Reagan effectively disarmed the nuclear freeze movement when, in his address to Congress on March 23, 1983, he introduced his plan for the Strategic Defense Initiative (SDI). SDI, Reagan argued, would not just limit nuclear weapons; it would develop a "leakproof population defense for the United States." Eventually, both the United States and the Soviet Union could have such a plan: "A global nuclear shield would reduce the risks associated with nuclear proliferation and accidental launches, while a freeze proposal does nothing to address these risks." By using this argument Reagan took the "moral high ground" away from the movement and attached it to his administration (189–190). As you can see, Bjork equates Reagan's persuasiveness with his reasoning. Her choice of an emphasis on persuasiveness and reason identifies her neoclassical assumptions.

In subsequent chapters each approach to criticism will be shown to have assumptions that dictate what data will provide the best interpretation. Each of these approaches makes different assumptions about what extratextual material (e.g., the immediate audience, the society in general, a prevalent ideology, the author) is most relevant in deciding which parts of the text are most important.

General Standards of Textual Analysis

The general standards for making a good critical argument are not much different from those necessary to construct any argument. As noted in Chapter 1, the critical claim must be useful and the argument supporting it must be carefully developed. The standards of carefulness examined here are language norms, consistency, generic appropriateness, and coherence.

Language Norms.   A good interpretation of a text must not violate the public norms of the language. Because such a rule permits considerable variation in possible interpretations, it includes that which might be literally and figuratively interpreted. This rule is also tempered by the realization that public use of the language changes. Our ancestors were not engaging in a version of puritan free love on houseboats when in the "Fundamental Orders of Connecticut" (1639) they said, "We . . . are now cohabiting and dwelling in and upon the River Conectecotte." So a legitimate interpretation of language has to be based on the meaning of words, but in their time, place, and circumstance.

Here is an example of close textual analysis by Hermann Stelzner (1966) that illustrates how a critic can interpret language norms. It is part of a criticism of Franklin D. Roosevelt's December 8, 1941 "Declaration of War against Japan." The interpretation quoted here is about the "last night" series in the section of the speech where Roosevelt said:

> Yesterday the Japanese Government also launched an attack against Malaya.
>> Last night Japanese forces attacked Hong Kong.
>> Last night Japanese forces attacked Guam.
>> Last night Japanese forces attacked the Philippine Islands.
>> Last night the Japanese attacked Wake Island.
>> And this morning the Japanese attacked Midway Island.
>
> Japan has, therefore, undertaken a surprise offensive extending throughout the Pacific area. The facts of yesterday and today speak for themselves. The people of the United States have already formed their opinions and well understand the implications to the very life and safety of our nation.

Stelzner's (1966) analysis of this short section of a short speech uses norms of language to explain what is happening and connects it to what Roosevelt said earlier and would say later in the speech.

> The "last night" series . . . supports the pace and quality of the attacks. Logically, last night, a part of yesterday, is illogical. The compressed "last nights," figuratively ticking off the clock, bring yesterday to a climactic end. The three "yesterdays" . . . spanned time and space: the night and the events in the night move faster. Simple declarative sentences present facts—actor, action, acted upon. The lengthy iteration is necessary to establish the magnitude of the Japanese thrust. However, had it been extended by the addition of only a few details, it would have been compromised, having its force, pace, and energy enervated. Finally, the verb "launched" more than attacks; it launched a series of sentences which structurally (i.e.: in form) harmonize with the acts embedded in them. The actions (i.e.: their substance) and the manner of describing them (form) are one. The syntax is itself symbolic of the fast moving military operations.
>
> The connotations from the cluster of "last nights" do more than support the emotional responses rising from "in the quiet of the night when all were abed and defenseless." The cluster is the turning point in a chain of emotive phrases. Prior to the "last night" series, descriptions are relatively mild and basically denotative: "suddenly and deliberately" . . ., "deliberately planned" . . ., "deliberately sought to deceive" . . ., and "false statements." . . . Following the cluster and supported by it is a chain of increasingly stronger phrases: a mild "surprise offensive" . . ., a slightly stronger "premeditated invasion" . . ., the strong "this form of treachery" . . ., and the vehement "unprovoked and dastardly" (429).

You can see here how all of Stelzner's points of analysis are based on norms of language. Specifically, he deals with what words will set a formal tone, when and how that changes to the less formal, but not the completely informal language of the streets. Pace is examined, number of details, the use of simple declarative sentences, connotations, and so forth. All are based on what the norms of language reveal. Because Stelzner chose to do a close word-by-word textual analysis of a relatively short speech, he was able to look in a detailed way at words, syntax, and figures, and to relate them to the communication situation.

For many texts, such tight analysis will not be necessary. Indeed, such analysis may not be possible because of the extensiveness of the text. But at particular points of emphasis it will be essential to look with care at specific passages. Furthermore, even when examining more extensive texts the interpretations made should be linked to the norms of the language whether to show representativeness or uniqueness.

Consistency.   A second general principle of textual interpretation is consistency. Perhaps the most powerful basis for rejecting any argument is inconsistency. Inconsistency means that the critic has advanced opposing claims, a far more serious error than missing evidence or than a misstep in reasoning. To be convincing, critical interpretation must be internally consistent; that is, what is affirmed in one part of the interpretation cannot be disconfirmed in another. For example, if a critic praises a docudrama for its accuracy, that same critic should not claim that the docudrama presents a character more interestingly than he or she was in real life. Similarly, to see a particular poem as ironic and then analyze parts of it literally can lead to the charge of inconsistency.

Inconsistency need not be a characteristic only of the text itself. If the critic's audience perceives that the criticism is inconsistent with what the audience knows to be true or factual, then that inconsistency must be clarified. Any perceived inconsistency will damage the credibility of the critic and, therefore, it is necessary to show the audience that what seems inconsistent is, on another level perhaps, quite consistent.

Generic Appropriateness.   Generic form is a context of any text. Certain classes of text will be defined as a genre because they follow the same conventions of "outer form (specific metre or structure) and inner form (attitude, tone, purpose—more crudely, subject and audience)" (Welleck and Warren 1970, 231). Thus, a critic cannot interpret a casual conversation with all of its loose syntax, fragmented sentences, and colloquial expressions as if it were a polished essay. Nor could a critic expect an article in a journal of experimental psychology to read like a detective novel.

The existence of genre provides the critic and the critic's audience with expectations that certain conventions will be followed. To expect that a message in one genre will have the characteristics of another genre is unfair and inconsistent. The objection that a particular soap opera on televi-

The end of an ERA

sion is not like a Broadway play is to question the value of that genre (soap operas), not the particular one studied.

Martin J. Medhurst and Michael A. DeSousa (1981) examined 749 political cartoons of the 1980 presidential campaign and identified what they called "six stylistic choices" that define what is available in that genre: "the *use of line and form*," "the *relative size of objects*," "the *exaggeration or amplification of physiognomical features*," "*placement* within the frame," "*relation of text*" ". . . to visual imagery, and rhythmic montage." The following is their interpretation of a Paul Conrad cartoon about President Ronald Reagan's objection to the Equal Rights Amendment.

These six stylistic choices offer cartoonists a wide range of tools with which to fashion their rhetorical invitations to the reader. Conrad, for example, often employs a wide, dark pen stroke to lend ominous tones to his political caricatures. [In "The end of an ERA"] he uses contrasts of line and form to convey his visual invitation to perceive Reagan in a certain way. There is the contrast of light (Reagan) and dark (shadow of elephant); the contrast of visual planes; and the contrast of graphic directions. Reagan as elephant immediately attracts the viewer's eye, but it is only as one compares Reagan to the shadow that one realizes the view offered is from the rear of the beast. Immediately the eyes return to the vertical plane where Reagan is seen peering backwards with two feet protruding from his mouth. There is the contrast of visual directions which emerges only as the reader's eyes decipher the internal rhythms of the form. Line is used to fashion the leather hide of the elephant which doubles as the facial wrinkles of an aging candidate. Not only does Reagan look to the past, he is a relic of it (212–213).

Sometimes the conventions of a genre are broken to provide a unique communication situation. Daniel Webster, the great New England orator, was regarded as a traitor by the antislavery advocates of New England when he supported the Compromise of 1850 with his speech of March 7. They regarded it as a sellout to the South, particularly because it called for the enforcement of the fugitive slave law. Henry Wadsworth Longfellow's poem "Ichabod" is a satire on the fallen "god-like Daniel." When Webster died two years later, Theodore Parker (1960) delivered a "eulogy" in the Second Unitarian Church of Boston that detailed the life of Daniel Webster, including an incredible climax that violates the conventions of the eulogy genre by attacking Webster for his actions.

Parker spoke of the greatness of Daniel Webster, probably the most revered man in New England, but he interlaced it with statements such as this:

> After the 7th of March, Mr. Webster became the ally of the worst of men, the forefront of kidnapping. The orator of Plymouth Rock was the advocate of slavery; the hero of Bunker Hill put chains around Boston Court House; the applauder of Adams and Jefferson was a tool of the slaveholder, and a keeper of slavery's dogs, the associate of the kidnapper, and the mocker of men who loved the right. Two years he lived with that rabble-rout for company, his name the boast of every vilest thing (244–245).

It is not just an attack; it is a masterful and awful analysis. The convention of not speaking ill of the dead is violated. But, the idea that there is a genre of the eulogy defined by a series of conventions is essential to the analysis of Parker's speech presented here. So, generic conventions are not always standards of judgment but they do help us to understand a text if only as a basis of the relationship of the unique text to the genre.

Coherence.   Coherence is a final general rule of interpretation. The interpretation or judgment of a text in its communication situation should "make sense." That is, all the subinterpretations should cohere in the claim being made. Although a multitude of interpretations can be made about any text, some observations will fit norms of language, be consistent and generically appropriate, and still not contribute to a coherent statement of a critical claim. In such a case, the observation should be deleted, for it only will draw a reader's attention away from the central claim.

In Chapter 1, we discussed what would seem to be such a case. Michael McGee (1984b) examined three interpretations to understand the Christian Fundamentalist's use of Judges 19–21. The first of these was an accurate interpretation that seemed to say that the events in Israel were irrational. The second looks past the events to the narrators of the story which ends dialectically with the interpretation that there is no authority in the land. This leads to an understanding of how Jerry Falwell could see in the Old Testament story a persuasive parallel to today when there is "no king in Israel." That is, divorce, homosexuality, drugs, pornography, and a host of other perceived moral evils make modern America as irrational as ancient Israel. Thus, three quite different interpretations come together; they have coherence. All are needed to make McGee's point.

Roderick P. Hart examined the nature of the American use of religion in his 1977 book *The Political Pulpit,* and showed how the seemingly inconsistent use of both separation of church and state and public religious statements and acts works in our society. This use has coherence, he argues, because in this country political religion is "safely ensconced in the realm of symbolic reality":

> Oh, yes, they will allow their preachers and politicians to talk about *the* national consensus, about *the* American ideal, and about *the* God-be-holdin'* American people; *but they will not easily forget, it seems to me, that all of this is talk.* Because it is talk, the American people can revel in it, carp at it, demand new versions of it, glorify it, dismiss it. But should some far-sighted prelate or politician fail to notice the fine print imbedded in the civil-religious contract and to misperceive its rhetorical nature, the American people will come a-marching (106).

These four general standards of interpretation—language norms, consistency, generic appropriateness, and coherence—are used to build the critical claim that a text is representative or unique. With these standards and the specific standards of the approach used in interpretation, the way is provided for making defensible judgments.

JUDGMENT

Like interpretation, standards of judgment are external to the actual text being examined. They are the product of the assumptions of the individual approaches to communication. However, as observed in Chapter 1,

conscious judgment is not necessary; a critic may choose to stop at interpretation. Nonetheless, for most critics, judgment is an important, virtually essential, part of the critical process. Judgment answers the "So
what?" question that ought to be asked of any piece of criticism. For many
critics, the following provides information on which a criticism could be
based although serving no critical purpose itself:

> A frequency count of the new and repeated docudrama quarter-hours,
> types 1 through 6 as defined in this analysis, clearly indicates a substantial
> growth of such programming on the commercial networks and public TV
> stations in the 12 television seasons, 1966–67 through 1977–78. But follow-
> ing the 1976–77 season there was a two-season down trend in the docu-
> drama quarter-hours except for NBC which substantially increased such
> programming by the 1977–78 TV season. The peak of docudrama pro-
> gramming from all four major "national" sources was the 1975–76 TV sea-
> son (Hoffer and Nelson 1980, 161).

The argument would follow that this conclusion gives information and limited interpretations useful to someone interested in the writers' purpose,
which was to explain a television trend, but it does not develop a significant critical claim of interest to readers of criticism. It is a quantitative, not
a critical, study.

   On the other hand, a study of crime on prime-time television between
1976 and 1981 used police statistics as an outside basis of comparison to
show that television overemphasizes violent crime such as robbery, as-
sault, and murder (as opposed to property crime) and overemphasizes
women and middle-class white victims. The authors also speculate that
such programming tends to increase viewer fear (Estep and Macdonald
1963). Recognizing that there is considerable argument about television's
effects, this study still provides a useful example of how judgments are
drawn. First, the interpretations are developed by contrasting the text with
an outside source—police statistics. A judgment is made (based on an interpretation of human nature) about what such programming does to audiences. Implied, but not stated, is an objection to inaccuracy and its possible
effects.

   This study involves at least two of the four possible areas of judgment.
It says that television crime shows are *inaccurate* and that they have the
effect of increasing viewer fear. Another kind of analysis would be necessary to make judgments about the *quality* of such programs—perhaps a
comparison to the aesthetic qualities of other genres. But, the study could
be part of an analysis of the *social role* of such shows. Even if inaccurate,
the television's portrayal of our society as one where violent crime against
women and middle-class whites is the norm might be seen as creating a
view in keeping with the natural biases of predominantly middle-class
America.

This chapter has emphasized the process and standards for analyzing communication situations and the texts embedded in them. Such analysis establishes grounds for interpretation and judgment of messages. The chapter has focused necessarily on general standards such as language norms, consistency, generic appropriateness, and coherence. The specific standards for textual analysis are rooted in the assumptions and procedures of the specialized approaches to criticism that are discussed in the next eight chapters.

CHAPTER THREE

Accurate Interpretation
Verifying Representation and Interpretation

Sergeant Christine Cagney on the television series *Cagney & Lacey* gets up quickly from watching a television police show. She stomps out of the room saying, "Those guys draw their guns more in one hour than I do in a week." With that statement she is not only an officer of New York's finest, she is a critic: an accurate interpretation critic. As such, she represents what is probably the most prevalent approach to criticism by amateur and professional alike.

The accurate interpretation approach to criticism is one of three which, taken together, are the oldest and predominant approaches to criticism. Until quite recently, they were virtually the only critical approaches to criticism. These three, accurate interpretation (Chapter 3), formal (Chapter 4), and neoclassical criticism (Chapter 5), represent a group that has been called "common sense" criticism (Belsey 1980, 2). They all begin with the assumption that the ordinary person with some essential knowledge can apply common sense to a text to depict its problems or virtues. The five chapters that follow the three just mentioned explain critical approaches that find common sense inadequate. They require that the critic deconstruct the text with knowledge of a special kind, such as the nature of social myth making, psychoanalytic interpretations of the human mind, or Marxist social theory.

No superiority of one over the other is suggested by listing them in this order. However, common sense criticism is the older and more pervasive. As such, much of deconstructive criticism draws from or reacts to the procedures of common sense forms. Therefore, in this chapter we will concentrate on common sense approaches, specifically the most basic of all: accurate interpretation. Sergeant Cagney says that real police work is not like what is portrayed on television. A social activist objects to cigarette advertisements because they glamorize a bad habit and ignore health and social consequences. A politician is criticized for making false and misleading statements about an opponent's record. In all these examples, and more, someone judges a text on whether it is an accurate representation of a situation.

WHAT IS ACCURATE INTERPRETATION?

These simple examples of criticism turn on the assumption that there is truth and it can be known. In the Bible this idea is stated, "Ye shall know the truth and the truth shall make you free" (John 8:32). Words such as *truth, fact, know, accurate,* and *objective* are the hallmarks of such criticism.

Although problems do arise with this approach—to be discussed later in the chapter—there is much to recommend it. Common experience and education provide people with a basis for behaving and thinking truthfully. If people are asked to abandon the idea that there are truths and facts that can be known, they seem to be asked to abandon all standards.

THE ACCURATE INTERPRETATION CRITIC

E. D. Hirsch, Jr. (1960) makes the argument to literary critics that a text must have a meaning of its own:

> The critic is right to think that the text should speak to *us*. The point which needs to be grasped clearly by the critic is that a text cannot be made to speak to us until what it says has been understood. . . . The text is first of all a conventional representation like a musical score, and what the score represents may be construed correctly or incorrectly. . . . If criticism is to be objective in any significant sense, it must be founded on a self-critical construction of textual meaning, which is to say, an objective interpretation (463).

The ability to interpret the meaning of a text accurately requires some objective understanding of its meaning. The words had to have some meaning to the author. Understanding meaning precedes interpretation, according to this point of view.

Similarly, any comment about the world has to be based on some understanding of objective reality. Think of all the things people live by and take for granted, assume to be true, or have learned are true. Isn't the United States in North America? Isn't water H_2O? Wasn't Abraham Lincoln president of the United States during the Civil War? Doesn't orange juice contain vitamin C? Won't the principle of gravity prevent objects from falling upward? There are multitudes of facts and truths that are acknowledged every day in words and behavior. It seems perfectly reasonable, therefore, to say that a text may be judged by common sense knowledge. If someone said that Abraham Lincoln was the president during the Vietnam War, that person would be judged as wrong—inaccurate.

Journalists frequently charged Ronald Reagan with inaccurate statements. "When he accepted his party's nomination in 1984," said Michael Wines (1984), "President Reagan told an ecstatic Republican National Convention that he had tightened the federal budget, vastly boosted middle class spending power and stopped poverty's growth almost dead in its tracks. . . . In what has become a tradition after the President's public statements, Administration critics charged that Reagan has juggled statistical truth. . . . Indeed, one critic, former Carter Administration economist Alfred E. Kahn, called some of the statements 'fraudulent' "(4). Obviously, the American people were judging Reagan by other standards because he was a very popular president. Nonetheless, we can see clearly the implications. A leader's credibility is challenged by the charge that he or she does not know, or distorts, the facts.

Journalists provided much of the criticism of President Reagan's statements, and that was appropriate because for journalists, accuracy is an essential standard. Not all journalists have followed the standard, but accuracy is dominant in both its professional standards and academic criticism. All journalists' codes of ethics begin with statements such as that found in the 1985 Associated Press Managing Editors (APME) code: "A good newspaper is fair, accurate, honest, responsible and decent. Truth is its guiding principle." A review of several years of *Journalism Quarterly*, the field's principal academic journal, reveals that most articles, whether descriptive, legal, or historical (the journal's principal orientations), are tied to the tradition of seeking out an accurate picture of what journalism is or has been.

Sometimes in historical analysis accuracy is used to question a previous interpretation. Ted Curtis Smythe (1980) examined the role of newspaper reporters from 1880 to 1900 for the influence they had on the news. Smythe did so to evaluate earlier interpretations of others for their accuracy:

> Yet the particular role of reporters during this period remains ill-defined, fuzzy. What contributions, if any, did reporters make to the news? Were they the linchpins of journalism, who influenced the news values of the day? Richard Hofstadter claimed they "brought to the journalistic life some of the ideals, the larger interests, and the sense of public responsibility of men of culture." Did their increasing status and glamour indicate that "The reporter had come into his own?" Or were they but menial factotums, commanded hither and thither at the whim of editor and publisher, with few rights and little standing except among peers? Were they nothing but clerks? Edwin Shuman claimed that the newspaper was like the department store. The publisher offered what the readers wanted, just as a merchant gave his customers calico if they wanted it instead of silk. The reporter," Shuman concluded, "must hand the goods over the counter." Which was the reality, which the myth? Or were both correct? (1).

This example from journalism history points to a broader observation that much historical writing, not just journalism history, aims at accurate

interpretation. We must remember that much of modern historical scholarship has its origins in the nineteenth century when the German historian,
Leopold von Ranke, led in the development of the theory of scientific history. This historian based his theory on the principle "let the facts speak
for themselves." This is an extreme statement, seeming to rule out any
interpretation; even von Ranke did not follow it slavishly (Smith 1966, 10).
Most subsequent historians have adopted some sort of a compromise between von Ranke's statement and Carl Becker's (1932): "Left to themselves
the facts do not speak; left to themselves they do not exist, not really, since
for all practical purposes there is no fact until someone affirms it" (233).

That compromise, for most historians, has preserved the accurate interpretation orientation. David Hackett Fischer's (1970) book on historical
method, *Historian's Fallacies,* emphasizes such matters as "factual verification," "factual significance," "semantical distortion," and "substantive
distraction." Journalists, some literary critics, and most amateur critics
have plenty of company here from historians in their emphasis on accurate
interpretation.

What has been called semantic criticism is also a variation of the accuracy approach. Although not popular currently, several years ago semantic
criticism was enthusiastically endorsed by many as *the* way to do communication criticism. In addition, its parent, general semantics, based on the
writings of Alfred Korzybski, S. I. Hayakawa, Wendell Johnson, Irving J.
Lee, and others, has influenced many critics who do not consider themselves general semanticists but have assimilated its point of view. For example, John Merrill (1981) calls his criticism of the Society of Professional
Journalists' Code of Ethics "a semantic analysis."

General semantics began with Alfred Korzybski's attempt to find a scientific language for a scientific age. Such a language, he argued, has to be
built on a structure similar to science; it has to be built on experiential facts.
Such a system seeks to identify what is real as opposed to mental. Since
"we cannot express the fullness of things, or even of one thing, in verbal
symbols," we need to find a way to explain the relationships among them
(Fogarty 1959, 98).

A significant part of understanding relationships is to understand how
people abstract through language. S. I. Hayakawa (1949) developed a "ladder of abstraction" by which we ascend from the thing to more abstract
statements. The example Hayakawa pesented was the perceived "cow"/
"Bessie"/"cow"/"livestock"/"farm assets"/"asset"/ "wealth"/ladder. Each
step on the ladder is more abstract and applies to fewer and fewer cows.
Human beings need to be conscious of this abstracting and not confuse the
levels ("Bessie" is not "wealth" if she is an old barren cow) (169).

This theoretical understanding of language problems leads to a number of principles, all variations on the standards of accurate interpretation.
Recall that the objective here is to move as close as possible to something
that approximates experiential fact. As a result, inexact language is approved of only when all or most people recognize the meaning suggested

or implied, for instance, such factually untrue statements as "the sun rises in the east." But, the communicator should, as a general rule, define a word by pointing down the abstraction ladder to a more concrete object rather than up, develop the habit of using terms that express reality as infinite and complex, index ("cow 1 is not cow 2"), use quotation marks (She is a "pretty" girl) to identify opinion, and use "etc." to show that there is more to reality than the language communicates (Fogarty 1959, 108–115).

This is a simplified statement of the general semantic position. Nonetheless, it is important to point out that although general semantic critics may see the language problem in a somewhat different way than journalists, literary textual critics, or historians, they have a similar objective—searching for a way to be as accurate as possible—and they criticize others who use language that distracts from maximum accuracy.

Another observation may be made about accurate interpretation. It is so deeply rooted in data as a base for an interpretation about accuracy and it is so clearly dependent on a traditional understanding of science that the steps—analysis, interpretation, and judgment, in that order—make perfect sense. Elise Parsigian (1987) suggests that a study of journalists shows that they claim to follow a social science analytic pattern. In many ways, then, the easiest kind of criticism stems from the critic's own knowledge. If critics follow the assumptions of accurate interpretation, knowledge and common sense are all they need.

To certain literary criticism which operates on the basis of objective interpretation can be added much historical analysis, general semantic criticism, and virtually all standards of professional journalism. Thus, accurate interpretation is a powerful approach to communication criticism. It also is the basis of much of today's ethical criticism.

ACCURATE INTERPRETATION AS ETHICS

It is easy to see how accurate interpretation becomes an ethical standard. Lying, fabricating evidence, distortion, and failure to report facts are all part of the Western ethical system that originated in numerous Judeo-Christian injunctions. "Thou shalt not bear false witness against thy neighbor" is one of the Ten Commandments and it speaks directly to those who prize accuracy as a communication objective. For journalism, the standards of accuracy are written in professional codes of ethics. One such code, the Society of Professional Journalists' (SPJ) Code of Ethics, is discussed in some detail later in this chapter.

Journalists are not alone in their use of accurate interpretation as a basis for ethical judgment. For instance, Karlyn Kohrs Campbell (1977), a critic from the rhetorical tradition, uses one of the three standards for differentiating good from poor criticism by stating, it "makes a contribution to the ongoing dialogue about the role of persuasive discourse in humane society. It deals with ethical and moral questions and gives the reader a glimpse of an 'ideal' rhetoric" (22). Campbell's ethical criticism can be found in her analysis (1972b) of a speech by President Richard Nixon on the Vietnam War, November 3, 1969.

At the time there was considerable controversy in the United States over continued American involvement in the Vietnam War. America was sustaining many casualties and protests were increasing on college campuses and within the general public. President Nixon went on national television to argue for his policy of Vietnamization: strengthening of loyal Vietnam forces, gradual withdrawal of American troops, and a search for a peaceful solution.

The president, Campbell (1972b) notes, ignored the actual positions of opposition spokespersons, who offered a variety of proposals, and instead positioned the choice he offered between himself and that of "a small minority of the peace movement [that] supported immediate, total withdrawal." She quotes Nixon:

> I am sure that you can recognize from what I have said that we have only two choices open to us if we want to end the war. I can order an immediate precipitate withdrawal of all Americans from Vietnam without regard to the effects of that action. Or we can persist in our search for a just peace through . . . Vietnamization.

"The misrepresentation of his opposition," Campbell argues, "makes the only apparent alternative to his policy as unattractive and radical as possible. This strategy may gull the audience, and it may make his speech more persuasive for some listeners, but the technique violates his earlier promise to tell the truth" (51).

In one sense all criticism is ethical if it makes a judgment about the worth of a text because it implies or states a judgment about the worth of the source that produced the text. But the ethical judgment referred to here is conscious and based on principles embedded in society about the ethical and moral quality of the source(s) of a text. And that kind of ethical judgment is an almost necessary component of accurate interpretation criticism. When we ask a speaker, journalist, historian, or a classmate to enlighten us and not deceive us, we are using a standard embedded in our ethical system and any judgment that we have been deceived is going to be read as an ethical judgment.

Contrast that with formal criticism (Chapter 4), which judges aesthetic beauty. An assessment that a play is badly structured or that a character is unrealistic may be an ethical judgment, particularly if the playwright sets out to create an unrealistic image of the world that would distort the viewer's understanding. But it is not automatically so. We do not charge people with being unethical simply because they cannot write well. Similarly, criticizing a text for its failure to persuade (Chapter 5) is based on judgments about the effectiveness of a message on an audience. Surely we could make an ethical judgment about a docudrama that convinced but misled an audience about a period in history. But we do not have to make an ethical judgment to claim that a message was or was not effective. An ineffective public speaker may be the object of our pity but not our ethical judgment. One might even argue that an ineffective communicator will seldom be charged with lacking ethics on a loose variation of the professional basketball axiom, "no harm, no foul."

Accurate interpretation is the only critical approach among the three commonsense approaches that has an ethical standard built into it. When critics operating from formal or persuasive critical standards make ethical judgments, they almost invariably use standards of accurate interpretation.

One kind of ethical criticism is unique, however. The judgments at its center originate in specialized ethical standards usually associated with religious or political groups, for example, Accuracy in Media (AIM). AIM is a politically conservative group that is "dedicated to promoting accuracy and fairness in news reporting by the major media." It investigates "complaints of media error, distortion and bias, and exposes them." Its most famous piece of criticism was the television documentary *Vietnam: The Real Story* narrated by Charlton Heston. It was aired on the Public Broadcasting System and designed to correct what AIM called "many of the serious errors and distortions in the PBS series *Vietnam: A Television History*" (Zeidenberg). Fairness and Accuracy in Reporting (FAIR) is AIM's liberal counterpart.

Note their names. The standards they most admire are accuracy and fairness. It is clear also from their statements that truth and freedom are elements of their standards. One may not agree with their application of those standards, as one may not agree with Professor Campbell's or other critics' applications. Just the same, accurate interpretation is the basis of their ethical judgments.

Religious ethical critics probably use the most specialized application of accuracy, and they still see their criticism as common sense. These critics differ from the secular accurate interpretation critics because, to them, the natural condition comes from God and is grounded in a text such as the Bible.

In August of 1988 a considerable storm was raised over Martin Scorsese's film version of Nikas Kazantzakis's novel *The Last Temptation of Christ*. Fundamentalist Christians picketed theaters and several theater chains agreed not to show the film. Most complaints focused on the last half hour of the film when a dying Jesus is visited by an Angel of Satan, who offers him the life of a human. Before rejecting it Jesus fantasizes two marriages and committing adultery. The fundamentalists' complaints are clearly focused on principles of accuracy. Said Jerry Falwell, "Neither the label 'fiction' nor the First Amendment gives Universal the right to libel, slander and ridicule the most central figure in world history" (Michaels and Willwerth 1988, 34). Such criticism is a variation on accuracy but its emphasis is on how the media distort the human potential.

Accurate interpretation criticism, therefore, is that criticism that seeks to judge a text and its sources by how well they conform to the facts. It is probably the most common approach to criticism being used by many different professional groups. In many cases it has a strong ethical component. Let us examine its assumptions more carefully.

THE ASSUMPTIONS OF ACCURATE INTERPRETATION

No critical system is assumption-free, and even though the standards of accurate interpretation are seen by their users as natural they are based on debatable assumptions. Accurate interpretation critics are influenced by assumptions they possess about how nature, human beings, and communication function. The following discussion identifies four assumptions that establish the foundation on which accurate interpretation is built.

Human Beings Are Essentially Reasonable

Humans are capable, through common sense, of understanding the difference between what is true and what is false. Because humans can reason, they can see errors in their own and in others' interpretations. This is not to imply that human reasoning is error-free. Bias may interfere with good judgment, and one's own advantage may color a judgment, but even the biased person is capable of rising above weakness and compensating for such bias. The critic's role is to identify errors and make public what errors of fact or reasoning appear in a message.

Reality Is External to Humans

Reality exists whether it is the product of God's actions or natural law. Reality is something that people cannot change although they may interpret it differently. Just as water is H_2O, something to float a boat on, or a life-giving liquid, so anything can be used differently by different people. But that does not, according to this assumption, change its fundamental nature. The evidence of this assumption in accurate interpretation criticism is in the most important words, mentioned earlier, that characterize it: *truth, fact, know, objective* and the word chosen here to represent the approach, *accurate*. All these words imply in their common sense meanings that there is an objective reality to be known and used to judge the accuracy of a text.

This assumption has a special application for certain literary critics who extend it to texts themselves. That is, the texts, Shakespeare's history plays, for instance, do not reflect historical events. But, while not historically accurate, a literary text, for critics such as E. D. Hirsch, Jr., has a meaning of its own. The critic then searches for this accurate interpretation of the text. Thus, for many accurate interpretation critics, reality is outside the text. For some critics, however, reality is in the text, integral with its content, style, and context, and is a natural precondition of any interpretation.

The Best Interpretation of Reality Is Systematic

If humans reason about how a message interprets reality, then humans must do so in a reasonable way via systematic observation.

Those persons who use this approach follow specific rules to guide their observations, and, therefore, to be more accurate. Journalists, for instance, look for two sources for a story so that one can confirm the other. Historians traditionally have followed a series of rules that they believe will result in greater accuracy; for instance, preference for documentary over oral evidence, witnesses or participants over persons with hearsay knowledge, and primary over secondary sources.

Its antithesis, the process to be shunned, is where a critic "leaps to conclusions," "substitutes personal opinion for facts," and "doesn't study the problem carefully." Such phrases and more represent the negative side of careful observational analysis. For the accurate interpretation critic, observational analysis is a given and following a whim or personal bias destroys reasonableness and fails to produce conclusions that conform to the natural condition.

There Can Be a Clear Separation of Fact and Opinion

The three assumptions already discussed point directly to another—the separation of fact from opinion, of textual meaning from textual interpretation. It is basic to the journalistic rule that newspaper stories should report the facts, and opinions should be confined to the editorial pages. The *Los Angeles Times* editorial section is called "Opinion," leading the reader to believe that the remainder of the paper tries, at least, to stick to the facts. One of the most serious charges that can be made against a newspaper is that it does not confine its opinions to the editorial page.

These four assumptions combine to set the bases for accurate interpretation as a critical approach. They should be kept in mind as we look at the standards by which accurate interpretation works.

STANDARDS OF ACCURATE INTERPRETATION

As noted earlier, accurate interpretation finds some of its strongest adherents among academic and professional journalists who also have done the most to codify its standards. There are many such codes, including the previously mentioned Associated Press Code, the Statement of Principles of the American Society of Newspaper Editors, and the Radio-Television News Directors Association Code of Broadcast News Ethics. Probably the most developed and well-known is the Society of Professional Journalists' Code of Ethics, first adopted in 1926 and revised in 1973, 1984, and 1987. It serves as a primary example of the standards of accurate interpretation. Even John Merrill (1981), its most aggressive critic, uses the standards of accurate interpretation to criticize the code, showing that it is inaccurate when it claims a "constitutional role to seek the truth," which Merrill says does not exist in the Constitution or the Bill of Rights (12).

The ethics section of the code is a collection of specific actions that journalists are expected to take in particular situations. With that section set aside, a few minor changes in wording such as substituting "freedom of the press, speech, and expression" for "freedom of the press" would make the SPJ Code applicable to all communication situations. As such, it provides us with six principles that are found in all the codes and can be used by the critic as standards for accurate interpretation: being truthful, communicating information, maintaining objectivity, treating others fairly, supporting freedom, and accepting responsibility. Let us look briefly at each of these.

Being Truthful

Following the assumption that reality is exterior to humans is the concept that such reality can be encapsulated in an accurate statement. It may be worth noting here that in the specialized language of scholars there is a difference between facts and truths: "The term 'facts' is generally used to designate objects of precise, limited agreement [water is H_2O] whereas the term 'truths' is preferably applied to more complex systems relating to connections between facts. They may be scientific theories or philosophic or religious conceptions that transcend experience [the principle of gravity]" (Perelman and Olbrechts-Tyteca 1969, 68–69). However, for accurate interpretation purposes they are quite similar and may be treated as part of the same phenomenon. Such critics see "the statement of a fact as a truth and that any truth enunciates a fact" (Perelman and Olbrechts-

Society of Professional Journalists

Code of Ethics

SOCIETY of Professional Journalists, believes the duty of journalists is to serve the truth.

We BELIEVE the agencies of mass communication are carriers of public discussion and information, acting on their Constitutional mandate and freedom to learn and report the facts.

We BELIEVE in public enlightenment as the forerunner of justice, and in our Constitutional role to seek the truth as part of the public's right to know the truth.

We BELIEVE those responsibilities carry obligations that require journalists to perform with intelligence, objectivity, accuracy, and fairness.

To these ends, we declare acceptance of the standards of practice here set forth:

I. RESPONSIBILITY:

The public's right to know of events of public importance and interest is the overriding mission of the mass media. The purpose of distributing news and enlightened opinion is to serve the general welfare. Journalists who use their professional status as representatives of the public for selfish or other unworthy motives violate a high trust.

II. FREEDOM OF THE PRESS:

Freedom of the press is to be guarded as an inalienable right of people in a free society. It carries with it the freedom and the responsibility to discuss, question, and challenge actions and utterances of our government and of our public and private institutions. Journalists uphold the right to speak unpopular opinions and the privilege to agree with the majority.

III. ETHICS:

Journalists must be free of obligation to any interest other than the public's right to know the truth.

1. Gifts, favors, free travel, special treatment or privileges can compromise the integrity of journalists and their employers. Nothing of value should be accepted.

2. Secondary employment, political involvement, holding public office, and service in community organizations should be avoided if it compromises the integrity of journalists and their employers. Journalists and their employers should conduct their personal lives in a manner that protects them from conflict of interest, real or apparent. Their responsibilities to the public are paramount. That is the nature of their profession.

3. So-called news communications from private sources should not be published or broadcast without substantiation of their claims to news values.

4. Journalists will seek news that serves the public interest, despite the obstacles. They will make constant efforts to assure that the public's business is conducted in public and that public records are open to public inspection.

5. Journalists acknowledge the newsman's ethic of protecting confidential sources of information.

6. Plagiarism is dishonest and unacceptable.

IV. ACCURACY AND OBJECTIVITY:

Good faith with the public is the foundation of all worthy journalism.

1. Truth is our ultimate goal.

2. Objectivity in reporting the news is another goal that serves as the mark of an experienced professional. It is a standard of performance toward which we strive. We honor those who achieve it.

3. There is no excuse for inaccuracies or lack of thoroughness.

4. Newspaper headlines should be fully warranted by the contents of the articles they accompany. Photographs and telecasts should give an accurate picture of an event and not highlight an incident out of context.

5. Sound practice makes clear distinction between news reports and expressions of opinion. News reports should be free of opinion or bias and represent all sides of an issue.

6. Partisanship in editorial comment that knowingly departs from the truth violates the spirit of American journalism.

7. Journalists recognize their responsibility for offering informed analysis, comment, and editorial opinion on public events and issues. They accept the obligation to present such material by individuals whose competence, experience, and judgment qualify them for it.

8. Special articles or presentations devoted to advocacy or the writer's own conclusions and interpretations should be labeled as such.

V. FAIR PLAY:

Journalists at all times will show respect for the dignity, privacy, rights, and well-being of people encountered in the course of gathering and presenting the news.

1. The news media should not communicate unofficial charges affecting reputation or moral character without giving the accused a chance to reply.

2. The news media must guard against invading a person's right to privacy.

3. The media should not pander to morbid curiosity about details of vice and crime.

4. It is the duty of news media to make prompt and complete correction of their errors.

5. Journalists should be accountable to the public for their reports and the public should be encouraged to voice its grievances against the media. Open dialogue with our readers, viewers, and listeners should be fostered.

VI. MUTUAL TRUST:

Adherence to this code is intended to preserve and strengthen the bond of mutual trust and respect between American journalists and the American people.

The Society shall--by programs of education and other means--encourage individual journalists to adhere to these tenets, and shall encourage journalistic publications and broadcasters to recognize their responsibility to frame codes of ethics in concert with their employees to serve as guidelines in furthering these goals.

CODE OF ETHICS
(Adopted 1926; revised 1973, 1984, 1987)

Tyteca, 69). Thus, for the accurate interpretation critic, being truthful and being factual are virtually the same.

In the SPJ Code, one can see that the words *truth* and *fact* are major terms beginning with the first statement: "Society of Professional Journalists, believes the duty of journalists is to serve the truth." Being truthful is not just important, it is a primary duty. By placement and emphasis it is the most important concern.

Oscar Patterson, III (1984), in his analysis of the news broadcasts of the Vietnam War, rejected as incorrect the generally accepted notion that television "projected into the American home night after night not only pictures of American troops dead and dying and killing, but of the terrible destruction American might was wrecking on a peasant society. . . . As a result, the war, with all its 'horrors' was fought in everyone's living room" (397). Patterson's analysis showed that a relatively limited percentage of the stories of the war carried such pictures (0–10.4%), leading him to the conclusion that "a form of selective perception (and more importantly selective retention) on the part of the general public of certain highly dramatic events has led to the projection of those events as characteristic of television coverage of the Vietnam war to a far greater extent than was actually true" (403).

Michael Osborn (1983) analyzed a local controversy in Memphis, Tennessee, over the building of an expressway through a mid-city park. The Overton Park controversy involved citizens' groups, *The Commercial Appeal*, and the *Memphis Press Scimitar*, and led, claims Osborn, to six major forms of abuse of argument. One of Osborn's claims is that both sides distorted and made the case melodramatic:

> In the melodrama that developed around the Overton Park expressway, both sides developed personae which featured themselves in heroic poses and draped the opposition in villainy. If you opposed the expressway, you might be labelled as unreasonable obstructionists who threatened "damage to the community" and who affiliated with "distant organizations." If you were not exiled in the role of "outsider," you might be depicted as a silly romanticizer, the sort of effete nature-lover who drove the Tennessee Lieutenant Governor to exclaim: "How much are these trees worth? What is their utility, except to build houses to house man?"
>
> On the other hand if you favored the park route, there was an equally ugly persona prepared for you. In the rhetoric of opponents of the expressway, the park was personified as a lovely, innocent, feminine victim of threatened sexual attack. Thus one official described the proposed route as "one of the worse rapes I've ever seen of a public park." In this melodrama proponents were identified in a male metonymy with bulldozers: those who would drive the "interstate bulldozer" into this lovely urban forest were violating our land under the banner of Progress (3–4).

Although Osborn only identifies the distortion, presumably a break with the truth, his argument implies that the distortion was deliberate, thus carrying his claim beyond untruthfulness to a more forceful ethical judgment. Sometimes, and as you read the quotation above you get a sense of it, the critic's statement of the interpretation is so strong that the reader cannot help making the ethical judgment that deliberate distortion has taken place.

Critical judgments about truthfulness can extend beyond distortion, accidental or deliberate. They apply also to omissions. *Extra* (1987), the newsletter of FAIR, criticized a *60 Minutes* report by Ed Bradley (May 3, 1987) about the Union Carbide, Bhopal, India, tragedy which "killed over 2,500 people and injured over 200,000 in December 1984." *Extra* claimed that "by focusing exclusively on India's deplorable record in caring for Bhopal's victims," the program "obscured the corporation's primary role in the continuing tragedy." A series of examples is then developed to prove the claim. According to this critical claim, *60 Minutes* was inaccurate because of its omissions from the full true story (Better Living . . . 6).

Communicating Information

The principle that information should be communicated is mentioned more often in the SPJ Code than any other principle. "The public's right to know," "carriers of public discussion and information," "the responsibility for offering informed analysis"—these are just three reflections in the Code of the principle that a text should communicate information.

Maurine Beasley's (1984) study of Eleanor Roosevelt's press conferences illustrates this standard. Her analysis of those press conferences informs the reader about the kind of information Mrs. Roosevelt presented to the assembled women reporters:

> A study of the transcripts shows she limited herself to areas traditionally considered appropriate for women: humanitarian and educational causes and services to the family. The legislation she endorsed pertained to broad social goals falling within this perview. Her advocacy of New Deal programs in a sense represented a wife's loyalty to her husband. Thus as a symbol of a new woman—a new kind of first lady—she did not move contrary to existing values except, possibly, by insisting on the right of married women to work (279).

Beasley's interpretation of the press conference transcripts is a straightforward explanation of the kind of information that was communicated. Sometimes, however, a critic makes an interpretation in a more figurative way. Accurate interpretation's concern for identifying the information communicated need not be purely descriptive. Sometimes a clearer explanation of a text can be made by the figurative characterization of information. For instance, Mary S. Mander (1984) examined the public debate about broadcasting in the twenties prior to the passage of the Radio Act of 1927, and found that "Three models and metaphors were used to conceptualize the use and development of radio: transportation, public utilities and the newspaper press." The public debate, she says, was a victory for the transportation metaphor:

> The over-arching model, rooted in the regulation of transport industries, was a market model, since the right to regulate broadcasting rested on the commerce clause. Thus from its inception broadcasting was not regulated as a symbol-producing, culture-maintaining medium, the purpose of which was art, intellectual exchange and the maintenance of a public sphere or community. Instead a market model prevailed. This way of visualizing the real world assumes a neutral society in which each individual is free to pursue his/her own interests and his/her own advantage as a natural right (184).

In this passage, Mander's essential investigative concern is to define working generalizations about the information in the debate. These generalizations are made clearer by characterizing them as models and metaphors.

Analyzing texts to see if they communicate information and what information they communicate may be judgmental as well as interpretive. For instance, Richard Corliss (1982) is scathing in his criticism of what television gave to its audience during the 1960s. He contrasts the reality of those turbulent times with the information about them projected through the television sitcoms:

> The sixties were no decade to laugh at—or through. The political and social impulses that shaped the Vietnam Era gave birth to a rancid, anarchic humor that gloried in what we'll call Radical Bad Taste, and shot its poison-tipped zingers into every open and concealed orifice of the American body politic. Meanwhile, back at the home, Mr. and Mrs. America ignored warnings from all the ships at sea and watched pallid, placid, plastic sitcoms whose concerns were relevant only to the Doris Day dreams of a generation before. . . .
>
> TV [ignored] in its "entertainment" programming, the insistent young who were making so much noise on the nightly news. Herewith A.C. Nielsen's ten top-rated shows of the 1967–68 season, whose highlights included the Tet Offensive, Lyndon Johnson's near-defeat in the New Hampshire primary and his subsequent announcement that he would seek no second term, and the assassination of Martin Luther King: *The Andy Griffith Show, The Lucy Show, Gomer Pyle U.S.M.C., Gunsmoke, Family Affair, Bonanza, The Red Skelton Show, The Dean Martin Show, The Jackie Gleason Show,* and *Saturday Night at the Movies.* While an important segment of Americans was sky-diving into the Twilight Zone, courtesy of S.D.S. and LSD, the rest of the country—this other, older colonial empire—was languishing in a time-machine placenta, the ever-popular womb with a view, whose umbilical cord was tie-lined to CBS and NBC (64–65).

Some will argue, of course, that television is a medium of entertainment and escape, but for the critic oriented to accurate interpretation every communication should convey accurate and useful information about the society it portrays. On these grounds, Corliss finds 1960s television wanting.

Maintain Objectivity

Robert A. Hackett (1984) has observed in recent years a growing challenge to the concept of objectivity, and its negative counterpart, bias. Yet these concepts have been central to much criticism, particularly in newspaper circles. "Objectivity," says Hackett, "has been described as 'the emblem' and 'keystone' of American journalism":

> Not surprising then, academics have also adopted bias and objectivity as organizing concepts in many studies of journalism. Students of news production, from Breed (1955) to Sigelman (1973), often took for granted the distinction between the biased editorial "policy" which may be enforced by newspaper publishers, and the ideal of journalistic objectivity—skeptical though they might have been of its realization in practice. Numerous content analyses have sought to evaluate the objectivity of news coverage of election campaigns, issues, policies, institutions, movements, or politicians (230).

Bias need not be a simple process of a communicator rewriting events so that they fit that communicator's personal view. Bias, the product of a person's experience and way of thinking, also may be unintentional and unconscious. A claim of unconscious bias is illustrated in an analysis of President Lyndon B. Johnson's characterization of the Vietnam War in his public statements:

> The symbols of peacemaker, savior, and enemy by which Johnson chose to characterize his policy evolved into a pattern of intense indignation, a rhetorical form conveying exclusiveness and the superiority of private values. In effect, the symbolic forms in Johnson's rhetoric contained the unstated, but crucial, assumptions that "because my intentions are virtuous, and because the values I endorse are good ones (who could argue against the motifs of peacemaker and savior?), then my claims should be accepted *ipso facto.*" Sincerity and virtue—as defined solely by a reservoir of private, and therefore non-debatable, values and experiences—became the chief criteria for deciding public policy. Yet, the connections between the private and public realms were never established. The messianic form of peacemaker/enemy/savior committed the President to an intransigent stance of indignation and superiority which itself mitigated against making such connections. In fact, no real awareness of the necessity to develop reasons for the benefit of a public emerges. Even at the end of his administration Johnson failed to comprehend the nature and significance of Vietnam as a public issue (Logue and Patton 1982, 327–328).

Treat Others Fairly

Much of what already has been said about truthfulness, informativeness, and objectivity implies that the communicator has an obligation to treat others fairly. Some would argue, however, that fairness is a more important goal than objectivity. If one believes that objectivity is difficult or impossible to achieve, one at least can argue for fairness (Goodwin 1983, 13). Both sides of a controversy should be shown.

The Associated Press Code calls this "integrity" and argues as follows:

> The newspaper should strive for impartial treatment of issues and dispassionate handling of controversial subjects. It should provide a forum for the exchange of comment and criticism, especially when such comment is opposed to its editorial positions. Editorials and other expressions of opinion by reporters and editors should be clearly labeled.

Thus, even if it is difficult to know what the accurate position is one can remove all obvious indications of bias and provide that all sides of a controversy are fairly shown.

In his analysis of the public park controversy in Memphis, Michael Osborn (1983) argues an important point that any critic interested in fairness must consider. The ability of the mass media to be silent constitutes a potential unfairness that is far more subtle than any deliberate bias:

> Silence has become a devastating new rhetorical option of our time. Too often we focus upon the positive power of mass media to communicate a message: we forget its negative power to deny visibility to an opposing position. The invisibility of one side is all the more profound because of the visibility of the other. Such imposed silence in effect denies identity and being: rhetorically, one simply does not exist. Freedom to speak then becomes only a hollow mockery, a right to address the wind in empty fields, a relegation to guerilla warfare in the great battle for the territorial possession of the public mind (9).

Therefore, although the critic must ask if both sides have been fairly represented, fairness itself is not so simply defined. It is complicated by intent, social attitudes, and the nature of the medium of communication. Nonetheless, fairness stands as a vital principle of accurate interpretation criticism.

Support Freedom

Providing people with facts, telling the truth, and being fair to all sides is closely linked to this understanding: The execution of such principles depends upon and supports individual freedom. Characteristically, the freedoms our society prizes most, freedom of the press and freedom of speech, have to do with communication.

Freedom is a central principle of accurate interpretation that can prove somewhat problematic. For example, a critic's support of freedom might conflict with other standards. Can one defend a newspaper's right to freedom of the press or an individual's right to freedom of speech and still insist on other standards, such as objectivity, which are also a part of accurate interpretation? "The strength of the American press is its diversity," said the executive editor of the *New York Times*, Abraham M. Rosenthal. "There are publishers I wouldn't dirty my hands with, but I don't want a code that would exclude them" (Goodwin 1983, 5). The accurate interpretation critic must continually be aware of this dilemma. Some people may exercise freedom in ways that violate accuracy. To resolve this dilemma, a judicious modification of all standards is necessary. Such a modification, Goodwin argues, is illustrated in the practice of the legal system:

> It must be understood that the First Amendment does not literally mean that no laws whatever can be passed abridging freedom of the press. Like all provisions of the Constitution, the free press provision has been interpreted and reinterpreted by the courts over the years, so that several restrictions on absolute freedom—libel and slander, for example—have been permitted (5).

This modification provided in legal procedure is used by critics to justify a modification of all standards to account for possible conflicts among them. Today, the standard used frequently involves extent. When freedom is seriously threatened, objectivity is widely ignored, or gross unfairness takes place, then the critic must call attention to the violation. One may recall from Chapter 1 that a good criticism advances a significant, not a trivial, claim. A significant critical claim looks for the major way or ways that standards are violated.

Accept Responsibility

Asking communicators to accept responsibility for statements they make is a corollary of earlier standards of fairness, objectivity, and freedom. When a person seeks to communicate to another person, that communication carries with it a responsibility to act in keeping with the standards already mentioned.

In 1981, Janet Cooke, a young reporter for the *Washington Post*, returned a Pulitzer Prize for journalism when it was discovered that she had fabricated the winning story of an 8-year-old heroin user. This serious violation of the ethics of accurate interpretation was treated in the journalistic community as a violation of trust, either by those who permitted it to happen (the editors) or Cooke herself. "The picture that emerged from much of the writing on Janet Cooke," says David Eason (1986), "is of a unified community of journalists betrayed by a person *Post* editor Benjamin Bradley referred to as a 'pathological liar'" (433–434). The critics using accurate interpretation standards placed responsibility for the event at the source. As noted earlier, that source is difficult to define in many cases. Is it the reporter, the editor, the television writer, the director, or the actor? But that difficulty does not prevent criticism from being source-centered. So, accurate interpretation is source-message oriented. It seeks to make judgments about the source based upon the accuracy of the message. In other words, the sender of the message must be responsible for the consequences of the message.

These six standards of accurate interpretation are not without their detractors. Nonetheless, they are important bases for many critical studies. So long as they are seen as guides but not absolute standards, and so long as they are seen as acting with and modifying one another, they can work as a foundation of criticism.

PROBLEMS WITH ACCURATE INTERPRETATION

Three major problems with accurate interpretation as a standard of criticism are pointed out by its opponents. One objection questions its assumptions. The other two are claims of inconsistency among standards and difficulties in applying them.

Like the other two common sense approaches to communication criticism, accurate interpretation has come under considerable attack because of the assumptions that govern it. Perhaps accurate interpretation is more susceptible to these attacks because of its strong commitment to the idea of reality as a standard of judgment. Its assumption that truth exists, and its literary counterpart that meanings are discoverable in texts, seem too simple when a text can be conceptualized as a social movement, a novel, a film, a TV docudrama, or the architecture of a building.

Those who question the assumptions of accurate interpretation usually do so from a deconstructivist's point of view, discussed in greater detail in Chapters 6 through 10. Briefly, the argument presents the thesis that what accurate interpretation critics call truth is constructed by authors, critics, or by the society those critics represent. They represent values, stories, or ideologies that, although widely or almost unanimously accepted, are still the product of the human mind, not some external reality.

The argument points out that words such as *truth, accuracy, fact, opinion, fairness,* and *responsibility* state values that humans support, not features of the world per se. These values constitute a human ideology that could be challenged by an alternate or contrasting ideology.

Similarly, to believe there is one meaning to a literary text is equally questionable. Literary theorist Steven Mailloux (1985) makes this argument against accurate interpretation's principles:

> Textual facts are never prior to or independent of the hermeneutic activity of readers and critics . . . not only is the interpreter's mind . . . active but . . . it is completely dominant over the text. There are no semantic or formal givens; all such textual givens are products of interpretive categories. This is a "build-down" model of interpretation. From this perspective, what counts as a correct reading depends entirely on shared assumptions and strategies, not autonomous texts . . . a text doesn't constrain its interpretation; rather, communal interpretation creates the text (622).

While Mailloux is speaking here of literary textual criticism, the approach is equally operative in other areas of criticism as the final five chapters of this book should show.

Although strongly linked to deconstructive approaches to criticism, Mailloux's complaint also is repeated by those who view communication as persuasion (see Chapter 5). It is rhetorical. That is, communication is concerned about what audiences see in messages. Such a point of view has a long tradition dating to Aristotle. It does not deny the assumptions of accurate interpretation that humans are reasonable and can find reality. It is audience response, more than truthfulness, that it emphasizes.

Neoclassical criticism, for the accurate interpretation critic, simply differs from accurate interpretation by emphasis. Those interested in persuasion and who argue from the point of view of neoclassical criticism claim that truth is essential to making the critic's search for effects ethical. In this light, Karlyn Kohrs Campbell (1972a) argues against persuasion as a critical standard. She states that "what we are to applaud as critics is highly skillful deception and concealment. As a critic, that is a bitter pill I cannot swallow" (452).

Deconstructive approaches are also not a serious challenge to accurate interpretation, according to their supporters. For, as Mailloux has observed, the deconstructive view and accurate interpretation, while differing radically on what establishes standards, both accept the presence of conventions. One set of conventions originates in a belief in objective reality and another in the society (or audience). But accurate interpretation critics do not see how conventions could serve as a challenge to the usefulness of the standards.

A second objection to accurate interpretation does not question the assumptions but finds difficulties in applying the standards. How do you maintain freedom, fairness, and truth all at once? Does not a communicator who wishes to preserve freedom need to act sometimes in a way that might be considered unfair? How does one link the "people's right to know" with the "protection of the individual"? Journalists are continually confronted with these dilemmas. Do people have a right to know about a political candidate's sex life, a potential judge's youthful indiscretions, or a professional athlete's personal finances? The answer, says the accurate interpretation critic, is in the standard that says the journalist should act responsibly. No doubt these are difficult decisions, but people of good judgment can make them.

Implied in the first two problems is the third. It can be argued that even if we believe there is truth, it is virtually impossible to know it or to apply it. There may have been a meaning to a literary text, and it may have been in the intent of the author, as E. D. Hirsch, Jr., claims, but who knows Chaucer's intent now? And, how do we know whether President Franklin Roosevelt knew that the Japanese would attack Pearl Harbor, or whether Ronald Reagan knew about the Iran-contra arms deal?

It is important to realize, however, that the proponents of accurate interpretation are not foolish. Despite the implied absolute standards of the SPJ Code and the implications behind the general assumptions of many literary critical theorists, most critics understand that accuracy has its relative aspects. They hold accuracy as a goal. They know that what appears to be true now may change later with new information. They realize that frequently their judgments must be tempered by the concept of probability. Believing, however, that an interpretation of the facts can be in error or that new interpretations are possible does not justify plunging into a swamp of relativism. As historian Gene Wise (1980) argued:

> [Carl] Becker was half wrong when he declaimed, "The historical fact is in someone's mind or it is nowhere." The historical fact is in someone's mind and it is in the world. Or at least some kinds of facts are. Regardless of our subjective dispositions, George Washington was born in 1732 and died in 1799, the Civil War broke out in 1861, the stock market crashed in 1929, and John F. Kennedy was shot in 1963. The same holds true for certain patterns of facts—like how many people voted Republican and how many Democratic in 1956, or how much of the federal budget goes to defense-related activities and how much to welfare, or what John Winthrop did publicly in response to the dual challenges of Roger Williams and Anne Hutchinson in the 1630's (39).

Furthermore, what, says the accurate interpretation critic, is the alternative? If you don't believe that in some probable way a critic can know what the text means or what the reality of the situation is, does that not return you to taste? Is every opinion as good as every other? If so, doesn't every critical method have equal weight and, if that is the case, doesn't that mean that the whole act of criticism is a waste of time?

Despite its detractors, accurate interpretation is probably the most common approach to communication criticism. It is the mainstay of journalists, historians, and most lay critics. It looks for accuracy, or at least fairness, in reporting the events or interpreting a text. To do this, its user has to assume that there is a natural world that can be known. A similar assumption motivates formal criticism, the subject of the next chapter, but formal criticism has a different primary objective: not accuracy, but aesthetic worth.

CHAPTER FOUR

Formal Criticism
The Aesthetic Worth of a Message

It is October of 1984 and a television viewer reaches a commercial break and sees "a grizzly, lumbering across a hilltop, crossing a creek, forging through underbrush. A drum slowly beats, haunting chords resonate. A voice-over says":

> There's a bear in the woods. For some people the bear is easy to see. Others don't see it at all. Some people say the bear is tame. Others say it is vicious and dangerous. Since no one can really be sure who's right, isn't it smart to be as strong as the bear? If there is a bear?

"As the announcer says this last line, we watch the bear walk slowly along a ridge, silhouetted against the sky; it looks up, stops, then begins to step backward. At this moment the camera pulls back to show a silhouetted man, gun slung over his shoulder facing the bear. The closing graphic reads 'President Reagan: Prepared for Peace'" (Muir 1988, 8–9).

The bear in the woods symbolizes the Soviet Union; man symbolizes a vigilant America, led by Ronald Reagan. The actions of the bear are not menacing; they reinforce the uncertainty. But surely the bear can be violent and dangerous. The sentences are simple, and evolve to questions that maintain the theme: preparedness. The theme is reinforced by the characters (the bear and the man), by the scene (the woods), and by the styling of words, music, and visuals. As political advertisements go, it is more than an argument: It is aesthetically pleasing. Such a judgment is the result of applying formal standards to a text. Formal criticism remains the prevailing approach among literary critics who have used it to judge a message for its aesthetic worth.

Even though formal criticism has been the specific province of art, music, film, and literary critics, it is not limited to them. Most deconstructive approaches discussed in the final five chapters of this book, while rejecting the assumptions of formal criticism, do examine formal characteristics to arrive at critical claims. In addition, formal standards frequently are part of other common sense approaches. For example, formalist characteristics can be found in the neoclassical, persuasion-oriented approach of speech criticism. The most comprehensive statement of the neoclassical critical approach uses formal notions of structure and style to judge the worth of a message (Thonssen and Baird 1948, 392–433).

Mary Strine (1978), in her study of William Styron's novel *The Confessions of Nat Turner*, is interested in the sociopsychological aspects of the race issue as imaginatively depicted by Styron. To get at them, she examines character development, a formal critical category, as one expression of the issue. Thomas Benson (1980), in his study of Fredrick Wiseman's film *High School*, seeks to show how the film develops its persuasive message that high school teenagers are subject to tyrannical power and sexual panic. To show how Wiseman achieves this persuasive purpose, Benson examines such formal categories as structure, coherence, and theme.

Frequently, formal criteria will be used together with another standard. Critic Michael Arlen (1979), in a *New Yorker* article, "Getting the Goods on President Monckton," mixed the standards of accurate interpretation and formal criticism about *Washington Behind Closed Doors* (the novel-for-television) based on John Ehrlichman's novel *The Company*. The characters were easy to identify as Richard Nixon, Lyndon Johnson, Henry Kissinger, and John Kennedy, for instance, and the events had a strong parallel to the Nixon years. Yet the events depicted were a mixture of accepted facts, rumors, and fancy. Says Arlen:

> There should be a place in our historical narratives for such a marvelously evocative though perhaps not precisely factual interpretation as [Jason] Robard's depiction of Nixon-Monckton's strange humorous humorlessness, where an actor's art gave pleasure, brought out character, and took us closer to truth. At the same time, for major television producers (in this case, Paramount and ABC-TV) to be so spaced out by the present Entertainment Era as to more or less deliberately fool around with the actual life of an actual man, even of a discredited President . . . seems irresponsible and downright shabby (167).

To "deliberately fool around" with a man's life is "irresponsible," but the formal evaluation is favorable of Robard's not "precisely factual" performance. Thus, although formal criticism can stand alone, it is frequently part of other perspectives. Formal criticism has a long tradition extending to the poetics of Plato and Aristotle and, as such, has established critical categories that even its detractors frequently cannot shake.

THE ASSUMPTIONS OF FORMAL CRITICISM

Like all common sense criticism, formal criticism uses some of the same assumptions as accurate interpretation, although they are altered by being linked to other assumptions and directed more to the nature of texts than to external reality.

Human Beings Are Essentially Reasonable

Although reasonableness is basic to both accurate interpretation and neoclassical criticism, it means more to formal criticism than to those approaches. To the formal critic, reasonableness is similar to educable. Formal criticism works from a set of standards that educated people have refined for several thousand years since their origin in ancient Greece. Humans are reasonable and, therefore, capable of learning how to do formal criticism. However, the rules of formal criticism are specific and cannot be entered into by just anyone.

Properties Are Inherent in Texts, Not Ascribed to Texts by Humans

Although there is considerable disagreement about how to find textual meaning, formal critics agree that textual meaning exists. Thus, the formal critic first must determine what a text means (interpretation) before judging it. In addition, the meaning of the text and the standards of analysis are derived from inherent properties of texts, not simply ascribed to texts by humans. The critic, therefore, strives to find the meaning and judge its development by formal standards based on established principles of aesthetic worth.

The Text Is Central to the Criticism

Formal criticism is usually associated with literary critics who became disillusioned with criticism that emphasized the historical (environmental) and the biographical (authorial) aspects of literary works. These "New Critics," as they were called, argued that historical and biographical emphasis ignored the essential object of criticism, the work itself (Welleck and Warren 1970, 139). W. K. Wimsatt, Jr. (1954) and Monroe C. Beardsley, in *The Verbal Icon,* attack both the "intentional fallacy" and the "affective fallacy" in two introductory essays (Wimsatt). The text itself, not its design in the author's mind or effect on a reader, is central to critical analysis. Such a view is not held exclusively by literary scholars. Charles Redding (1957), a critic from the tradition of neoclassicism, lamented that too much criticism of public address is concerned with external factors, and he called for more attention to the intrinsic elements of communication.

New Criticism in several manifestations was the dominant force among literary critics between the 1940s and the 1960s. Even today, most literary critics who are unwilling to go to the extreme of ignoring intent or effect recognize the necessity of some means of formal "close reading" to unveil the internal aspects of the work as a central function of criticism. R. S. Crane (1953) was a leader of the literary neo-Aristotelian movement which emphasized the relationship of the text to the reader. Yet his emphasis is on the form of the text (165–166).

Even the primary target of the New Critics, the literary biographers, acknowledge the importance of a fuller understanding of the works of an author and defend biography only if it reveals something of what makes one author's works different from another (Simonson 1971, 83). Formalism's case against biographical criticism is based on the fear that such biography will interfere with textual understanding.

The farther one moves away from text, as was noted in Chapter 1, the less likely that the product of such study can be called communication criticism. This illustrates again that formal principles are pervasive even among critics who would not be called formalists.

Artistic Merit Is the Aim of Formal Criticism

Because formal criticism has been developed by artistic and literary critics, it tends to emphasize aesthetic excellence. It concentrates on genres of communication that can be more clearly defined aesthetically than others. Much of the theory of literary criticism is about poetry, the most concentrated and condensed form of literature (Perrine 1987, 3). Consequently, much of what has been written is less applicable to public address, the television documentary, or protest pamphlets.

In addition, formal criticism usually is applied to works that are seen as having quality. Selection processes make it unlikely that television commercials, speeches, or editorials will be examined. Formal criticism assumes a sophisticated reader, educated in aesthetic standards, and is, therefore, less likely to explain how messages relate to a general audience.

Formal literary criticism shares with neoclassical criticism an emphasis on verbal language. Therefore, it is not so easily adapted to the criticism of the visual. James Steele Smith (1962), educated as a literary critic, has observed:

> Writing or speaking about visual forms, the critic can make only rough, often misleading distinctions between visual phenomena—colors, shapes, textures, lines, spaces. Word comments about visual differences are always approximate—and very roughly that. Color vocabularies, for instance, are exceedingly vague and unhelpful; even the most carefully worked out color vocabularies of such color specialists as physicists and painters permit much variance of meaning and so room for confusion (249).

Like any approach, if formal criticism is not slavishly or mechanically applied, it can be useful. Any "cookie cutter" criticism, where the critic dissects messages and can only find a list of independent items, is not good criticism. "Look! Here is a metaphor, an image, a metre, a genre." Certainly, formal criticism can degenerate to this, but it need not, and intelligently used it can provide useful insights into the formal aesthetic components of the communication situation.

Form and Content Are Separable

Formal criticism emphasizes the nature of the forms that a message may take. As such, it directs attention to the traditional division between form and content. Content refers to "the ideas and emotions" communicated by a message and form includes "all linguistic [and visual] elements by which the content is expressed" (Welleck and Warren 1970, 140).

Much of the popular criticism of television indicts it for beautiful words and pictures without substance. Here is a short analysis of two soap operas from *TV Guide's* "Cheers 'N' Jeers" section to illustrate this kind of criticism:

> Jeers to CBS's *The Young and the Restless* for its unrealistic, soft-soap depiction of an AIDS sufferer. Jessica (actress Rebecca Street) is afflicted with the deadly disease but walks around most days looking the very picture of robust health. By way of contrast, ABC's *All My Children* chose to bring verisimilitude to a similar storyline, educating—and moving—its audience in the process.

Because of its emphasis on form, formal criticism has been said to lack interest in the content of the message. But this is not so, as René Welleck and Austin Warren (1970) point out:

> As we shall use it [form] here, it names the aesthetic structure of a literary work—that which makes it literature. Instead of dichotomizing "form-content," we should think of matter and then of "form," that which aesthetically organizes its "matter." In a successful work of art, the materials are completely assimilated into the form: what was "world" has become "language" (241).

Probably the most influential modern statement of the formalist position was Cleanth Brooks's and Robert Penn Warren's (1960) *Understanding Poetry,* because of its extensive use in university English classes. Brooks and Warren focus specifically on the form of the poem, ignoring its biographical and historical relations. In emphasizing the form a poem takes, they argue that it is an organic system of relationships.

> Certainly, it [a poem] is not to be thought of as a group of *mechanically*
> combined elements—meter, rhyme, figurative language, idea and so on—
> put together to make a poem as bricks are put together to make a wall.
> The relationship among the elements in a poem is what is all important;
> it is not a mechanical relationship but one which is far more intimate and
> fundamental. If we must compare a poem to the makeup of some physical
> object it ought not to be to a wall but to something organic like a plant
> (16).

Those who follow the dictates of formal criticism, then, do not ignore
content. However, critical judgment is concerned with what the artist does
with content, not an evaluation of its worth (Simonson 1971, 25). The quality of the form is judged by the ability of the artist to make it an organic
whole that integrates form and content. Says David Daiches (1956): "The
work which combines the communication of profound insight with the
satisfaction of formal perfection (*Hamlet* or *King Lear*, for example) is greater
than the work which demonstrates only the latter quality (such as a perfect
detective story)" (38).

Formal criticism, therefore, has these assumptions: that humans are
reasonable, that properties are inherent in texts, that the text is central to
criticism, that artistic merit is its aim, and that form and content are in
some sense separable. The significance of these assumptions will be clearer
when we examine the principles that guide formal criticism.

THE PRINCIPLES OF FORMAL CRITICISM

What does a formalist critic look for in judging a work? Aristotle (1951)
identified a six-part division of tragedy: "plot, character, diction [style],
thought, spectacle, and song" (25). The first four have been the primary
concern of most formalist critics because of their preferences for written
texts such as poems, novels, short stories, or plays. For Aristotle, the last
two were examined, because in his day most literature was performed as
a part of plays or pageants. Spectacle and song take on added significance
today because of the growing importance of television, radio, motion pictures, video, and records.

Aristotle's term *mythos*, or plot, includes not only the simple narrative
line of actions but the development of a theme that reveals general human
experience. In this sense, and for our purposes, plot is both too broad and
too narrow. It is too broad because it contains the idea of theme that we
will separate for purposes of analysis. It is too narrow because it refers
to the story form only. Therefore, the term *structure* will be used in our
examination of five formal features: theme, structure, character, style, and
spectacle.

Theme

To a formal critic, any subject matter is potentially worthy of communication. What differentiates worthy from unworthy texts is not the subject matter but the theme. Theme is what the communicator carries into the subject matter; it is the recurring, unifying idea, motif, or value of the message. Given any subject matter—teenage pregnancy, inflation, a presidential campaign, AIDS—the issue is clear: What theme does the communicator find in the subject matter?

The television series *M*A*S*H*, for example, is about a medical unit in the Korean War. Now historically 40 years behind us, that war has little sense of immediacy in and of itself. But *M*A*S*H*'s success and critical acclaim come from its ability to provide more general insights. Its themes are about such general matters as personal relations among people, racial prejudice, war, and brutality, all of which have applications far beyond the Korean War alone.

General Applications.   A first standard of formal criticism is the extent to which the communication provides insights into themes that are not bound to the particular situation. Consider, for instance, a travel film about trout fishing in the California Sierra Nevada mountains. There are people riding horseback into a wilderness area, tall cliffs, towering trees, rushing water in beautiful rivers, and placid lakes at sundown. Fish are caught. People are happy. They sit around the fire frying fish in a pan. They enjoy eating the fish. The theme is immediate pleasure, perhaps wonder, at what they had seen. However, the theme is mostly transitory; it does not propose general questions because it is designed for the moment. It does not provide insight into the character of human beings, the relation of human beings to nature, or even the issue of conservation.

An examination of the dialogue on Sunday afternoon television fishing shows reveals this weakness most clearly.

> *Speaker 1:* Hey, I got a strike.
> *Speaker 2:* Be careful; he looks like a big one.
> *Speaker 1:* Oh, oh, there he goes; look at him jump.
> *Speaker 2:* That's a nice fish, there.
> *Speaker 1:* He's an old heavy job, isn't he?
> *Speaker 2:* What are you going to do with him?
> *Speaker 1:* I don't know.
> *Speaker 2:* There he is; get him up there, easy, that's better.

Such dialogue is repeated with minor variations on similar shows over and over again. Such programs are only for escape.

The formal critic would give the higher evaluation to a message that went beyond both of these examples. Ernest Hemingway's *Old Man and the Sea* is a story about catching a fish, but there the similarity to the previous example ends: "Hemingway's theme, expressed in the apparently simple, yet actually intricately designed plot of Santiago's adventure with the marlin and sharks, is man's capacity to withstand and transcend hardships of time and circumstance" (Jobes 1968, 2).

Probability.   A second standard for judging theme is the level of probability established. No communication can reveal a situation in its totality. Messages reflect a sender's interpretation of a situation. A speaker or writer selects words and a receiver interprets their meaning in a speech or newspaper report. The very nature of language dictates that everything cannot be said. In film, the viewer is shown what the camera is aimed at. The level of focus, the distance, and the lighting all select what will be seen.

Probability, however, is not a standard to be applied simply on the basis of whether something happened or is likely to happen. It is not predictive but rather a judgment of the lifelike characteristics of plot. The historical novel, for instance, may be inaccurate but still reveal a vital theme. In Part One of *Henry VI*, Shakespeare kept Joan of Arc alive for 20 years after her death so that she could participate in the battle of 1451 (Campbell and Quinn 1966, 336). However, it is not argued that the play developed an improbable theme.

There is also the concept of the probable impossible; that is, something that could not happen but is quite probable on an imaginative level. Simple examples of this abound in children's cartoons. The Roadrunner is being chased by Wile E. Coyote toward the cliff. The Roadrunner makes a sharp turn—Wile E. Coyote does not. He runs out five or six steps over the edge of the cliff, realizes what he has done, puts his hand down, and feels for the ground. Now it is clear in his mind; he has violated the laws of gravity. He turns in panic and falls, making a deep coyote impression in the ground from which he crawls, much the worse for wear, but able to recover and chase again. It is impossible, without aeronautical assistance, to defy gravity. But, as a representation of Wile E. Coyote's mental state, the scene is quite probable.

Density.   A third standard for evaluating theme is in what Horace Newcomb (1987) calls density (622). It relates to the literary principle stated by Cleanth Brooks that "the general and the universal are not seized upon by abstraction, but got at through the concrete and particular" (Simonson 1971, 33). It is encapsulated in the dictum "show, don't tell." The critic looks for detail that is adequate in amount and quality to develop the theme.

Certain media and genres have a distinct advantage over others in providing density. Novels are usually long enough to be detailed. For example, James Michener's *Centennial* builds its theme on large doses of detailed description of people and places, which detail helps to build probability for the theme.

Here is an example of density from Franklin D. Roosevelt's speech on September 11, 1941, on "Freedom of the Seas." In it he eventually announces that "if German or Italian vessels of war enter the waters, the protection of which is necessary for American defense, they do so at their own peril" (1946, 304). But first, he sets up five examples of which this is the first:

> The Navy Department of the United States has reported to me that on the morning of September fourth the United States destroyer Greer, proceeding in full daylight toward Iceland had reached a point southeast of Greenland. She was carrying American mail to Iceland. She was flying the American flag. Her identity as an American ship was unmistakable. She was then and there attacked by a submarine. Germany admits that it was a German submarine. The submarine deliberately fired a torpedo at the Greer, followed later by another torpedo attack (298).

Notice how Roosevelt uses short sentences, each containing a specific to set the basis for density, and this is only one of five examples he uses to support his point.

Television news, on the other hand, has been widely criticized for its lack of density. "What is striking, of course, is how thin and how much the same all this video news is," says Lawrence Lichty (1982). "The half hour evening news show has room for 17 or 18 items in 22 minutes (commercials eat up eight minutes). Eight or nine of these items are film snippets lasting from a few seconds to one and a half minutes" (52).

In summary, a key concern for the formal critic is theme. The critic looks for richness of theme and its ability to exceed the immediate situation to reveal general principles that can be applied to other times, people, and circumstances. These principles must be developed so that the reader or viewer has a strong sense of probability and the detail necessary to make the richness of the theme apparent.

Gilbert Highet's (1954) analysis of the theme in Abraham Lincoln's "Gettysburg Address" illustrates how a critic might show that a theme had these characteristics:

> Analyzing the Address further, we find that it is based on a highly imaginative theme, or group of themes. The subject is—how can we put it so as not to disfigure it?—the subject is the kinship of life and death, that mysterious linkage which we see sometimes in physical succession of birth and death in our world, sometimes as the contrast, which is perhaps a unity, between death and immortality. The first sentence is concerned with birth: "Our fathers *brought forth* a *new* nation, *conceived* in liberty."

The final phrase but one expresses the hope that: "This nation under God, shall have *a new birth* of freedom."

And the last phrase of all speaks of continuing life as the triumph over death. Again and again through the speech, this mystical contrast and kinship reappear: "those who *gave their lives* that this nation might *live,*" "the brave men *living and dead,*" and so in the central assertion that the dead have already consecrated their own burial place, while "it is for us, the *living* rather to be dedicated . . . to the great task remaining" (88–89).

Structure

For most formal critics, structure is even more important than theme. However, disputes over the relative importance of theme and structure should be avoided. Both are linked together—structure is a vital part of defining the theme—and can be separated only for purposes of discussion. Two factors contribute to adequate structure: order and unity.

Order.   A communicated message should reveal some sense of order. In the simplest terms, we look for a message to have a beginning, middle, and end. In the most traditional rhetorical forms such as essays and speeches, a message will introduce the subject, develop its main points, and bring the subject to a conclusion. In the development of main points, the formalist critic looks for some rationale for putting one point before another. Speeches typically are patterned in chronological, spatial, topical, cause and effect, or problem-solution formats. Such patterns also will be found in TV documentaries, travel films, newspaper editorials, and all other means of communication that attempt to convey specific information to advance an argument.

Some communication follows a narrative rather than an argumentative form, however. Narrative form is rooted in the chronological but will sometimes break with it. The novel *Ordinary People* by Judith Guest (1976), from which the award-winning film was made, follows a narrative chronological pattern. The author chooses to follow the main characters in a troubled family through a chronological series of events. Nonetheless, Guest's chronology is not rigid. She uses flashback to return to past experiences. Note that flashback does not violate narrative order here because it explains the background of what is happening in the general frame of this chronological story.

Sometimes order can be overdone. *The Love Boat* is an example of this phenomenon. Its order and theme are thoroughly predictable. It follows a formula. Cathy Schwichtenberg (1987) calls *The Love Boat* an "empty structure inflated with banality":

The Love Boat, as a purely formulaic show, invites . . . critical barbs. Its plotline is repetitive and deals with the love problems of old and young,

married and unmarried passengers (the featured guest stars), in three in-
terwoven playlets which are parallel and alternate. Unifying the show are
the crew of regulars. . . . Crewmembers either involve themselves directly
in the "dramatic" action or help to mediate and resolve their passengers'
love problems. By the end of the cruise, the passengers in all three playlets
find their love problems resolved and leave the ship as a reunited family
or as a couple which has "family potential."

   Thus, from an aesthetic point of view, *The Love Boat* presents an essentially empty tri-part structure unified by the ship and crew, and inflated
with the problems of banal love situations (126–127).

For the formal critic, there must be a sense of discovery. A text should
develop in an orderly way to tell the receivers something they hadn't
known or understood before. The repeated formula order eliminates the
discovery that should make sense. It should tell us more than we could
anticipate but it should do so by seeming to be the sensible outcome of a
narrative order.

   Unity.   Much of what has been said about order involves the second
critical standard for judging structure: unity. Judgments about unity concern how well a text coheres so that its receivers can understand the theme.

   Terry Gilliam's motion picture *Brazil*, a black comedy, reminiscent of
1984, about life in a postmodern society, is a good example of unity without order. The film centers on Sam Lowery, who seeks work in the Department of Information Retrieval so that he can locate a woman, Jill Layton,
who keeps appearing in his dreams. The plot jumps from one location to
another. Characters appear and disappear. It is difficult to tell what is
dream and what is not, or if the Robert De Niro character, Tuttle, actually
exists. Everything is fragmented. No one seems to have any individual
identity. But all the scenes point to the uniting theme of people losing
identity in a society that dehumanizes the individual in a flood of gadgets,
regulations, and, above all else, paperwork. It is "with his dreams," the
source of seeming disunity, "that Sam actually does defeat the bureau-
cracy" (Rogers 1990, 40). The pieces develop the theme and the confusing
mixture of reality and dream holds together in a different and vital way.

   Hill Street Blues, the award-winning television series about a big-city
police precinct, has several subplots and switches back and forth among
them. An individual program gets its continuity, not from some clear notion of order, but from an overall sense of unity. Indeed, part of the show's
strength is the way in which movement from one subplot to another helps
to convey the disorganization and frantic nature of the unending struggle
with crime. Captain Furillo stands as a central organizing character in the
scene, but he too has his problems with his subordinates, his superiors,
and the women in his life. Without him all sense of unity would be lost.
However, he is only a touchstone for this unity. He contrasts with the
disorganization around him and, thus, gives it a unified meaning. The

Furillo persona is, therefore, a device that emphasizes the unity of the themes of disorganization and frustration.

As illustrated by these two examples, the principle of unity specifies that theme can be found by examining all elements in the message. If individual subplots, scenes, or characters do not contribute to the theme, unity is damaged.

A second principle of unity is that actions should arise out of the plot. Nothing should be included that pulls the attention of the receiver away from the central unity of the piece. In 1948, President Harry Truman concluded his presidential campaign with a speech at Madison Square Garden on the economy—the central focus in his campaign. Inserted into the speech was a paragraph on his support for the state of Israel. Politicians knew that he inserted that paragraph because New York was an important state with a large Jewish vote. In addition, Jews across the country were being wooed by the Progressive party of Henry A. Wallace. Standards of persuasion would make such a decision necessary, but from a formal standpoint it flawed his speech by weakening its unity.

Cleanth Brooks, in his "articles of faith" for New Criticism, says "that the primary concern of criticism is with the problem of unity—the kind of whole which the literary work forms or fails to form, and the relation of the various parts to each other in building up the whole" (Simonson 1971, 33).

Character

In formal criticism, how the author deals with a subject, what form the author gives a subject, is more important than the subject itself. The critic's search is for the coherent poem, narrative, or play that reveals general themes through formal characteristics. As such, the characters in a particular message must support the theme. For Aristotle (1927), the characters are less important than the structure but still important:

> But most important of all is the structure of the incidents. For Tragedy is an imitation, not of men, but of an action and of life, and life consists in action, and its end is a mode of action, not a quality. Now character determines men's qualities, but it is by their actions that they are happy or the reverse. Dramatic action, therefore, is not with a view to the representation of character: character comes in as subsidiary to the actions. Hence the incidents and the plot are the end of a tragedy; and the end is the chief thing of all. . . . The Plot, [theme and structure] then, is the first principle, and, as it were, the soul of a tragedy: Character holds the second place (25–29).

Now this perspective does not diminish character development, which remains an important way to establish the theme the structure reveals. But well-developed character must do more than be interesting or believable. The character must aid in establishing the theme by what he or she does or does not do, an idea we will return to. Still, here are three questions on which character development can be judged: (1) Does the character have an appropriate role? (2) Does the character reveal an approach to life? (3) Is the character believable?

Does the Character Have an Appropriate Role?   Because all characters in a story must contribute to developing the action and from the action the theme, it is important that each character play a part. If a character is missing, part of the action is missing. Or, if there are too many characters, then extraneous and unnecessary actions will confuse the theme. Soap operas clearly focus on characters. Their plots move slowly—so slowly that viewers can discontinue viewing for a period and still understand what is going on when they resume. The story lines are repetitive, lack physical action, and depend on dialogue among characters to explain them (Cantor and Pingree 1983, 19–24). The slow pace probably makes it possible for viewers to get to know and develop a sense of intimacy with the characters.

This sense of intimacy that viewers develop with such characters may make them popular. Unfortunately, the emphasis on characters does not lead to a very favorable formal response, because formal critics are looking for the development of general themes. Soap opera themes tend to be limited to the particular characters in the series. Horace Newcomb (1987) commends *Dallas*, a prime-time soap opera, for its "sense of place" and its characters who represent that "place" (221–228). But does *Dallas* develop themes of general applicability? Probably not. *Dallas* has power but not for formal critics. Says Newcomb:

> The power of *Dallas* lies in this extraordinary accomplishment of the oldest pop-culture trick. It has recycled a cluster of America's most basic images and polished them into a financial success. Probably without knowing it, the show's creators pump nourishment into audiences' veins. Their timing is perfect. As a nation we are actually growing older and developing the caution that comes with age. It is a time of decline, of recession and restriction, a time of real trouble. The grand old cities of the East and the Midwest are burdened with financial failure and bitter winters. Small wonder that the Sunbelt flourishes and *Dallas* leads the ratings. Small wonder, too, that J. R. has become a national symbol, replacing the mellower, resigned, saddened Archie Bunker (226).

So, J. R. is interesting and entertaining. In one sense the character develops an appropriate role, however shallow it is. His character does not lead a viewer beyond an immediate fascination for what is happening to an understanding that encompasses more general themes.

Does the Character Reveal an Approach to Life?   Humans respond to their experiences. When taken together, such responses constitute a view of the world. Some would say each person has a psychological make-up, a point of view, an attitude about self and others that may be called an approach to life. To the formalist critic, each character should reveal such an approach. Some characters will be appealing; others will be reprehensible with numerous alternatives in between. However, a character is more than someone who is or is not appealing. Each character has a specific role to play in unfolding the plot. Russell Conwell (1988) was enormously successful as a nineteenth-century lecturer with his speech "Acres of Diamonds." He told people that they had a right to be rich and that wealth could be found at home. The speech is little more than a collection of stories headed by the title story of a man who sold his farm and searched the world over to find diamonds. After he died in poverty, the farmer who bought his land found diamonds on it. The character in this story is not very believable in other ways but he surely represents an approach to life shared by others: the desire for riches.

Is the Character Believable?   Each of the previous two principles of character development leads to believability. If a character has an appropriate role that reflects a way of life, the character will be believable. Initially, believability can be defined as true to life. It means that the character is physically and psychologically plausible, but believability does not mean "realistic." Bugs Bunny, Mickey Mouse, the Roadrunner, and many other cartoon characters are not realistic but they are believable. They are believable in ways that the characters in *Masters of the Universe* are not. They display characteristics that permit them to personify important themes, albeit at the level of a child's understanding.

Rambo is the adult equivalent of the characters in *Masters of the Universe*. He does no more impossible things than Bugs Bunny; but, Rambo is serious, Bugs is not. For a closer comparison consider the difference between Sean Connery or Roger Moore as 007 and Sylvester Stallone as Rambo. 007 does impossible things but with a certain sense of humor which seems to say, "This is all in fun, you know." In the formal sense, that makes him more believable than Rambo, who is forever serious about his impossible feats.

Therefore, in judging the characters in a story, the critic tries to determine if they are believable: if each has a role appropriate to the story and if that role reflects an approach to life. To be formally useful, characters must do more than create interest. They must be an integral part of the process of developing a theme that carries the reader, listener, or viewer beyond the immediate story to general insights.

Style

Style is far too complex a subject, linked to other formal characteristics, to be fully covered here. Therefore, we will emphasize its central standards. Since antiquity, theorists have agreed that to develop a theme language should be used in correct, clear, appropriate, and impressive ways.

Correctness.   In its simplest form, correctness in language refers to standard rules of formal grammar, syntax, and pronunciation. Such rules are useful for the beginning writer or speaker. However, they are virtually automatic to the writer of most of the texts the formal critic examines. Frequently, formal grammatical "errors" are not errors in correctness; the standards of correctness will vary depending upon the voice with which a particular writer or character speaks.

A character who is portrayed as a well-educated professional would be expected to speak according to the rules of standard grammar and pronunciation. Such language represents the use by that person of the conventions of educated language. A speaker from another social situation would be expected to speak from its conventions. Judgments about correctness are not rooted in universal rules but in the conventions of the social situation.

Alice Walker's (1982) *The Color Purple* is the story of an uneducated, southern, rural African American woman. Celie's story of her growing self-awareness and independence is told through a series of letters she writes—first to God and then to her separated sister, Nettie. It is a powerful story and, as befitting the character, the letters are written in dialect:

> The only thing keep me alive is watching Henrietta fight for her life. And boy can she fight. Everytime she have an attack she scream enough to wake the dead. Us do what you say the peoples do in Africa. Us feed her yams every single day. Just our luck she hate yams and she not too polite to let us know (213).

Clarity.   In general, clarity is more important than correctness. Many speeches, for instance, fall between conventional systems. Speakers, even those who are well educated, may speak in nonstandard English to create effects or to provide emphasis. Therefore, grammatical forms representing different convention systems can be used. In such cases, the more important question asks: Is the message understandable? On April 23, 1964, Malcolm X (1965), the Black Nationalist leader, spoke in Cleveland to a principally African American audience. His speech, "The Ballot or the Bullet," has many passages that mix conventions of correctness but, as the following illustrates, are quite clear:

> And now you're facing a situation where the young Negro's coming up. They don't want to hear that "turn-the-other-cheek" stuff, no. In Jacksonville, those were teenagers, they were throwing Molotov cocktails. Negroes have never done that before. But it shows you there's a new deal coming in. There's new thinking coming in. There's new strategy coming in. It'll be Molotov cocktails this month, hand grenades next month, and

something else next month. It'll be ballots, or it'll be bullets. It'll be liberty, or it will be death (31–32).

Clarity requires that there be precision in language use so that a receiver can understand the developing themes. Ambiguity, where the language can mean more than one thing, is usually seen as an impediment to clarity. Humorous examples of such ambiguity abound:

My children like our dog more than me.

I'm sorry to hear that you are recuperating from your operation.

Texas is famous for its beef from its ranches and its oil fields.

Utah, a pretty, great state.

Because such ambiguities threaten the unity of the message, they are to be avoided. But ambiguity also can provide for formal beauty where different views of the language may work into the plot and add to the theme. William Empson (1970) identifies seven types of ambiguity. For him ambiguity is "any verbal nuance, however slight, which gives room for alternate reactions to the same piece of language" (1). These possibilities for "alternate reactions" may be used to enrich the interpretation. This is particularly true of poetry because it is so compressed and metaphorical.

"Civil rights" as it was used in the 1960s meant the black civil rights movement. But the term has subsequently been used to apply to women, gays and lesbians, Hispanics, and others. It is ambiguous in a way that makes the term richer. It has become a theme that is applicable in more than one situation. As such, even in formal criticism, or perhaps especially in formal criticism, clarity is not an easy standard to enforce. Ambiguity that on occasion destroys clarity also can enhance a message by making it richer.

Appropriateness.   From correctness and clarity comes appropriateness. It is necessary to understand, however, that there are many special vocabularies involved. It is only to poke fun at a middle-aged father that an author would have him speak the language of his adolescent daughter, for example. In addition, communication is impaired for the uninitiated when a writer or speaker orients the message to a special shoptalk that the reader or listener does not know. In our culture such problems are common.

A significant source of humor on the original *Cheers*, the situation comedy about characters in a Boston bar, is the specialized (and out-of-place) jargon of Diane Chambers. In one episode, Woody Boyd, the young bartender, may have to return to Indiana because his father feels that Boston is a dangerous place to live. Diane scripts and attempts to shoot a video intended to persuade Woody's father otherwise. The following excerpt illustrates the language problem:

Diane: Please, a little more reverence for the words I've written. Stick to the script, and try to be spontaneous.

Norm: You know, when the average Joe, like me, gets off work he needs to come to a place like this where he can sort of unwind with his surrogate family.

Cliff: Took the words right out of my mouth, Norm. But it feels as if a crucial part of our support system is missing.

Sam: You're right. What do you think that would be, Carla?

Carla: Could it be that bucolic ray of sunshine from Indiana? This is stupid. This whole thing is stupid, Diane.

Diane: People, people. Work with me. Work with me.

Sam: I hate that "people, people . . ."

Diane: Please, Sam.

Sam: All right. You're right, Woody's not here. The place isn't the same without his smiling countenance.

Woody: Hello, everybody.

All: Hello, Woody.

Sam: Come over and join us for some male bonding.

Woody: Well, that sounds good but first I have to call my mother.

Norm: Sure is refreshing to see a son being so considerate of his mother, isn't it, Carla?

Carla: It's stupid.

There are two immediate problems with shoptalk and jargon: The uninitiated may not understand it and it soon becomes trite. Sportscasters labor under this problem all the time. They look for "momentum," "the Big M," "Old Mo." They believe in the "home court advantage." They want more recognition for "the men down in the trenches." They know a "sack," a "blitz," a "two-on-one advantage" when they see them, and they know when "someone got burned." The problem is that they say these things so many times that the expressions become boring and less appropriate, even though they are clear.

To illustrate the principles operating here, let us turn to Cicero, ancient Rome's greatest orator, who identified the general classifications of low, middle, and grand style. Low style, he said, was appropriate to instruction, middle was for pleasure, and grand was for persuasion. The competent orator must be able to use all three, even in the same speech. But the orator must know on what occasions and on which parts of a speech to use what style (Clarke 1953, 81–82). These styles were differentiated by the complexity of the vocabulary, the extensiveness of the figures of speech, and the elaborateness of the sentence structure.

Herman Melville's (1964) *Moby-Dick* is a classic treasure, but it is a product of another time and more elegant language than one would expect today. Consider the following excerpt:

When on that shivering winter's night, the Pequod thrust her vindictive bow into the cold malicious waves, who should I see standing at her helm but Bulkington! I looked with sympathetic awe and fearfulness upon the man, who in mid-winter just landed from a four years' dangerous voyage, could so unrestingly push off again for still another tempestuous term. The land seemed scorching to his feet. Wonderfullest things are ever the unmentionable; deep memories yield no epitaphs; this six-inch chapter is the stoneless grave of Bulkington (148).

William Faulkner (1946) uses a plain style because the voice that is speaking in *The Sound and the Fury* is Benjy, a mentally retarded boy:

"What is it." Caddy said. "Did you think it would be Christmas when I came home from school. Is that what you thought. Christmas is the day after tomorrow. Santy Claus, Benjy. Santy Claus. Come on, let's run to the house and get warm." She took my hand and we ran through the bright rustling leaves. We ran up the steps and out of the bright cold, into the dark cold. Uncle Maury was putting the bottle back in the sideboard (27).

These are quite different styles: the first is high in figures of speech, vocabulary, and complex sentences—a grand style; the second is short on figures of speech, uses simple sentences, and vocabulary—a plain style. Each is adapted to the situation; each is appropriate.

Impressiveness.   *Impressiveness* is the term we give to the extent to which a message moves toward, or adopts, the grand style. Writers and speakers will use many devices to provide greater emphasis and imagery. More complex sentence structure and greater variety in sentence structure is one device. Also used are such syntactical forms as repetition, climax, antithesis, and rhetorical questions. However, the most prevalent device used today is metaphor.

For many critics, metaphor is more than a device. Metaphor, because it draws an analogy among situations that are unrelated (e.g., "the war on drugs," "a marriage of convenience," "loan sharks"), is a way to create new thought through language use. Thus, it is central to making sense through language. A poem can be thought of as an extended metaphor that relates human experience to general principles. For example, Robert Frost's (1946) "Mending Wall" is not simply about two men repairing a wall (the obvious meaning) but repairing relations, or perhaps, in the words of Louis Untermeyer, "the clash of two forces: the spirit of revolt, which challenges tradition, and the spirit of restraint, which insists that conventions must be upheld, built up and continually rebuilt, as a matter of principle" (Frost, 111). Also, a story is always about something more than the details of its telling. For a non-believer, the Bible is a collection of stories, but for the believer, those stories are metaphors that reveal general truths as applicable today as then.

Therefore, metaphor takes on special significance. At the very least, it is a powerful figure of speech, at the most the basis of all communication. Again, to illustrate the value of metaphor, let us turn to the last eight lines of Frost's "Mending Wall":

> . . . I see him there
> Bringing a stone grasped firmly by the top
> In each hand, like an old-stone savage armed.
> He moves in darkness as it seems to me,
> Not of woods only and the shade of trees.
> He will not go beyond his father's saying,
> And he likes having thought of it so well.
> He says again, "Good fences make good neighbors" (113).

There is a simile here: "like an old-stone savage armed." Then a metaphor, "He moves in darkness," which is weakened somewhat by "as it seems to me." Is the poet not so sure of himself? Or is he just being polite? His point of view is made clear by the metaphor of "savage" and "darkness." But by the end of the poem its dominant metaphor is final: "Good fences make good neighbors." What fences, what neighbors? Surely not just rock walls between New England neighbors where "He is all pine and I am apple orchard." It is friends, family, neighbors, colleagues, perhaps nations.

Spectacle and Song

For Aristotle (1927), spectacle and song were the least important formal aspects:

> Of the remaining elements, Song holds the chief place among the embellishments. The Spectacle has, indeed, an emotional attraction of its own, but, of all the parts it is the least artistic, and connected least with the art of poetry. . . . The production of spectacular effects depends more on the art of the stage machinist than that of the poet (29–31).

Although Aristotle was speaking at a time when the means of producing spectacle were limited, his formal priorities remain important. Formalist critics come primarily from literary backgrounds where even plays are frequently seen as written documents to be read by actors. To such critics, core aesthetic values are in language.

The formal critic's reservation about spectacle as a contributor to aesthetic worth is reinforced by others. On July 27, 1988, the day before the Democratic National Convention, Garrick Utley on the *Sunday Today* show said: "The fact is that conventions and television were made for each other—substance and spectacle. . . . Why should you watch? You already know the score [which candidate will win]. You watch because you want to know how the players will perform." That might be a basis for judging the political conventions worth watching, but not by formal standards.

Perhaps if Aristotle were alive today he would not argue quite so negatively against spectacle. What William Shakespeare's plays could never do on stage they can do on film and video. As a college student, I recall hearing a professor in a theater literature class say of Laurence Olivier's films *Hamlet* and *Henry V*, "Shakespeare wrote his plays for the motion pictures." Certainly, in terms of realism such a claim is true. Placing the ghost at the Castle at Elsinore is no problem for modern technology. The ghost can walk right through the castle wall or disappear in an instant. Henry V can fight the Battle of Agincourt against the French in a realistic fashion never possible on the stage. Indeed, Shakespeare (Winston edition, 1926) opens the play with a call to the viewers to use their imaginations. The Chorus says:

> Think, when we talk of horses, that you see them,
> Printing their proud hoofs i' the receiving earth;
> For 'tis your thoughts that now must deck our kings,
> Carry them here and there, jumping o're times,
> Turning the accomplishments of many years
> Into an hour-glass (539).

While realists prefer to see horses, ghosts, and kings, others argue that the human imagination possesses more value than any realistic rendering. However, this debate is of some complexity and will not be resolved soon. For even other critics, modern visual techniques provide an opportunity unique to itself: the visualization of ideas and feelings.

Production effects, the visual elements of modern technology, also can help to establish a sense of intimacy impossible even in a stage play. Horace Newcomb (1987) has pointed out that intimacy is a primary characteristic of the television aesthetic and he illustrates it with an examination of the show *Ironside*, the main character of which is a physically handicapped police chief:

> In some shows, such as *Ironside*, the redesigning of space in keeping with the needs of the character takes on special significance. Ironside requests and receives the top floor of the police headquarters building. In renovating that space he turns it not only into an office but into a home as well. His personal life is thereby defined by his physical relationship to his profession and to the idea of fighting crime. He inhabits the very building of protection. He resides over it in a godlike state that fits his relationship to the force. The fact that it is his home also fits him to serve as the father figure to the group of loyal associates and tempers the way in which he is seen by criminals and by audience (616).

Not only do the words, actions, and revealing camera close-ups depict intimacy, but also in *Ironside* the set in which the story is shot provides an intimate screen through which the plot develops.

Robert K. Tiemens (1978) examined the 1976 presidential debates between Gerald Ford and Jimmy Carter and found that generally the "differences in camera framing and composition, camera angle, screen placement, and reaction shots seemingly favored Mr. Carter" (370). Here is one example of his analysis:

> Two-shots [where both candidates are shown] used in the first and third debates showed a difference in screen height which favored Ford. This is not surprising in light of the fact that Mr. Ford is three to four inches taller than Mr. Carter, . . . In the second debate, however, analyses of the two-shots from both sides of the stage made Carter appear taller (368).

Of course, these are only a few of the ideas that have been developed from the careful examination of the physical factors of modern electronic media.

Although examination of the visual (television and cinema) is in its early stages, attempts at standards that provide interesting differences have been made. James Monaco (1977) calls film a "quasi-language" and argues that the viewer must develop a visual literacy "to fully appreciate it" (121). Although Monaco defines categories of analysis that reflect analogy with language (denotative and connotative meaning, metonymy, synecdoche, and syntax, for instance), he also looks to codes that, at first glance, have no relation to language at all ("the framed image," "perception of depth," "proximity," "planes") (130–192). Herbert Zettl (1973), on the other hand, approaches the visual from its own scientific language specifically to avoid analogy with verbal language. He is interested in how light, color, depth, timing, and motion interact.

On this subject, there is far more to say than is possible here. The combination of the visual and the auditory in music videos would require a chapter of its own. It is good that serious critics are examining more carefully the formal visual aspects of communication. Their importance to formal criticism, however, will always be linked to how well such forms can lead to general principles of human existence. Any kind of visual aesthetics must, like style and character, contribute to that objective or else they are interesting, perhaps even spectacular, but not particularly important to formal criticism.

PROBLEMS WITH FORMAL CRITICISM

Formal criticism reveals many of the same problems as accurate interpretation, based as they are upon two of the same assumptions. For example, some critics argue that formal criticism is incorrect in assuming that there is an objective interpretation of the text, ignores the historical dimensions of communication, and assumes a sophisticated reader or viewer.

Arguments that deny the possibility of an objective interpretation of a text were reviewed in the previous chapter. For example, some critics believe that the interpretation of a message is set by the conventions of a society, not by some general notion of the "true" meaning. Those who have tried to defend the notion of accurate interpretation have frequently turned to intention (Hirsch 1960, 467–468): The intention of the author is revealed through the text and determines meaning. Still, how do we know the author's intention? Even if we knew the author's intention, what do we do with interpretations that other persons and other ages might bring to a particular text? Even where formal critics are willing to accept alternate interpretations, their separation of form and content leads to narrower focus than is possible with other approaches to communication criticism.

If there is no possibility of accurate interpretation, the formal critic would argue, then any interpretation is legitimate and criticism becomes a matter of taste. In addition, even if we grant the difficulty of accurate interpretation, it is significant to note that many divergent approaches still use formal categories.

Formal criticism's orientation to the development of general themes that transcend the story makes texts ahistorical, and, it is argued, not particularly useful to contemporary readers. Once again, as in the complaint against accurate interpretation, the disagreement is over fundamental assumptions. Formal criticism in its most pure form, New Criticism, came about because of a belief that the literary text was being lost in historical and biographical studies. Today, formalist critics can argue that deconstructive approaches to criticism are losing the text in politics and sociology. Critics who emphasize history, politics, and receivers may lose track of what the text says on its own.

But the social condition is an important part of life and needs to be understood. If formal criticism is carried to an extreme, it would deny to the text any relevance to the nature of contemporary society and the way people live in it. How, then, could people use texts to help them understand further or resolve their problems? Many readers want texts that help them decide which candidate to support in an election, how to be a better spouse, how the welfare system should be administered, and so on.

In response, the formal critic would point out that such recommendations are expressed although not specifically. Again, formal criticism provides general principles of aesthetic and moral worth that can be applied to specific situations. Messages that provide timely answers alone are trivial; they do not reveal universal themes. Chapter 5 will discuss another common sense critical approach that seeks to know about specific answers and their effect on audiences—neoclassical criticism. To the formal critic, however, much of that approach is frivolous, more concerned with advertising and which soap to purchase than anything more. Therefore, while formalist critics are faulted for being uninterested in the social dimensions of texts, they argue that that is the only way to reveal what is essential in texts—the general principles.

Although formal criticism is a common sense approach, the skills necessary to use it are not as common. Unlike accurate interpretation that requires only some research skills to find information and check it against the information presented in the message, formal analysis requires an understanding of sophisticated elements such as plot, character, and language.

Whereas any reasonably well-educated person can function as an accurate interpretation critic, the formalist critic requires considerable special training, particularly in literary studies. The need for special training becomes especially true for poetry, the subject of much literary theorizing. Poetry is highly compacted, emphasizes metaphorical language, and is much more difficult to unravel.

Formalist critics recognize this problem but regard it as a necessary condition. Interpretation will be difficult when trying to understand general themes in a language that argues by metaphor. However, it is just such study that will reveal the essential elements of meaning in a text. Other easier approaches, such as accurate interpretation, are more trivial in their objectives.

Formal criticism is one of the oldest and most developed approaches to criticism. Its aim is to discover the aesthetic value in a message. It is not easily mastered because it depends on a sophisticated reader, listener, or viewer. Consequently, it is perhaps the most demanding common sense approach to criticism.

CHAPTER FIVE

Neoclassical Criticism
Communication as Persuasion

On the morning of April 13, 1963, the Reverend Martin Luther King, Jr., sat in a jail cell in Birmingham, Alabama, and wrote his "Letter from Birmingham Jail." He had deliberately disobeyed an injunction of the Alabama Supreme Court against demonstrations, and he had disobeyed it on a symbolic day: Good Friday. His letter was in response to a letter published in the *Birmingham News* by eight white Birmingham clergymen, arguing for an end to protest activities.

The letter, begun on the margins of the newspaper and on small scraps of paper, had a major impact on the civil rights movement of the sixties and on subsequent audiences with different issues. Designed as a refutation to the argument of others, it is a persuasive document with a clearly defined audience. It emphasizes

> clarity and logic. . . . Its structure makes it both readable and thorough. Its refutative stance makes it alive with the fire of heated but courteous controversy, and the dual nature of the refutation makes it simultaneously persuasive and logically compelling. Its stylistic variety and nuance portray a personality in print, manipulate a reader's emotions, and create a union of reader and rhetor (Fulkerson 1979, 136).

This interpretation of King's letter for its persuasive characteristics illustrates neoclassical critical argument. Neoclassical criticism has been the dominant critical form for examining speeches, although it also has been applied to other persuasive message forms, principally essays, pamphlets, editorials, and advertisements. It even has been extended to messages previously considered the province of accurate interpretation and formal criticism such as docudramas, news reports, films, novels, and letters.

During the past 20 years or so, the neoclassical approach has experienced a series of changes. Within the field of public address criticism, neoclassicism was attacked with some success for reasons that will be discussed later (Black 1965b). These attacks caused many critics to examine alternative approaches to the study of speeches. At the same time, a growing number of critics from fields such as journalism, history, and literature usually associated with accurate interpretation and formal approaches to criticism became more interested in persuasion (Glasser and Ettema 1987; Megill and McCloskey 1987, 221; Fish 1980, 365; Eagleton 1983, 205).

Therefore, at the very moment when neoclassicism seemed most in danger, it gained in popularity. In addition, G. P. Mohrmann's 1980 survey of articles in public address criticism showed that many of the alternate approaches and "innovations" contain neoclassicism's principles if under different labels (266–267).

Neoclassical is used to characterize this approach because, although it has strong links to Aristotle's *Rhetoric*, it is more flexible than *neo-Aristotelian*, which carries the negative connotations ascribed to it by Edwin Black (1965b, 27–35). *Neo-Aristotelian* also can be confused with the Chicago School of formalist critics, such as R. S. Crane (1953). *Neoclassical criticism* is a more useful designation than *neo-Aristotelian* also because it is based on more than a narrow interpretation of Aristotle's *Rhetoric* (Mohrmann and Leff 1974, 459). Although this chapter will focus on the most traditional approach in order to more easily differentiate it from its deconstructive offspring in later chapters, neoclassical criticism remains a coat of many colors.

THE ASSUMPTIONS OF NEOCLASSICAL CRITICISM

Early writers on rhetoric did not write about criticism per se. Rather, they attempted to explain to citizens how to give speeches. In ancient Greece, where citizens had responsibilities in legislative affairs and were required to speak for themselves in a court of law, the ability to give a speech was an essential skill. Because public speaking was a practical art, rhetorical criticism derived from principles of application. However, in describing practical arts, classical writers also described them within a philosophical system. For this reason, we are able to determine the assumptions of neoclassical criticism.

Humans Are Essentially Reasonable

"The function of man is an activity of the soul which follows or implies a rational principle," said Aristotle (1941, 1098a). The actions of human beings, including what they say, can be explained as a part of a reasoning process. To be reasonable, however, does not mean the same as to be logical. Logic is a specialized form of reasoning that does not explain how a person uses common sense reasons. Some persuasion-oriented critics have tried to adapt the rules of logic to their critical method, but none expects a message to meet the rules of logic (Mudd 1959). To Aristotle, humans act in ways that follow or imply rationality, but they do not live by logic.

Chaim Perelman (1979) notes "the existence of two adjectives, 'rational' and 'reasonable,' both derived from the same noun, and designating a conformity with reason," that have quite different applications because rational means a "conformity to the rules of logic" while reasonable means that persons make judgments "influenced by *common sense*" (117–118).

Thus, the reasonable argument will have a persuasive effect on a particular audience. Unlike formal critics, the neoclassical critic does not claim to find general principles to find what should be accepted. Neoclassical criticism is message-environment oriented. It seeks to find what arguments will be seen as reasonable by particular audiences.

Even with the most sophisticated research methods, any argument (for example, the argument that the Soviet Union can be trusted) can only be made as a probable case. The meaning of the term *trusted* is not absolute, but a matter of common sense interpretation. The same is true of the statistical and anecdotal evidence that is available to prove the claim. Many believe the claim but they have not found truth; they have accepted probability as reasonable.

This same first assumption characterizes accurate interpretation with this difference. Accurate interpretation emphasizes a belief in objective truth while neoclassical criticism emphasizes an audience's understanding of what is probable. The audience of reasonable human beings sets the standard for what is believable, and to the neoclassicist one audience will differ from another in what it accepts.

Neoclassical Criticism Is Concerned with Audience Response

Neoclassical criticism is concerned with the ways that messages provide probable arguments to reasonable human beings. Thus, the effect of messages on audiences is preeminent. The phenomenon of effect, however, has a variety of interpretations.

The strictest understanding of effect, quoted in Chapter 1, was Herbert Wichelns's 1925 statement. It emphasized that a speech is "a communication to a specific audience, and holds [criticism's] business to be the analysis and appreciation of the orator's method of imparting his ideas to his hearers" (35).

Wichelns's statement and the further codification of neoclassical criticism in Lester Thonssen and A. Craig Baird's (1948) *Speech Criticism* served for a quarter of a century as the central orientation of the approach. But Wichelns's statement is more an assertion of liberation from formal aesthetic standards than a basis for criticism. In that regard, Thonssen and Baird in their chapter on the subject identify six different bases for judging effectiveness, "long-range effects upon the social group" being one of them (455–459). In addition, effectiveness is measured not by the actual changes in the audience, then or later, but how well the speaker did considering the circumstances. The Reverend Jesse Jackson failed to gain the Democratic nomination for president in 1988. He received less than 30 percent of the delegate votes at the convention. Yet, he is a clergyman, a black, a person without previous political office, and a social liberal. The critic of Jackson's campaign must consider these and other circumstances in assessing his effectiveness.

This point of view is supported by Aristotle's (1932) definition of rhetoric "as the faculty (or power) of discovering in the particular case what are the available means of persuasion" (7). So, the means of persuasion are available in the audience and must be found. A critical judgment, therefore, is over how effective the speaker was in finding what was available.

Aristotle's Athenian audience was a comparatively homogeneous group with similar values that limited the potentially effective arguments. In our complicated modern society with diverse interest groups contending with one another, the small Athenian audience cannot serve as a model. Consequently, the contemporary communicator's audience is not a whole nation but a "target audience" (Hill 1972, 375). Thus, a neoclassical critic could find communication effective with one target audience but ineffective with others.

Two studies of American communism illustrate this difference. Carl R. Burgchardt (1980) examines Communist pamphleteers in the 1930s, and observes that despite the favorable conditions of the Great Depression, they had no success with the non-Communist public because of what the audience perceived as "shrill name calling" and "bluntness in presenting communism's uncompromising goals" (379). Richard J. Ilkka (1977) shows how the early American Communist rhetoric was "both exciting and confirmatory for those already involved within the movement. After all, when the view of a world turning on a revolutionary axis was joined with those dramatizations of the emerging Communist hero as revolutionary activist, the result must have been an irresistible directive, the chance to be heroes in a conflict whose triumphal resolution was historically inevitable" (427). Here are two studies on the same subject but quite different in the judgment of effectiveness, not just because they used different texts, but mostly because they are interested in different audiences.

Some would argue that a neoclassical critic cannot address the effects on an audience unless reasonable assumptions are made about the speaker's intent. Such a criticism is oriented source–message–environment, and the critical question is stated: How effective was the message in achieving the intended result? But intent is not essential. Most critics from a neoclassical approach are interested in the impact of a message on an audience, whether intended or not (Sillars 1976, 76–77).

Messages Are Judged by the Arguments They Make

With the attention paid to reason and audiences, it is not surprising that the neoclassical approach should emphasize the arguments made in messages. The persuasion-oriented critic finds it useful to consider a message as a series of arguments aimed at gaining the adherence of the audience. But this series of arguments does not stand alone. Aristotle (1932) said that "rhetoric proves opposites" (6). Not only does an arguer find arguments that will be probable to an audience, but another arguer could use similar arguments to prove the opposite claim. Therefore, opposing arguments must be considered in determining the effectiveness of any claim. In the contest to gain audience adherence, unstated and opposition arguments are potentially part of a debate and must be considered.

Looking at a message as an argument made up of a series of claims and their support addressed to an audience requires that the critic examine the context in which the audience receives the message. Are there arguments, stated by opponents or known to the audience, that a message does not address? If so, a critic may have reason to find the message nonpersuasive. In a previous chapter, the 1988 controversy over the motion picture *The Last Temptation of Christ* was discussed. Fundamentalist Christians opposed it because of what they considered a false portrayal of Christ. Some extreme opponents made their argument an anti-Semitic one without considering opposition arguments:

> The debate has been ugly. Jerry Falwell predicted the film would create "a wave of anti-Semitism," and to an extent he's been proved right. Fundamentalist Baptists picketing Universal Studios enacted a "Jewish businessman" stomping on the back of a blood-splattered Christ. They chartered a plane that flew the banner: "Wasserman Fans Jew Hatred with Temptation." (Lew Wasserman is the chairman of MCA, which owns Universal.) It is unlikely that such thoughts would have occurred to anyone were it not for the fundamentalists, since none of the creators of the movie was Jewish. The original author was Greek Orthodox, the director Roman Catholic, the screenwriter, Paul Schrader, Dutch Calvinist (David Ansen, et al. 1988, 56).

The neoclassical critic is concerned about the quality of the arguments addressed to the audience and emphasizes what Aristotle (1932) called "artistic proof" rather than "nonartistic proofs." Artistic proofs are provided by the communicator at the moment of communication; they are what the communicator says or does to have an effect on an audience. Nonartistic proofs are those that might influence an audience but are "not supplied by our own efforts, but existed beforehand, such as witnesses, admissions under torture, written contracts, and the like" (8).

Today, admissions under torture have little to commend them as proof but the principle can be extended to those items that might be persuasive regardless of what the speaker says. Sometimes, in a court of law, clients win despite the ineptness of their attorneys. In 1980, Jimmy Carter lost the presidential election to Ronald Reagan. His defeat was influenced by several events over which he may have had no control: the Soviet invasion of Afghanistan, the Iranian seizure of American hostages, the oil shortage, and subsequent high inflation. In 1952, Dwight D. Eisenhower won the election although most commentators described him as a poor communicator. Nonetheless, his role as Commander of the Allied Forces in Europe in World War II may have been all he needed to be elected.

Although nonartistic proofs can be quite persuasive, and the neoclassical critic will not ignore them, of greater importance are artistic proofs; that is, those constructed by the source of the message. Aristotle (1932) identified three artistic proofs. "The first kind resides in the character [*ethos*] of the speaker; the second consists in producing a certain attitude in the hearer [*pathos*] the third appertains to the argument proper [*logos,*] in so far as it actually or seemingly demonstrates" (8).

Logos, ethos, and *pathos* are closely related to rhetorical organization, delivery, and style. How a speaker organizes a talk can contribute to *logos,* delivery can influence an audience's perception of a speaker's *ethos,* the language used can enhance an audience's emotional response to values (*pathos*), for instance. Thus, in a very real sense, these methods of proof are integrated one with another.

While *logos, ethos,* and *pathos* are the substance of rhetorical proofs, they are combined together, says Aristotle (1932), in two argument forms: the enthymeme and the example (10–11). The enthymeme is a rhetorical deduction based on audience-accepted warrants that yield probable conclusions. The example is what Aristotle called "a rhetorical induction" (10); that is, examples are used to demonstrate how a generalization is applicable to their lives. For years Democrats used Herbert Hoover and the Great Depression as examples of what happens when Republicans run the economy and, since 1980, the Republicans have used Jimmy Carter, inflation, and loss of prestige abroad to generalize about Democrats.

In December of 1988, when the University of Oklahoma football program was placed on three years probation by the National Collegiate Athletic Association (NCAA), a sportswriter argued that it was no surprise, but rather represented "the sorry state of college athletics." He argued by enthymeme: "Tell me, when Oklahoma won the national championship three years ago, did any college football fan in the country believe for a minute that all the Sooners' scholarship players at the Orange Bowl coronation on January 1, 1985 got there without ever receiving a single illegal inducement?" The answer he claimed was "no" because of an unstated basic principle that no school can win the national championship without violating national rules. To further prove the "sorry state," he used other schools charged with violations—Texas A&M, Houston, Kansas, Kentucky, Southern Methodist, and Nevada, Las Vegas—as examples (Hemphill).

There is much more to be said about how these two argument forms can encompass such modern forms of argument as analogy, sign, or cause (Perelman 1979, 26–27). For now these two Aristotelian categories can serve us well. To summarize the nature of rhetorical arguments and the relationships we have discussed, let us look at a diagram developed over 50 years ago by James McBurney (1936, 52):

Aristotle's Rhetorical System

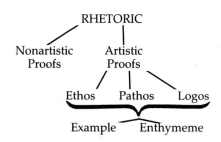

After J. H. McBurney.

This diagram illustrates much of what we have already noted. Rhetoric has both nonartistic and artistic proofs but the artistic proofs are most important.

How can a general principle be justified by as few as one example or how can one reach an acceptable deductive claim without meeting the tests of logic? The diagram tells us the answer: because enthymematic arguments and arguments from examples have *ethos* and *pathos* as well as *logos* to justify them (Grimaldi 1972, 136):

An argument which did not contain all three factors is an impossibility. The critic might find one factor emphasized over another in a given argument but would not find any missing. For instance, in Richard Nixon's defense of himself in his 1952 vice-presidential campaign he used many arguments to build his *ethos*. Here is one: "I joined the Navy and served in the Pacific Theater. Oh, I guess I earned a few battle ribbons but I was no hero. I was just there when the bombs were falling" (78). Although the appeal to *ethos* is obvious it does not function unless an audience is disposed to believe it reasonable that modesty and serving one's country in wartime are signs *(logos)* of patriotism *(pathos)*.

Neoclassical criticism shares with its two common sense cousins the assumption that humans are essentially reasonable. But the second and third assumptions of neoclassical criticism are what clearly separates it from the other two. The audience (listener, reader, viewer, society) sets the standard by which persuasiveness is measured. Messages are made up of arguments directed at audiences. Their nature—a combination of *logos*, *ethos*, and *pathos*—makes them different from what arguments would be thought of in any other context. These assumptions must be kept in mind when looking at the application of neoclassical criticism.

NEOCLASSICAL ANALYSIS

To describe the full array of procedures of neoclassical criticism would require more space than is available here. However, some main areas of analysis can be identified. This section, then, will identify what the critic looks for. The following section explains how the criticism is organized. Neoclassical analysis involves finding issues, understanding the audience, discovering the structure, identifying arguments, values, *ethos*, and examining style.

What Are the Issues?

James R. Andrews (1983) calls this stage of analysis constructing "an argumentational history of issues" (22). The critic must discover what the potential issues are in the communication situation. To do this, the critic examines the subject matter of a message and asks questions such as: what have others said about the subject? What arguments are likely to be raised against the position developed in the message? The critic must also study what others have said and what recent events are likely to influence the receivers of the message. From this analysis the critic finds the claims that are likely to influence the target audience. When these claims are placed in opposition to one another, they identify the issues.

In 1990, Nelson Mandela, the 72-year-old leader of the African National Congress (ANC), was released from a South African prison. That country, under the leadership of President Frederik W. de Klerk, seemed to be moving away from apartheid, the policy of racial separation and white dominance, toward greater freedom for native Africans, but most restrictive laws were still in force.

In June of 1990, Mandela came to the United States and was honored with a tremendous reception in cities like New York, Detroit, Atlanta, and Miami. He hoped to encourage the United States to continue sanctions against South Africa until the political system there was reversed. Some Americans, however, wanted sanctions relaxed to encourage the de Klerk government to do more.

Some people were disturbed by Mandela's friendly attitude toward Yassir Arafat, Muammar Qadhafi, and Fidel Castro in response to their support of the ANC when he was in prison. Each of these leaders was seen by one American group or another as opposed to human rights ("Living under a hero's mantle," 1990; and Johnson and McLeod, 1990).

As Mandela toured and spoke in America, the issues that took shape for most people were not opposition to apartheid, support for human freedom, or Mandela's personal courage. The important issues, the potential points of clash, could be defined with statements like the following:

> Will continued sanctions against South Africa help or delay racial democracy?
> Are conditions improved by nonviolent protest or must violence always be a factor?
> Can Nelson Mandela improve human rights while he accepts the support of Arafat, Qadhafi, and Castro?

To find the issues, critics must examine the history of the disagreement to discover what claims others have made to which this message might be expected to respond. If an analysis of the message reveals that it did not respond to the issues, a critic must take that failure into account in determining its effectiveness.

What Is the Nature of the Audience?

Already suggested above is the audience's role in determining which issues could or must be addressed. For instance, the 1980 presidential campaign was influenced by the fact that Iran had seized 57 American hostages. Neither Jimmy Carter nor Ronald Reagan could claim to know a means of freeing them for fear of being called upon to provide it. There was no issue over their desire to free them. But the situation posed a particular problem for Carter because it was during his presidency that the hostages had been seized. What he could say was limited by the situation. Reagan could claim that the Carter administration was responsible for the seizure and make an issue of it. As such, issues were limited by what the audience knew or believed (Bitzer 1968).

By combining the analysis of issues found in the argumentational history with an understanding of what the audience knows and believes, the critic can see what limits and opportunities are available to the arguer; these will define the "available means of persuasion." A first step in that process is to look at contemporary audiences.

Target Audience.   In a large and diverse society, talk about the mass audience can be rather useless. In the United States, there is diversity in economic status, religion, and racial and ethnic background. Consequently, messages are addressed to target audiences.

"Overall, the evening TV news audience," says Lawrence Lichty (1982), "is disproportionately older (especially over 65), female (53 percent) and less well educated than are newspaper readers or the population as a whole." Consequently, network news has to adapt to the knowledge level of that group. Neoclassical critical judgments will take that information into account either in evaluating how well the networks adapt to that target audience or to speculate on why other groups are less interested in it.

Forbes Hill (1972) in his analysis of Richard Nixon's speech of November 3, 1969, on the Vietnam War defines the target audience this way:

> The primary target was those Americans not driven by a clearly defined ideological commitment to oppose or support the war at any cost. Resentment of the sacrifice in money and lives, bewilderment at the stalemate, longing for some movement in a clearly worked direction—these were the principal aspects of their state of mind assumed by Nixon. He solicited them saying "tonight—to you, the great silent majority of my fellow Americans—I ask for your support" (375).

Knowing the target audience is a first step. Then it is necessary to know what the characteristics of that audience are.

James R. Andrews (1983) has identified three audience variables that will influence the communicator's limits and opportunities: *knowledge*, *group identification*, and *receptivity* (31). These three provide a reasonable basis for understanding the role of audience in any communicative situation.

Knowledge.   The potentials for persuasion are limited by what the audience "knows" about a situation. Audience knowledge includes knowledge that the critic may consider erroneous. If an audience "knows" that foreign goods are hurting the American economy, it does not matter that the critic disagrees. That knowledge will limit the rhetorical efficacy of a speaker who argues for free trade. This is one of the clearest points of difference between the neoclassical critic and the accurate interpretation critic. The critic who wishes to see communication as persuasion must begin where the audience is, not where the critic would like it to be.

Television newsmagazine programs such as *60 Minutes* or *20/20* introduce subjects about which their audiences know little—an Illinois power plant, a religious group in Florida, or a suit against the Mormon Church in Utah. Therefore, what information they provide is a part of their persuasion. Their technique is to appear to be objective, to merely give information, to increase the viewer's knowledge. However, the information they choose to introduce and what they leave out must be analyzed by the critic.

Philip Kipper (1987) argues that television news is persuasive. As an example he cites a *CBS Evening News* story in January of 1987 about television evangelist Oral Roberts telling his viewing audience that unless he received $4.5 million for his medical center he would be "taken away" by

God. The news story by Harry Smith, Kipper shows, emphasizes how Roberts has become pessimistic, is in financial trouble, is criticized by clergy and citizen alike, is losing viewers, and puts money over faith. CBS News persuades its audience by providing information, implying that Oral Roberts is more interested in money than faith (17–22).

Group Identification.   A target audience will also be influenced by the groups it identifies with and those from which it disassociates. The critic needs to know about these group identifications or may be led astray in assessing persuausibility. The popular situation comedy *All in the Family* and its sequel *Archie's Place* were produced by Norman Lear and the star as Archie Bunker was Carroll O'Connor. Both Lear and O'Connor are political and social liberals. Norman Lear and others believed that a humorous portrayal of an ignorant Archie Bunker who was right wing in his politics, a racist, and sexist in his social views, would counter such views. However, for viewers who held similar views, Archie Bunker became a kind of folk hero who said exactly what they wanted to say (Vidmar and Rokeach 1974, 47). As a result, the neoclassical critic who examines the persuasiveness of *All in the Family* must recognize that part of the audience identifies with, and part rejects, Archie Bunker.

The Thorn Birds, a television miniseries about a Catholic priest who falls in love and fathers a son was, at the time, the second most popular miniseries in television history. It also aroused the ire of Catholic groups, who objected to the theme and the fact that it was aired during the Easter season. For those Catholics with a strong group identification as Catholics, the series's effectiveness was limited.

In a 1976 presidential debate with Jimmy Carter, President Gerald Ford said, "There is no Soviet domination of Eastern Europe and there never will be under a Ford Administration." In answer to a follow-up question he said, "Each of these countries is independent, autonomous, it has its own territorial integrity and the United States does not concede that those countries are under the domination of the Soviet Union." His opponent replied, "I would like to see Mr. Ford convince the Polish Americans that those countries don't live under the domination and supervision of the Soviet Union behind the Iron Curtain" (Carter and Ford, 36). That exchange was widely regarded as an element in Carter's victory.

Important for the critic here is that people frequently do not think of themselves as being in a particular group until an issue is made of it. Thus, Americans of Eastern European heritage may not have thought of themselves as such until Ford made the statement and Carter pointed it out. The critic will be interested in what potentials exist for group identification and then observe how the message calls up such identification.

Receptivity.   Even when the issues at hand are part of an audience's knowledge and related to its group identification, audiences will differ in receptivity, depending on the extent to which the issues are seen as important. The issues around nuclear war are important in society today in a general sense, but are they important at the moment people receive the message? They may not be, for instance, to unemployed workers whose concern is more immediate: the need to get jobs.

The critic must discover what issues are most important to a target audience and determine to what extent the message is linked to those issues. Even on specific topics where several issues exist side by side, one particular issue may be more important than another. In the recession of 1982–1983, President Reagan could argue that taxes had been cut, inflation lessened, and government spending reduced, but because unemployment had increased at the same time that increase could not be ignored. In his 1982 "Speech to the Nation on G.O.P. Policy and the Economy," Reagan began with the problem of unemployment and argued that the control of other factors was a sign that unemployment would be controlled.

The critic of that speech must think clearly about its target audience and the knowledge, group identification, and level of receptivity of that audience. Such an examination will set the basis for determining the effectiveness of the president's message.

What Is the Structure of the Message?

Although most rhetorical principles of structure are discussed in more detail in Chapter 4, two general principles are unity and order. Therefore, look for indications that all arguments are united around a single theme in such a way that each argument relates to every other and to the central theme. The introduction of elements that distract the audience from the central thesis is to be avoided. The critic will look for order that introduces arguments in such a way that each succeeding argument builds on each previous argument.

Ronald Reagan's 1982 speech on the economy presents a good example of such building. The problem, he told his audience, was unemployment. Then he said, "Now let's look at what's behind this bad trend in unemployment. What's been causing it for over a decade?" His answer? "Inflation, and the high interest rates it leads to." And the cause of high interest rates and inflation? "Mistakes of the past," "quick fixes," and "government spending." Then he turned to solutions reversing the cause and effect order. He cut government spending, interest rates and inflation came down, and unemployment was soon to follow. So, let's not return to the "quick fix." We need "courage to see it through." "Stay the course." Part of the rhetorical effectiveness in the speech was how the problem of unemployment in 1982 was put into a problem-cause-solution order, and in each section, individual arguments were structured so that each argument was linked to the argument before and the argument following (Sandeen and Sillars 1983).

The critic also will look for the specific means by which unity and order are maintained. The critic will ask what transitions are used between points to make unity and order clear to the particular audience. Note this example of the transition from problem to causes in Reagan's speech:

> Getting Americans back to work is an urgent priority for all of us—and especially for this administration. But remember, you can't solve unemployment without solving the things that caused it—the out-of-control government spending, the sky-rocketing inflation and interest rates that led to unemployment in the first place (6).

As noted in the previous chapter on formal criticism, Harry Truman, in the campaign of 1948, broke the order of his speech in New York City on the economy because of the need to deal with an issue about Israel. That was a case where the available means of persuasion were more important than the formal structure. Although formal conventions of structure will usually be more persuasive because they help to clarify an argument, there are times when they may be broken to aid persuasion.

Malcolm X was a powerful speaker for black revolution in the 1960s. Yet his famous speech, "The Ballot or the Bullet," seems to some to be a string of stories and charges, each one of which can stand alone. In Chapter 2, we saw how one could uncover its themes; but it does not build one argument upon another. It seems only to be a string of examples. It is not quite clear what central claim is being argued. Malcolm X seems to argue that blacks should be permitted to vote, but it is not clear how that will solve the problems of blacks as he portrays them. Yet some young blacks found the speech a powerful message, perhaps because, although short on solutions, it amplified the problems they felt. So, it is probably the case that other available means of persuasion were more important to this target audience than formal structural standards.

What Arguments Are Used in the Message?

The critic will want to know what arguments are developed and how they are supported in the message. Arguments will be evaluated by how well they set the issues that the audience believes are most important, how the message develops issues that were not known to the audience, and what issues important to the audience are ignored.

Even the simplest claim will use argument to support it. Consider, for instance, a short TV commercial. A long-running Crest toothpaste series features a mother and her child who has cavities. The mother is distressed; Mr. Goodwin, the local druggist, tells them that they have not been using the correct toothpaste ("That's not Crest"). Crest, he tells them, has fluoride and is endorsed by the American Dental Association. "Proof, not promises," he tells them. At a later meeting, the child, who has now been using Crest, announces a "good checkup." The druggist beams knowingly. In 30 seconds, a policy claim is advanced—"You should buy Crest." It is supported by two claims of fact, "Crest has fluoride" and "Crest is endorsed by the American Dental Association."

The arguments can be diagrammed for analytical purposes by using the Toulmin model. By this model, a message will provide grounds to support the claim and a warrant that justifies as reasonable the move from grounds to claim. All parts of the argument will frequently not be introduced but where they are omitted they must be part of the audience's knowledge so that they will fill in the missing parts.

Arguments also will need to be backed by evidence if the audience might not accept the statements made. The amount of backing necessary will be determined by the potential for audience distrust of the statements. Let us look at the three arguments in the Crest commercial.

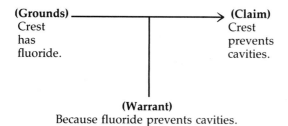

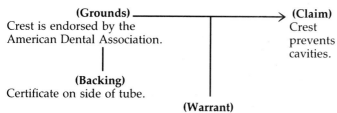

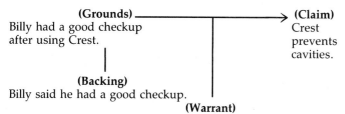

Note that none of the warrants is stated. The producers of this commercial believe they will be understood. Note also that the arguments are enthymemes of special kinds. The first and third are enthymemes based on cause and effect, the second, based on authority. In addition, only the first of these arguments has backing. It could have been backed with statistical evidence showing the amount of fluoride, what is needed to prevent cavities, and so forth. The second enthymeme does have a specific statement from the American Dental Association. The third is backed by Billy's statement. To believe this argument, we must trust Billy. We also have to believe that one example is sufficient proof. It could have been more strongly grounded and backed with statements from Nathaniel, Tommy, Jolene, or Carmen. Thus, backing can be identified generally by three forms of support: statistics, testimony, and examples.

The three factual claims developed in these arguments can be combined to justify a policy claim that the viewer *should* use Crest (see the figure below).

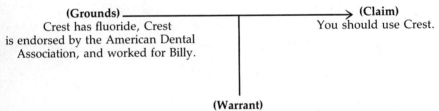

(Grounds) —————————————————→ **(Claim)**
Crest has fluoride, Crest   You should use Crest.
is endorsed by the American Dental
Association, and worked for Billy.

(Warrant)
Because everyone should use a toothpaste that has fluoride, Crest is
endorsed by the ADA, and works.

This argument is never fully developed because the producers of the commercial believe that such a conclusion will be obvious to the viewer from the development provided. To analyze these arguments we have to ask some questions:

1. Will the viewer have additional issues? Example: The Aim commercial, running at the same time as the Crest series, argues that it also tastes good, causing the child to brush more often. How does Crest taste?
2. Will the viewer believe the argument is reasonable? Example: How does Crest compare with other toothpastes on these issues?
3. Will the viewer believe the argument is adequately supported? Example: Is one example adequate to prove it works?
4. Will the viewer accept the message's values? Example: How important is preventing cavities (the value of health)? Does the viewer consider the unmentioned cost value important?

5. Will the viewer accept the message's *ethos?* Example: Is Mr. Goodwin the kind of person we believe?

In this brief examination, we have emphasized the area of argument
form and support, such as statistics, testimony, and examples. Yet, it is
clear that arguments involve, as we noted earlier, more than these elements. They also involve values and *ethos.*

What Values Are Developed in the Message?

No matter how complex or simple, each message is based on certain
values that account for its social force. In the Crest commercial, health in
the form of fewer cavities is clearly basic. If parents do not care whether
their children have cavities, they could hardly care about the argument.
There may also be, for some, an implied value of cost. That is, if a child
has "good checkups" there is less cost for filling cavities. Cost also could
be a negative value if viewers believe that Crest costs more than other
toothpastes.

It is important to examine the message for its stated and unstated values that warrant the claims and determine whether or not those values
will be important to an audience. In Chapter 7, we will look at values in
greater detail. There, values are seen as the basis of an entire approach:
value analysis. But they are important to the neoclassical approach as well.
Although Aristotle did not use the term *social values,* he came close when
he defined happiness as the object of all human action. He went on to
define the constituents of happiness as good birth, children, wealth, good
repute, honor, health, beauty, strength, size, a good old age, friends, good
fortune, and virtue (1932, 24–29). These do not define all of today's values
but they overlap today's value systems. And, of course, values will differ
from one target audience to another.

Values are the source of *pathos* in arguments. They either are the warrants for arguments or serve as backing for the warrants. In that sense, all
messages depend for their effectiveness, eventually, on a link between the
values they state or imply and the values of the audience.

What Ethos Is Developed in the Message?

Aristotle (1932) said that he "might almost affirm that his [the speaker's] character [*ethos*] is the most potent of all the means of persuasion" (9).
"It is a cause for persuasion," he said, "when the speech is so uttered as
to make [the speaker] worthy of belief; for as a rule we trust men of probity
more, and more quickly, about things in general, while on points outside

the realm of exact knowledge, where opinion is divided, we trust them absolutely" (8).

The qualities that define *ethos*, Aristotle (1932) said, are "intelligence, character and good will" (92). The contemporary term *competence* may be better than *intelligence* because it is broader. It might mean formal education to one audience and practical experience to another. Similarly, the contemporary term *trustworthiness* is probably more useful than *character*. Is this someone the audience can put its trust in? It is reminiscent of the question posed by opponents of Richard Nixon, "Would you buy a used car from this man?"

Thus, the critic will want to observe what is indicated in the message to show that communicators are competent and, therefore, worthy of belief because of the knowledge they reveal. The critic also will want to see if messages show that communicators can be trusted to reveal the competent decisions they discover. It is also necessary for communicators to provide evidence to the audience that they have the best interests of the audience in mind (have *goodwill* toward the audience).

Contemporary research has revealed a number of other qualities that provide proof through *ethos*, but the results are rather mixed. That is, sometimes such qualities are there in audience perceptions, sometimes they are not. The most prominent of these qualities is dynamism. Dynamism, however, is problematic in that it is not always positive; rather it is responsive to a situation. Audiences would always want a speaker to be trustworthy, competent, and have goodwill but may find dynamism, as in the case of the overly aggressive salesperson, a sign of lack of trustworthiness.

A critic must also recognize the distinction between reputation and *ethos*. The neoclassical critic is interested in what is encoded in the message. Aristotle (1932) said, "This trust, however, should be created by the speech itself, and not left to depend upon an antecedent impression that the speaker is this or that kind of man" (9). Reputation is a kind of nonartistic proof, so to evaluate a message by the prior reputation of a speaker is to ignore the impact of the actual message. *Rocky II* may have been successful because of the great success of *Rocky* but that does not make it effective in its own right.

Of course, this is the most traditional point of view. Note how such neoclassical judgments sound like judgments a formal critic might make about the artistic merit of a work. Obviously, a critic need not ignore the effect of nonmessage-related factors such as reputation. However, most neoclassical critics would caution that carrying the practice too far will produce noncriticism; that is, it will produce criticism that does not deal with text. Therefore, the artistic development of *ethos*, what the communicator does to enhance it, is generally considered most important.

One useful way of viewing *ethos* is through the concept of *image*. What image of the communicator is created in the message? Image permits the critic to combine the qualities in a general picture. Thus, it is possible to ask what image a campaign created of a particular candidate.

Image is also easier to extend to a wider variety of messages than speeches. There are movements, like the environmental movement, the consumer movement, the gay and lesbian movement, that develop images. There are actors and other celebrities who add their images to products (e.g., Linda Ellerbee and Willard Scott—Maxwell House Coffee; Karl Malden—American Express; Linda Evans—Clairol Ultress Haircolor; Phylicia Rashad—Yoplait Yogurt; Bill Cosby—Jello Pudding; Michael J. Fox—Diet Pepsi).

Furthermore, since neoclassical criticism is oriented to arguments and issues, a comparison of the image communicators construct of themselves as opposed to images they construct of opponents is useful. In each persuasive situation there is not only a clash of arguments and values but of images. Each persuader not only attempts to construct a positive image for person or product but also constructs (if ever so subtly) a negative image of the opposition. When Ronald Reagan said in 1983 that the anti-missile demonstrators were "unknowingly doing Moscow's work," he was questioning their competence, trustworthiness, and loyalty (good will).

By examining the argument proper, the values to which those arguments are linked, and the *ethos* of the speaker, the neoclassical critic can see the kinds of proofs that were addressed to the audience and move toward an evaluation based upon the extent to which the speaker exploited the communication situation by finding the available means of persuasion.

What Is the Verbal and Physical Style of the Message?

Many of the questions of language use discussed in formal criticism are also appropriate in neoclassical criticism. Questions of appropriate word choice, grammar, sentence structure, and figures of speech must be examined. Here, appropriate language use must mean appropriate to the audience, not to some external standard. Thus, violation of the formal principles is not automatically poor language use. Such violations may be used effectively with a particular audience. For example, there is a general formal injunction against mixed metaphors, yet one of the most highly regarded speeches of recent years, Martin Luther King, Jr.'s (1964) "I Have a Dream," begins with a mixed metaphor:

> Five score years ago a great American, in whose symbolic shadow we stand, signed the Emancipation Proclamation. This momentous decree came as a *great beacon light of hope* to millions of Negro slaves who had been *seared in the flames of withering injustice* (44).

Technically, the combination of a beacon light as a way out of flames is mixed because that is not the usual purpose of a beacon. But in the context of an audience intent upon righting 400 years of injustice, the figure has a power far beyond any formal questions of language.

In addition, the neoclassical critic will examine the physical factors of delivery such as voice, tone, pitch, gestures, eye contact, and bodily action in judging the effectiveness of a speaker.

With the advent of sophisticated media, the problem of judging style and delivery has grown more and more complicated. With new technologies come new considerations. For instance, the ability to project the voice was once a vital part of public-speaking success. If speakers like William Jennings Bryan, Albert J. Beveridge, or Robert M. La Follette had not had powerful speaking voices, they could not have been heard by large groups and so would not have been effective. Today, that quality is less important and, beginning with Franklin D. Roosevelt in his "Fireside Chats," presidents have used a conversational mode of delivery on radio and television to communicate with large numbers of people. Some, like Ronald Reagan, have been particularly commended for their ability to speak to audiences via television as if they were sitting and talking to viewers in their homes.

Thus, while media have made some qualities of delivery and oral style less important, a variety of new problems that a speaker must solve now exist. When the neoclassical critic moves beyond the single speech to examine more complex media productions such as news, docudramas, and media campaigns, a host of production questions must be addressed as well. What is the effectiveness of a speaker who is seen in a close-up shot for long periods of time? Is the credibility of a speaker weakened by having visuals interrupt the direct contact between speaker and audience? What is the influence on the reception of a speech when it is interspersed with shots of an audience in the room with the speaker or with other viewers around the country? These are but a few of the problems of evaluating media effectiveness.

ORGANIZING THE NEOCLASSICAL CRITICISM

In the foregoing section, we followed a rather traditional pattern that, with a final discussion of effectiveness, might be used to organize the written criticism:

1. Rhetorical situation
2. Nature of the audience
3. Structure of the message
4. Forms of argument
5. Values
6. *Ethos*

7. Style and delivery
8. Assessment of effectiveness

This sequence corresponds closely to what Edwin Black (1965b) found in his study of neo-Aristotelian criticism (29). By the most traditional arrangement, assessment of effect will be revealed after a complete analysis is made. One part will be more developed than another because it is more important to the final analysis, but none will be slighted. Still traditional but somewhat modified is an organization Black also noted in 1965, where some studies "employ only one or two Aristotelian canons to serve for the entire critical apparatus" (28). *Strategy* is a term that becomes useful here. That is, the critic will look for the strategy of the communicator implied by the argument and will organize the criticism to interpret and evaluate that strategy. Only those elements that are important to explaining the strategy of a message need to be explored.

However, the same principle of selection, to use those critical precepts that throw light on the effectiveness of the strategy, might lead a critic to organize the criticism differently. Michael C. Leff and Gerald P. Mohrmann (1974) organize their analysis of Abraham Lincoln's address at Cooper Union by the structure of the speech. That is, after a short section on the rhetorical situation and the audience at the beginning of the criticism, they moved through the three sections and the conclusion to the speech in the order of their presentation. Their emphasis is on the development of the arguments and the relation of the arguments to the audience, but they also discuss values, Lincoln's attacks on his opponents, *ethos*, and style.

Why do Leff and Mohrmann choose to organize their neoclassical critique by the structure of the speech? It is not a casual decision; it is dictated by the thesis of the criticism. Leff and Mohrmann wish to disprove the established claim that, strategically, Lincoln's speech was organized in three sections to address three different audiences. Their claim is that it is a united attempt to appeal to one audience, Republicans, so that Lincoln could identify himself as their best possible candidate for the presidency. Leff and Mohrmann seek to show that the speech has unity, and moving through the speech from beginning to end is the most reasonable way to show it.

Critical studies also may be organized around the particular form of proof that is most important to the analysis. David Zarefsky (1984) examined "Conspiracy Arguments in the Lincoln-Douglas Debates." He did this to show that the Lincoln-Douglas Debates, frequently held up as the "exemplar of public political debate, masterpieces of statesmanship, eloquence, and argument from high moral principle," had the negatively viewed "conspiracy argument [as] the predominant argumentative pattern" (63). Zarefsky identifies five conspiracies: the plot to abolitionize the

Whigs, discredit Lincoln, make slavery national, exploit federal patronage, and deny Kansas a referendum. Zarefsky then discusses the implications about the nature of conspiracy arguments, for example:

> Interestingly, neither man really came to grips with the other's pattern of support. Lincoln dismissed Douglas' documents by contending that the writers were not qualified to speak or that they themselves had no evidence. Douglas dismissed Lincoln's inferences as speculations and conjecture unsupported by any evidence. He denounced the charges as lies and waited for Lincoln to prove them (74–75).

Thus, neoclassical criticism, while having a traditional format, is not limited to it. It does not always involve an equal treatment of all the proofs or always require that all parts of the traditional model be covered. Within the basic objective of seeing the relation of the message to the audience, the critic selects what to cover and in what order to cover it, based on the need to prove the critical claim. In short, the critic is governed by his or her own critical purpose, not any traditional order, categories, or communicator practice.

PROBLEMS WITH NEOCLASSICAL CRITICISM

Neoclassical criticism has been the subject of considerable complaint. Five early studies come to mind: Donald C. Bryant (1937), "Some Problems of Scope and Method in Rhetorical Scholarship"; Irving J. Lee (1942), "Four Ways of Looking at a Speech"; S. Judson Crandall (1947), "The Beginning of a Methodology for Social Control Studies in Public Address"; Loren D. Reid (1944), "The Perils of Rhetorical Criticism"; and Ernest J. Wrage (1947), "Public Address: A Study in Social and Intellectual History." The most significant and developed attack is Edwin Black's (1965b) *Rhetorical Criticism: A Study in Method*.

It has been over 25 years since Black wrote that book, and in that time not only have a number of alternate approaches taken hold but the neo-Aristotelian criticism Black identified has adapted to some of the charges Black and others made. Those adaptations are reflected in this chapter. As mentioned earlier, G. P. Mohrmann's (1980) analysis of critical studies since Black's book reveals that many studies claiming to be alternative approaches still have the neoclassical approach embodied in them but without the traditional terminology. He notes that (as in this chapter) "ethos becomes image. . . . Critics have become even more adroit at transcending logos and pathos. Inductive and deductive processes clearly are passé, as are immediate emotional connections. Now one encounters tactics and strategies and appeals to cultural or societal values" (269).

Those changes may blunt some of the earlier complaints, but do not

eliminate them. So, the four problems with neoclassical criticism I will discuss do not follow Black (1965b) exactly, but are strongly influenced by his
arguments: (1) it cannot be recreative, (2) the attention to effect makes it
too narrow, (3) its emphasis on reason is limiting, and (4) it is circular.

Black (1965b) developed the argument that neo-Aristotelian criticism
could not be "recreative." Says Black, the critic "approaches the work already convinced of the irrelevancy of his own response" (48). In making
this argument, Black contrasts neo-Aristotelian criticism with formal criticism, which permits the critic to have individual moral and aesthetic responses to a speech. For Black the culprit is the audience orientation of
neo-Aristotelian criticism. Any judgment, he argues, must be "empirically
confirmed in a way that aesthetic reactions cannot be—namely with reference to the audience rather than to the object of criticism" (48).

It is clear that Black is responding to the narrowest interpretation of
neo-Aristotelianism in this charge. We have already seen how audience is
considerably broader than this criticism implies and how effectiveness,
how well one did with what was available, blurs Black's harsh definition
of neo-Aristotelian criticism. Surely this would be a reasonable answer for
a neoclassical critic to give. Still it is true that attention to audience, like
attention to standards of accuracy and formal excellence, limits what the
critic may say. The question might be asked, can any common sense criticism be recreative? One might also ask how far should we go with individual recreation?

Closely related to the recreative argument is the general criticism of the
special narrowness caused by the effect orientation of neo-Aristotelianism.
How does one justify looking at ineffective messages? (Black 1965b, 49).
Messages are ineffective if they do not succeed in having an effect on present or even future audiences. But sometimes such failures may be judged
to be aesthetically valuable. One might call that effect but it is more of
a formal approach oriented to the receiver than an approach oriented to
persuasion.

Another limiting factor for neoclassical critics is that their orientation
to effects puts them in the difficult position of not being able to render
moral judgments. When such a critic examines John C. Calhoun's "Slavery, a Positive Good," the critic must evaluate it by the standards of the
antebellum South Carolina power structure. Thus, even though the critic
found Calhoun's argument morally repugnant, such a judgment would
be irrelevant. Furthermore, even if the critic knew that the receivers were
uninformed and were being lied to, such a judgment would be secondary,
at best, in neoclassical criticism.

In response, it could be argued that effect is a difficult standard to
uphold but probably no more so than accuracy or formal standards. In
addition, there are numerous examples of situations where critics have imposed neoclassical and ethical standards at the same time. Bert E. Bradley
and Jerry L. Tarver (1970) examined the case of John C. Calhoun, men-

tioned above, and noted that he followed an "expository method." "He deliberately elevated expository speaking above ordinary argument" (172). In addition to a careful study of Calhoun's expository speaking strategy, Bradley and Tarver assess it with mixed neoclassical standards:

> Calhoun spoke meaningfully, however, only to those who could not "safely or logically deny" the component parts of the system he defended. He was effective only with those to whom his descriptions, definitions, narrations, and analogies were considered indisputable. His addresses were finally little more than revelations of his conclusions in a form easily adapted into a catechism for the faithful. Thus he turned his intellect inward; he constructed a rationale for partisans, an argument for those who already believed.
>
> The distorted and single-minded view of the truth held by John C. Calhoun had tragic results. His explanation of slavery which could not carry the Senate flourished only in its one natural habitat; the South embraced his exposition and used it in vigorously protecting slavery. His analytical prowess provided bits and pieces of argument to sustain an unworthy cause for a decade after his death (188).

At the beginning of this chapter we noted that a number of journalists, historians, and literary critics have become interested in persuasion. It would seem that the accuracy, aesthetic quality, and effects standards are moving closer together. One prominent alternative has been to abandon all common sense approaches for deconstruction. But, even there, Terry Eagleton (1983), an ideological literary critic who will figure prominently in the last two chapters of this book, calls for the rescue of literary theory by expanding what should be considered literature to all discourse and "reading it to see how its discourse is structured and organized, and examining what kinds of effects these forms and devices produce in particular readers, in actual situations. . . . It is, in fact, probably the oldest form of 'literary criticism' in the world, known as rhetoric" (205). Thus, there are those who paid effect no attention earlier who now find it less limiting than their previous objectives.

The principal problem with defending an effects orientation for criticism comes from Wichelns's (1958) statement and his dedicated followers who limit effect to immediate effects on immediate audiences. I have argued elsewhere "that much of the energy spent attacking the application of the effect of messages as a criterion of rhetorical criticism has been misspent because no theorist since Wichelns has insisted that the rhetorical value of a message is determined only by its immediate effect—physical or philosophical, tentative or complete" (1976, 75).

A third major problem is the emphasis that neoclassical critics put on rationality. According to Black (1965b), such emphasis provides a restricted view of human behavior (113). By emphasizing messages that are clearly argumentative, neoclassical critics fail to account for many messages that are oriented to emotional appeal (108–109). If this criticism is applicable to speeches, it is even more applicable to messages which are more narrative in their orientation. One might be able to see an argumentative development in some novels, plays, films, or television dramas. *M*A*S*H* comes to mind, as do the novels of Sinclair Lewis and films such as *Apocalypse Now* or *The Deer Hunter*, but what of those dramatic productions that are not clearly argumentative in their purpose? How does a neoclassical approach account for these without distorting them?

Such questions may be legitimate. However, a neoclassical approach that translates reason into reasonableness and sees the union of *logos, ethos* and *pathos* as expounded by McBurney (1936) and Grimaldi (1972) can respond to a broader spectrum of message than the narrowly rationalistic neo-Aristotelianism to which Black objected.

Finally, there is the concern that the neoclassical approach may be circular in its reasoning. Forbes Hill (1972), for instance, found the target audience Richard Nixon had in mind by looking at Nixon's speech. "An examination of the texts shows us which groups were eliminated as targets, which were made secondary targets, and which were primary" (375). Thus, the message is used to define the audience and then the message is evaluated by its persuasiveness to that audience. Although one might argue that the definition of the audience is general while the analysis of the proofs in the text is specific, such a procedure is dangerously close to circular reasoning. Neoclassical criticism can become a kind of self-fulfilling prophecy. The neoclassical critic can protect his or her analysis from circularity, however, by careful study of the environment (or audience) to better understand its nature as verified independent of the message.

Such criticisms as those presented here certainly point to the limitations of neoclassical criticism. Anyone who wishes to accept Wichelns's statement that effect on a specific audience is the singular emphasis of all rhetorical criticism will have difficulty getting past these limitations. But the neoclassical approach is not used that rigidly by most critics. Even Forbes Hill (1972), whose examination of the Nixon Vietnam War message is the most Aristotelian of the neoclassical criticism used in this chapter, acknowledges other approaches, claiming only "for my part I think we will write more significant criticism if we follow Aristotle *in this case*" (386).

There is no question but that the critic should recognize the limitations of neoclassical criticism. Today, plurality in critical approaches is the general condition. The critic of public address can thank the detractors of neo-Aristotelianism, particularly Black, for exposing its weaknesses and forcing a reconsideration. But the same can be said of formal criticism. The strong pull of New Criticism has been broken among literary critics and diversity of approach is the watchword in communication criticism. The neoclassical approach alone, or in combination with others, has a place if it is defined and properly used.

Neoclassical criticism rounds out the common sense approaches. It focuses on persuasion, the relation between message and audience, although it contains elements of the other two common sense approaches. There are numerous ways in which these three are alike and borrow from one another. They also, because they are the oldest approaches perhaps, have had a significant influence on the deconstructive approaches that will be discussed in subsequent chapters.

CHAPTER SIX

Semiotics
The Turn to Deconstruction

In what was assuredly one of his most stupefying lectures, titled "Consciousness and Language," [delivered] over one hundred years ago, [C. S.] Peirce raised the question: "What is man?" His decisive answer was that man is a symbol. Peirce elaborated and deepened his argument by comparing man with some other symbol, to wit, the verbal sign *Six,* and showed that, "remote and dissimilar as the word and the man appear, it is exceedingly difficult to state any essential difference between them." Elsewhere Peirce claimed that "my language is the sum total of myself," a view tantamount to asserting that man is a string of signs, a process of communication, or, in short, a text. Nor is man uniquely endowed with the property of life, "For every symbol is a living thing, in a very strict sense that is no mere figure of speech" (Sebeok 1977, 180–181).

This view of humans introduces a radical departure from the common sense understandings discussed in the previous three chapters. In this and the next four chapters, approaches to criticism quite different from common sense approaches will be examined. Not only do they not agree that there is a natural state, they posit a world that is essentially unknowable so that terms such as *knowledge, truth, reality,* and *natural* become subject to interpretation.

Critics who use common sense approaches follow essentially process models. They see communication as a process by which messages are transmitted from one person to another. Those who use deconstructive approaches see meaning not as moved, with more or less success, from one person to another, but as generated by the interrelation of a person and a message (Fiske 1982, 42). In such a system, there is little difference in what the participants are doing. Speaker and listener, for instance, are seen as "users" (46). One person does not pass meanings on to another, making one the sender and the other the receiver. Rather, together they generate meaning from the text. The critic, therefore, is interested in the text not for its accuracy, beauty, or effect, but for how it is used by people.

These alternative approaches recognize the text "as a *construct* . . . to treat it as available for *deconstruction*" (Belsey 1980, 104). The critic does not analyze the text, its context, and its audience; the critic deconstructs from these the social meaning the text has for those who use it to make sense of their world. So, even the common sense approaches we have discussed are constructed and, therefore, are subjects for deconstruction. They are "rooted in a specific historical situation and operating in conjunction with a particular social formation. In other words, it is argued that what seems obvious and natural is not necessarily so, but that on the contrary, the 'obvious' and the 'natural' are not *given* but produced in a specific society by the ways in which that society talks and thinks about itself and its experience" (3).

Deconstructive thinking originated in a theory of language variously known as semiology or semiotics, the science of signs. American philosopher Charles Saunders Peirce and Swiss linguist Ferdinand de Saussure remain the two major sources of these theories. Nor is there much difference philosophically between the two or their British alternatives, C. K. Ogden and I. R. Richards. The basic assumptions are the same. Semiotics has been influential on other approaches to criticism and, for some, it is regarded as an approach in and of itself. As such, it deserves a brief description here, at least to establish a basis for understanding the chapters to come.

WHAT IS SEMIOTICS?

Semiotics is the study of signs: "A sign is something physical, perceivable by our senses: it refers to something other than itself; and it depends upon a recognition by a user that it is a sign" (Fiske 1982, 44). Notre Dame Cathedral, rock music, and a southern accent all are signs provided only that someone recognize them as such. Saussure, perhaps because he was a linguist, recognized language as the most important sign system, and communication critics generally do also. Although other systems, such as the visual, may be more dominant at times and other systems of signs will frequently play an important role (as pictures do in a child's storybook) semiotics emphasizes language-oriented sign systems.

For Saussure, language is not a way of naming things that already exist; language is what creates the things by making a differentiation. The word *man* is not different from the word *woman*. Rather, these two words make "the world intelligible by differentiating between concepts" (Belsey 1980, 38).

Each sign is made up of a physical image (print, sound, pictures) and a concept: the "signifier" and the "signified." The most important point to observe here is that the word is related to a concept, not a thing. You will recall from Chapter 3 how General Semantics tries to find a way to solve the problem that "the word is not the thing." Semiotics solves the problem by ignoring it. For semiotics, word and thing can be identified with one another only through social convention.

The critic who utilizes a semiotic approach seeks to learn how different individuals and social groups construct different meaning from the same signs. These signs are the stuff of the values, myths, and ideologies by which human beings explain the world and their place in it. So, the interest of the semiotic critic is to assess not how accurate or effective a political leader is but how leaders and followers socially construct their worlds.

It may be useful here to emphasize in what way semiotic critics use the term *meaning*. "Meaning is not an absolute, static concept to be found neatly parcelled up in the message," says John Fiske (1982). "Meaning is an active process, semioticians use verbs like create, generate or negotiate to refer to this process. Negotiation is perhaps the most useful in that it implies the to-and-fro, the give-and-take between man and message" (49). Because it is a process, not a thing, some prefer Peirce's term *semiosis* or Saussure's term *signification*. We will use the term *meaning*, but in the deconstructive process-oriented sense, different from its common sense interpretation.

To better understand semiotic criticism, we will look more carefully at its assumptions and then the procedures the critic follows. Finally, we will look at some expressed reservations about such analysis.

THE ASSUMPTIONS OF SEMIOTIC CRITICISM

The brief section on the nature of semiotics already has suggested the assumptions behind a semiotic approach to criticism. This section will expand on those assumptions. Four assumptions govern semiology and are fundamentally different from the assumptions that govern common sense criticism.

Human Beings Are Sign Users

This assumption, expressed in the words of Kenneth Burke (1966), "man is the symbol-using animal" (3), is in direct contrast with the common sense idea that humans are reasoning animals. As such, it is an essential first step in deconstruction. Although common sense approaches to criticism point to the human condition as accessible via reason, deconstructive approaches see language use as the defining characteristic of humans. The implications of this assumption are profound. When you make symbol use the core of humanness, symbols take first rank in any theory of criticism. In that sense, text becomes more important than in other approaches to criticism. "Semiotics, then," says John Fiske (1982), "focuses attention primarily on the text. The linear process models give the text no more attention than any other stage in the process" (43). That may be an overstatement, but no one can deny that semiotics makes the text central, not only in expressing ideas about outside factors, but in defining the human condition itself. Because sign using is basic to human existence, a human society must have a language system. According to Belsey (1980), "Social organization and social exchanges, the ordering of the processes of producing the means of subsistence, is impossible without the existence of a signifying system. Language therefore comes into being at the same time as society" (42).

Signs Are Arbitrary

Although humans are the users of signs, there is no necessary relationship between the physicality of the sign and the concept it signifies. True, some signs seem to have this relationship, such as the symbol on the doors of men's and women's restrooms or the road signs that warn of deer crossing with a picture of a deer or of a curve with a curved line. As we shall see later, these are said to be *iconic* and, therefore, less arbitrary. But these are less arbitrary only because there are conventions so deeply embedded and generally accepted in our society that a stick figure seeming to wear a dress is taken to be a woman or an animal with antlers is seen as a deer. We know that not all women wear dresses and those who do, don't do so all the time and not all deer have antlers, but we accept such signs and even alter our behavior because of them.

There Are No Distinctions in Nature Until Humans Make Them

By this reasoning, nature is all of one piece. Human beings use language to categorize things, ideas, and feelings; thus, there is no knowledge before language. Language is, therefore, basic not only to the individual human but to society and all that individuals and society understand. Is not the difference between a dog and a cat obvious? Obvious to whom— an infant? A person who has never seen either? No, obvious only because we have been taught the difference, and the first person who observed the difference gave the difference a name: "dog and cat." "House pets" or "animals" could suffice without a difference. Our understanding of the difference, or that there is a difference, exists only because language that embodies the difference is accepted as a convention.

What of a word like *democracy*? Is America a *democracy*? If so, must all *democracies* be *capitalist* as well? Many people think so. If so, what are the socialist democracies such as Sweden or the "people's democracies" such as the People's Republic of China? One could argue in the common sense

tradition that a democracy is a state with certain characteristics such as elected leaders, opposition parties, and guaranteed freedoms. By such reasoning, a "people's democracy" is indeed a misnomer. From the standpoint of semiotics, however, what you have is an ideological clash over how the language may be used, not a conflict over the nature of reality.

Meaning Is Socially Constructed

Because signs are arbitrary, they cannot have a fixed meaning. Their meaning must be negotiated among the parties who use them. What a sign will mean will be determined by the particular persons who use it. Catherine Belsey (1980) suggests that "while the individual sign is arbitrary there is an important sense in which the signifying system as a whole is not. Meaning is public and conventional, the result not of individual intention but of interindividual intelligibility. In other words," Belsey continues, "meaning is socially constructed, and the social construction of the signifying system is intimately related, therefore, to the social formation itself" (42).

A semiotic approach does not imply, as the idea that signs are arbitrary might seem to imply, that every individual is at liberty to make signs stand for whatever he or she chooses. Indeed, far from it. As the next four chapters will show, semiotics is involved significantly in the way in which social conventions of values, myths, and ideologies control the users' understanding of a particular text. But the potential is always there for alternate values, myths, and ideologies. Meaning is always potentially plural because of changes in the source or the audience of the message, or the context in which it is viewed. This plurality permits semiotic critics to enter the communication situation at a number of points. To illustrate: Neoclassical criticism, like semiotic criticism, is interested in the relationship of the environment to the message. But a semiotic analysis of Margaret Thatcher addressing Parliament is not limited by what seems to be the target audience, or the idea of a reality at which her speech is aimed, nor is the critic constrained in the point of view he or she takes. The approach, therefore, provides the basis for fierce disagreement over what the socially constructed meaning of a text is. The critic is, after all, a part of the social process of constructing that meaning.

These four assumptions, which point to signs as the way in which human beings define their world and make sense of their experience, establish the foundation on which all semiotic systems are built. Before we look at specific applications of semiotic criticism, however, we must look more carefully at semiotic theory and the kind of analysis it predicts.

SEMIOTIC ANALYSIS

In order to understand semiotics, one needs to be more familiar with various types of signs, how their meaning is governed by codes, and some of the factors that influence across codes.

Nature and Type of Signs

To understand more about signs, let us turn to Charles Peirce's distinction among the three types of signs: icon, index, and symbol.

An *icon* is a representation that bears a resemblance to an actual object. A picture of Mt. Rushmore is an icon for it. A caricature of President Reagan (such as the one in Chapter 2) is an icon; so is a map of New Jersey. And John Fiske (1982) notes, "it may be verbal: *onomatopoeia* is an attempt to make language iconic. Tennyson's line, 'The hum of bees in immemorial elms' makes the sound of the words resemble the sound of the bees. It is iconic" (51). Music such as "The Orange Blossom Special" or "The Wabash Cannonball" is iconic because it imitates the sounds and the rhythm of a railroad train.

An *index* is a sign in the conventional argumentative use of the term *sign*. An index implies its meaning. Smoke means fire. A "For Sale" sign outside a home means that the home is for sale. "Men" or "Women" on a door indicates a public restroom. These two, icons and indexes, are parts of the semiotic process that help people to explain their world.

A *symbol* bears no relation to the object or concept it represents. Most words are symbols and are, as noted earlier, arbitrary. That your name is Tara and not Margo, Sharon, Maria, Rebecca (or Kyle, for that matter) is an arbitrary decision based on social convention. For a semiotic critic, these are the most important kinds of signs. Because they are arbitrary, they are considered the most highly developed and less constrained by outside factors as icons and indexes are.

Arthur Asa Berger (1982) developed the table on page 116 to explain the relation among icon, index, and symbol. The most important point to be observed is the process section because, while people can see an icon, and figure out an index, they must learn the meaning of a symbol. Once again, this emphasizes that the meanings of the most important signs are arbitrary and must be negotiated in society. However, even icons and indexes, like the figures on restroom doors that differentiate men and women by pants or dresses, although easier to understand, still have socially negotiated meanings. Perhaps the greatest usefulness of this tri-part division is to demonstrate that some signs are more constrained than others.

	Icon	Index	Symbol
Signify by	Resemblance	Causal connections	Conventions
Examples	Pictures, statues	Smoke/fire, symptom/disease	Words, numbers, flags
Process	Can see	Can figure out	Must learn

From Berger 1982, 15.

Conventions

These signs, whether iconic, indexical, or symbolic, are governed in their meaning by social conventions. Some we know as formal conventions (Fiske 1982, 57), for example, rules of grammar. That a sentence needs a subject and a predicate is not some law established by nature but a social convention. Indeed, grammar changes with the social situation and the group involved. An African-American friend, having just returned from visiting his mother in Philadelphia, saw a toy store Toys "Я" Us and commented, "You know in North Philly we have a store called We 'ᗺ' Toys." When I told the story to a white friend, he suggested that I not tell that story again because it is "something approaching a racial slur." To see it as a racial slur, one must see language as having set rules with variations of the standard pattern a sign of inferiority. From a semiotic perspective, alternate grammars and dialects such as the African-American dialect represented here are not inferior—only different.

Nonetheless, there are certain formal conventions that can be identified and generally accepted by all language users of a particular group. There are also many less formal conventions, such as the practice followed by soap opera directors of using the close-up to imply intimacy. Asa Berger (1982) has developed a short list of various camera shots and editing techniques that help to illustrate these informal conventions (facing page).

It is probably readily apparent that such informal conventions are far more numerous than formal conventions. The formal designation of a person who says "He ain't got no hammer" as uneducated, and someone who names a store We "ᗺ" Toys as a speaker of an African-American ghetto dialect, are less frequent than the informal conventions of meaning.

Informal conventions also are more important to the critical analysis because they provide greater possibilities to challenge that analysis. The more informal the convention, the more sophisticated must be the critic's ability to judge what meaning will be negotiated by the users of the text.

In the late 1950s and early 1960s following the successful launch of Sputnik I by the Soviet Union, the United States made its manned space program into a "quest for national purpose." Michael L. Smith (1983) examined the language used in this project. In the following excerpt it is easy to see how Smith found in the informal conventions of language a far more

Camera Shots

Signifier (shot)	Definition	Signified (meaning)
Close-up	Face only	Intimacy
Medium shot	Most of body	Personal relationship
Long shot	Setting and characters	Context, scope, public distance
Full shot	Full body of person	Social relationship

Editing Techniques

Signifier	Definition	Signified (meaning)
Pan down	Camera looks down	Power, authority
Pan up	Camera looks up	Smallness, weakness
Zoom in	Camera moves in	Observation, focus
Fade in	Image appears on blank screen	Beginning
Fade out	Switch from one image to another	Simultaneity, excitement
Wipe	Image wiped off screen	Imposed conclusion

From Berger 1982, 38–39.

flamboyant meaning to space exploration than simple explanation might have offered:

> Long before the first astronaut left the launch pad, space enthusiasts ex-
> perimented with the analogies and associations that might be attached to
> the event. The editors of *Newsweek* saw rejuvenative powers in space
> travel. "[T]he moral energies that drove America to true greatness lately
> seem diluted," they warned at the outset of "The Sixties: Decade of Man
> in Space." For too long no new arenas of conquest awaited at the national
> horizon. Now, however, "Man is embarking on the supreme adventure;
> he is heading into the universe."
>
>   For those who stressed the restorative powers of this "supreme adven-
> ture," the presence of helmsmen in space was an essential aspect of the
> enterprise. Only when the first "awe-struck pilot" experienced "the giddy
> buoyancy of weightlessness" would man "break free of his terrestrial
> bonds." Projection of the national imagination into space required a hu-
> man emissary so that "all mankind may ride along vicariously." The first
> astronaut's "epochal adventure," *Newsweek*'s "Space and the Atom" edi-
> tor asserted, "will signal, as no satellite could, the dawn of the space age."
> "Machines alone will not suffice if men are able to follow," a columnist
> observed in *The Nation*. "The difference is that between admiring a wom-
> an's photograph and marrying her" (199).

Signs vary from the iconic to symbols that are totally arbitrary. Their meanings are governed by conventions that vary between the formal (those governed by explicit rules) and the informal (those that are less gen-erally understood). But the arbitrary signs with only informal conventions are the most numerous and also the most important in a semiotic critical analysis. Their further analysis, together with the more iconic signs and more formal conventions, require that we see them not in isolation but in combination, in codes.

Codes

Signs do not stand alone; they are organized into codes. These codes link signs together in ways that reflect a particular interpretation of a community's system of values, myths, and ideologies. To make sense of this statement, some basic understandings of semiotics are in order. The critic does not look for how signs reflect a known system of values. If that were the case, the critic would be arguing from a common sense point of view. To the semiotic critic, signs are the basis for defining the community. A sign system may not be shared by many people, but it is a way of understanding the code of the group of people who do share it.

A friend sees a television news program about a proposal to censor books in a small-town public library. The reporters illustrate the controversy by choosing an obese, plain, middle-aged male, with little ability to use formal grammar, to represent the censorship position. To represent the anticensorship position, they choose a good-looking, young, articulate, female American Civil Liberties Union (ACLU) lawyer. This is an example, says the friend, that the media biases the news against positions with which they disagree. They select people who will be judged through codes of appearance and speech. Of course, the media industry pretends to be objective in showing both sides. Several objections could be made to this interpretation, however. Perhaps these were the only spokespersons available, or obese men have just as much right as anyone else to act as spokespersons. However, such objections are irrelevant to semiotic analysis. The important thing is that we see how the friend, and presumably many others, interprets the media through social codes that might not be readily apparent to a critic oriented to accurate interpretation.

Codes and Society

Codes perform a dual, interactive function. They reveal the view of society a person has, and simultaneously they help to determine what that view will be. Persons learn how to talk from their peers. They imitate those around them but the language they adopt does not come to them free of value or ideology. The language they learn shapes the values they hold, and the values they hold cause them to choose a certain language.

This difference can be illustrated many times over by noting the problem of translation from one language to another. The phrase "it loses something in translation" is common enough in our society. Other languages reflect other cultures and, therefore, cannot be translated literally.

Even among English-speaking peoples the idiomatic expressions, specialized vocabulary, and forms reflect a difference in social outlook. In America, the differences are great from one social class and ethnic group to another as the following expressions signifying police officers will illustrate: "men in blue," "safety officials," "officers of the law," "traffic officials," "police personnel," "cops," "the brass," "the fuzz," and "pigs" (Ehninger et al. 1982, 228). And to this may be added many adjectives that further reflect different social meanings ("crooked cops," "New York's finest").

The codes into which language is organized (including the Code of the Society of Professional Journalists discussed in Chapter 3) define a view of society. Thus, the standards of a critic are negotiated in the society and not given to the critic from some common sense standard. Catherine Belsey (1980) illustrates how the language reveals a view of society with her examination of the Sherlock Holmes novels:

> The project of the Sherlock Holmes stories is to dispel magic and mystery, to make everything explicit, accountable, subject to scientific analysis. The phrase most familiar to all readers—"Elementary, my dear Watson"—is in fact a misquotation, but its familiarity is no accident since it precisely captures the central concern of the stories. . . .
>
> The stories are a plea for science not only in the spheres conventionally associated with detection (footprints, traces of hair or cloth, cigarette ends), where they have been deservedly influential on forensic practice, but in all areas. They reflect the widespread optimism characteristic of their period concerning the comprehensive power of positivist science. Holmes's ability to deduce Watson's train of thought, for instance, is repeatedly displayed, and it owes nothing to the supernatural. Once explained, the reasoning process always appears "absurdly simple," open to the commonest of common sense (111–112).

Belsey contrasts the central meaning of the romantic ode with the central meaning of Sherlock Holmes. Where Holmes seeks to "*dispel* mystery in the interest of science the romantic ode seeks the quite antithetical one of *revealing* the mystery at the heart of things." Odes such as "Wordsworth's 'Intimations of Immortality,' Coleridge's 'Kubla Khan,' Shelley's 'Ode to the West Wind,' and Keats' 'Ode on a Grecian Urn,' all to varying degrees attempt to isolate the moment of vision which is itself the source of poetry, and to meditate on the meaning and value of the vision-as-poem" (118).

Thus, two quite contradictory interpretations of society are made by these two genres of English literature. One extolls science as the explanation of human life, the other rejects it by extolling its opposite, mystery.

Types of Codes

The semiotic literature identifies a number of different types of codes that are not so important here so long as you understand that codes may be specific to social groups, as already observed. They also may be specific to certain communication situations. There are interpersonal codes, literary codes, public-speaking codes, and mass media codes to mention but a few. Some codes are subcodes; that is, while we can identify that public speaking calls for certain social conventions, a sales presentation reveals a subcode quite different from that of a sermon. There are visual codes for television news such as positions of anchors, camera shots, and angles. There are also subcodes of pace, camera movement, editing, and color (pastel not white shirts, for example).

Thus, signs are organized into the many, complex systems called codes and these social codes determine meaning for a text. To understand their application to a text, it is useful to look at the factors in a text that influence its negotiated meaning through codes.

FACTORS INFLUENCING MEANING

Certain factors are more important than others to help the semiotic critic explain meaning: connotation, metaphor, metonymy, token, value, myth, and ideology. Each is the potential central factor in negotiating the meaning of a sign system. For instance, a critic might see in a text a dominant metaphor, the generalized myth of a group, or an implied ideology.

Connotations

Connotations are probably the most obvious language factor with semiotic implications. Because signs have no meaning of their own, denotative language is impossible. Some situations may be less arbitrary (more iconic or indexical) but, as already observed, even these have arbitrary characteristics. "Connotations," says John Fiske (1982), occur "when the sign meets the feelings or emotions of the user and the values of [the] culture" (91). Connotations are found in the language that names things: "jock," "foreigner," "slum," "bureaucrat," "professor," "leader," "criminal." They are also found in adjectives: "crooked politician," "shyster lawyer," "intelligent woman," "happy man," "fierce competitor." Critics using a semiotic approach look for a pattern of connotation. In this pattern they try to identify the general connotation implied by the text.

The Golden Girls, a popular television sitcom about four older, widowed, or divorced women who live together in Miami, ties together visual and verbal symbols that all carry connotations of a helping and loving middle-class retirement. Virtually all the action takes place inside their comfortable and spacious home. The show opens with a view of the outside of a large ranch style home surrounded by tropical and semitropical gardens. The theme song revolves around being friends: "Thank you for be-

ing a friend." "You are a pal and a confidant." The story line on one program is about how Rose's daughter Kirsten visits and falls out with Rose
because she learns that her father's fortune had been "squandered" by
Rose. Rose finally tells Kirsten the truth: her father, Charlie, was a "won-
derful man: kind, warm, and caring, never willing to let a neighbor struggle through hard times alone, but he was also the worst businessman who
ever had to balance a checkbook." Rose and Kirsten make up and go out
arm in arm.

The dialogue includes statements such as "of course it's our business,
we're friends," "Dorothy, I want you to know that having friends like you
really helps me get through times like this," and the closing, "Isn't it amaz-
ing how things always work out?" Insults provide much of the humor of
the show but the responses are not negative. It is clear that, like poor de-
parted Charlie, all the connotations of the show are kind and caring in a
comfortable, middle-class setting.

Metaphor

Metaphor is an analogous relationship in which one concept is related
to another to create a new way of seeing the first concept. Using a semiotic
approach, the critic may find in the text a metaphor that best characterizes
its meaning for society.

For example, a critic could argue that the guiding metaphor of Abraham Lincoln's (1953) presidential campaign in 1860 was that of the house
divided: "A house divided against itself cannot stand. I believe this government cannot endure, permanently half slave and half free" (II, 461). All
of Lincoln's arguments are designed, one could say, to placate the growing
abolitionist sentiment in the Republican party and in the nation, and to
do this without taking an outright abolitionist position. Home and family,
familiar and important to the society, are used to characterize the government and nation. But families do not fall apart or change their ways quickly
and so the word *permanently* is used to characterize the then current state.
The change from the current state to a future alternative is made to seem
indefinite. The signs, Lincoln's words, metaphorically signify that there is
a society in which slavery must end but not in the near future.

Metonymy

While metaphor makes words usually associated with one plane of
meaning work on another plane, metonymy associates two meanings
within the same plane. It is a condition where one word or phrase substitutes for another ("White House"—"president," "Hawkeye"—
"Iowan," "physicians—doctors"). Most commonly, metonymy character-

izes the whole by a part or a part by a whole (synecdoche). When the government is called "the president" or "the administration," the Queen of England the "Crown," television the "media," and all writers "poets," that is metonymy.

John Fiske (1982) illustrates metonymy with the example of a picket line at a strike. Although images of a lawful and quiet scene are available, television chooses to focus on a confrontation between picketers and police. Viewers see this violence as the metonymy for the strike. Nonetheless, even if those pictures were not chosen, the same condition would hold because "all news films are metonymies and all involve an arbitrary selection" (98).

To select a scene of peaceful picketers playing cards would be negotiated by viewers as a quite different meaning (peacefulness). Suppose the scene shows picketers playing cards while heavily armed police stand by just watching. Here, perhaps viewers will find an antigovernment or anticapitalist meaning. Simply, it is impossible to offer an accurate interpretation of the story of a picket line. Human choices have to be made and the choices made will reflect a socially defined meaning. Different choices negotiate different meanings.

Tokens

Tokens refer to objects that through conventions come to stand for concepts. The flag stands for the nation. A Cadillac stands for wealth. The cross stands for a Christian church, the Star of David, Judaism. The ram indicates a California professional football team while a cub represents a Chicago professional baseball team. Tokens have negotiated meanings that go far beyond the mere denotation that might seem implied here. At times an entire critical analysis might be built around such tokens.

Athletic teams such as the Bulldogs, Lions, Rams, Tigers, Cowboys, Utes, Seminoles, Crimson Tide, and Rebels all are read by their supporters as tokens of strength and ferocity. So what do we do with the Georgetown Hoyas, Pomona Sage Hens, Temple Owls, or U.C. Irvine Anteaters? Are they jokes or leftovers of an earlier time when athletic teams were named for other purposes? What do these tokens tell us about the cultural meaning of athletics?

Values

In the next chapter we will look at values more carefully, but let us note for now that values are expressions in the language of general conceptions of what is and is not good. Freedom-slavery, rich-poor, health-sickness, true-false are just a few of the positive-negative words that reflect the way a culture is defined by those who use them. These values may be directly stated or they may be implied in the language: "Exercise is good for you" (health), "Work hard to get ahead" (financial success), "God bless America" (religion and patriotism). A critic may look to the values stated or implied in the text to find the value system that is constructing a culture in the text.

Myths

A myth is a story that the members of a particular culture use to explain themselves. It derives from Aristotle's term *mythos* which has been translated as "plot." It is an imitation of action. In its common usage, the word *myth* means a falsehood, something untrue as in "the myth of American invincibility." As it is used in semiotic criticism, however, it is neither true nor false but a useful explanation. In our society we tell stories of Paul Bunyan, Davy Crockett, Kit Carson, Jim Bridger, and the like. Some lived, some never did, but the stories told about them create an image of a strong, bold, adventurous America. Each of these persons acts in a story that when joined with other stories creates what might be called the American myth.

Every subculture has its myths (stories) by which it defines itself. The groups you belong to all have stories about themselves and their members, told over and over to explain who and what they are. Consider your family. Are there not stories that explain what your family culture is about? Do not these stories have meaning for you and other members of the family about your relationships? And is there, perhaps, one story that, if you thought about it, might stand for the central myth of your family?

Ideology

Ideology is a term used to refer to specific beliefs of a culture that are revealed in messages. While values are general conceptions of what is good, an ideology is a representation of a specific political position. Critics who view ideology as the final product of all deconstructive criticism are called ideological critics. For them, myths, values, tokens, metonymy, metaphor, and connotation are all ideological. For them, myths such as "God's chosen people," values such as freedom, tokens like the American flag, metonymy as in "we the people," and metaphors such as "the scales of justice" all unite to support the ideology of our current political order.

In this book, ideology will be used in a somewhat narrower focus as a particular commitment to a political point of view. Although its use is not limited to Marxists, they do tend to see it as their personal possession; a critical tool that, as they have developed it, has considerable influence on its use by others. For instance, Marxists, from their commitment to the dialectic as interpreted by Marx, have influenced others to view ideology as a dialectical process. As a result, the emphasis in ideological criticism tends toward polar opposites: power versus powerlessness, workers versus capitalists, citizens versus politicians, men versus women, blacks versus whites.

However, as strong as this dialectical tradition is, all semiotic critics need not follow it in looking for ideologies. Most important is that beyond values, tokens, and myths are specific ideologies, which are commitments to a particular conception of the society that becomes negotiated in the society through texts. Critics search for these ideologies.

On Wednesday, July 13, 1977, there was a blackout in New York City during which mobs of people set fires and broke into and looted stores. Such scenes were shown on television. On Sunday, July 16, 1977, the *New York Times* editorialized about the event. Edwin Black (1984) examines that editorial in detail and notes how the looters became victims. Said the editorial: "These people are victims of economic and social forces that they sense but do not understand." Says Black, "Beginning with rage and anguish, we then are invited to discern the conditions that legitimate them. To accept this pattern is to accept the implicit claim of this text that the looters were actuated by judiciary and socioeconomic considerations—considerations that they sensed but did not understand." Black finds in the text "the discourse of liberal politics" (149–150). Black's interpretation is not some general idea about what is valuable but a specific ideology that explains events and defines the culture.

Ideology is like myth and value in the sense that it is an interpretation of the society. Nonetheless, the critics who find it are far more specific in identifying its ramifications. For example, if a critic sees in a text the ideology of a male power dominance over women, that critic will probably argue that the ideology illustrates a general ideological bent in the society.

These, then, are factors that influence meaning: connotations, metaphor, metonymy, token, value, myth, and ideology. As critics examine the language and visual action of the text to see what meanings are negotiated, they pay particular attention to them. Critics also look to them as the possible central concepts structuring the meaning of the text. The value system, defining metaphor, repeated myth, or central ideology can be the organizing principle of deconstruction criticism.

THE TEXT IN DECONSTRUCTION

Frequently, when critics make the change from common sense criticism to deconstruction, they attempt to redefine the text. The critic who follows a common sense approach will most likely choose as a text a rather specific verbal or visual experience, for example, a novel, situation comedy, political speech, or horror film. A deconstructive critic will more frequently go beyond such specific texts to a broader view of what can define a culture. Such a critic is more likely to unite texts of different kinds by different authors at different places and even different times. In their cultural studies, deconstructive critics are not so much interested in what a particular author or genre has produced as they are in defining the diverse aspects of what is frequently referred to as a movement.

Deconstructive critics also will more likely choose a wider variety of artifacts to constitute a text, including informal conversation, the architecture of a football stadium, the musical background of an event, the signs on a highway. In short, deconstruction is frequently more inclusive than common sense criticism in what it regards as a text because the idea of signs is more inclusive than the idea of language.

Cultural studies expand text in another way. The text may be of the critic's own construction in the form of field notes.

For example, the study conducted by Michael Pacanowsky and some of his graduate students was designed to discover and define the culture of a suburban police force. The participants in the study rode with the officers in their patrol cars and after a four-hour shift, went home and wrote detailed descriptions of what was done and said (O'Donnell-Trujillo and Pacanowsky 1983, 240–241). These descriptions then became the text that the participants, now serving as critics, analyzed. The text is constructed from memory after the event by the critic. Although such a text is questionable in common sense terms, its appropriateness to a deconstructive critic is clear. The meaning of a text is in the interaction of the critic and the text, not in some objective standards of accuracy or formal excellence. The same conditions would hold for the cultural critic who chose to examine a literary text such as Joseph Wambaugh's (1970) novel *The New Centurions*. The cultural critic always has a part in constructing the text.

This difference points to a major distinction between common sense and deconstructive criticism. Common sense critics relate their analyses to a reality "out there," beyond the critic. Avoiding bias or inaccuracy is one of their important attributes. The deconstructive critic, on the other hand, believes that the critic will always be part of the critical process. To return to Rosenfield's categories, there can be no purely objective criticism of the Source-Message-Environment, or Source-Message, or Message-Environment varieties. All of these imply some objective standard by which the communication situation can be measured. In deconstruction, a critic might concentrate on the Environment or the Source to define the culture, or look at both as part of the culture defined, but the critic will alway intrude, so criticism will be Source-Message-Critic, Message-Environment-Critic, or Source-Message-Environment-Critic. Semiotics is concerned with how people use signs and, the argument goes, the critic is as much a user as a person who generates or receives a message.

Does that mean that critics can put whatever interpretation they wish on a communication event? Of course not. Then what controls interpreta-tions? Each critic makes an argument that embodies a critical claim, grounds it in the text and context, and warrants it by the assumptions of a critical approach. It is the reader who grants or denies adherence to the argument and tests its reasonableness. Even though signs are arbitrary, there are limits to what they can mean. Social convention restricts the meaning of signs and, therefore, the interpretation of the text.

PROBLEMS WITH SEMIOTICS

If there is no reality for the text to reflect or for the critic to interpret, then many critical judgments available to common sense criticism are not available to the semiotic critic. Semiotic criticism in one sense can be only interpretive. It can only explain how the meaning of a text is negotiated by its users and how they use it to interpret the society. Berger (1982) points out, for instance, that "in its concern for the relationship of elements and production of meaning in a text it ignores the quality of the work itself" (39). The same could be said about judgments of effect or accuracy. Given the assumptions of semiology, it is difficult to imagine how such criticism could go beyond an identification of social role. The basic assumptions of semiotics, that meaning is arbitrary and negotiated, that language con-structs nature and not the reverse, lead to a strictly interpretive criticism.

Interestingly enough, this has not been the case in actual practice. Par-ticularly, ideological criticism has been highly judgmental. Nor is ideologi-cal judgment limited to Marxists. When Marxists see the dialectic between the powerful establishment and the powerless individual, there is no ques-tion that they favor the individual. Such predisposition in Marxist analysis and, to a lesser extent, feminist ideology can be accused of causing self-fulfilling prophecies. One begins with an ideological assumption and, of course, finds it in the text.

Ideological critics defend such action by the claim that all criticism is ideological. In short, designation of ideological criticism as a subcategory of communication criticism reveals an ideological perspective, an ideologi-cal critic would say. And to charges such as Berger's (1982) that the study of formal or aesthetic characteristics is lost to analysis (39), one could reply that the very basis of semiotics is formal criticism. At base, semiotics is interested in the relationship of one sign to another. Indeed, it could be argued that the formal relations of language are more important in ideolog-ical than in formal criticism because they are the basis of all knowledge, not just narrow aesthetic judgments.

As is typical of most controversies, the disagreement between common sense and deconstructive approaches based on semiotic understandings seems to be an argument between extremes. For example, the issues seem to be articulated by the most dedicated accuracy buffs and formal analysts on one side and the most ideological Marxists on the other. A more open reading of contemporary criticism on both sides indicates a good deal of borrowing. Perhaps it is here on this middle ground that we can leave the general discussion of semiotics as the turn to deconstruction and examine specific applications of deconstructive criticism to value analysis, narrative, psychoanalytic, and ideological criticism.

CHAPTER SEVEN

Value Analysis
Understanding Culture in Value Systems

"This convention has shown to all America," said Republican presidential candidate Ronald Reagan in his 1980 acceptance address, "a party ready to build a new consensus with all those across the land who share a community of values embodied in these words: family, work, neighborhood, peace, and freedom" (642). Perhaps no candidate in recent years has made so much use of values in a campaign. This practice was carried into his presidency and subsequent campaigns in 1982, when he campaigned for Republicans in the House and Senate and in his 1984 campaign for reelection (Sandeen and Sillars, 1983, 20). Indeed, in 1984, values became a campaign issue, as the Democratic candidate, Walter Mondale, struggled to identify his own values and Republicans chided Democrats for scurrying to find them. Said Ronald Reagan at the Republican Convention: "We didn't discover our values in a poll taken a week before the convention. And we didn't set a weather-vane on top of the Golden Gate Bridge before we started talking about the American Family" (706).

Ronald Reagan's campaigns portrayed a steady and direct reference to values, running the gamut from Lee Greenwood's top of the charts campaign song, "God Bless the USA," to statements made by the candidate himself. And such direct reference to values can be found in many of the messages of our society; witness even a television commercial such as Chrysler Corporation's "Born in America."

But talk about value is considerably more pervasive than these obvious cases. The deconstruction of messages for value statements is a complex process that requires analysis of the ways people give meaning to messages. Before looking at the specific techniques of value analysis, however, it is necessary to understand the special way that the term *values* is used in this chapter and some of the assumptions that underlie value analysis.

VALUE ANALYSIS AS DECONSTRUCTIVE CRITICISM

All criticism, common sense or deconstructive, has some relation to value. In Chapter 5, for instance, we noted that all arguments are warranted by stated or implied values and are effective because the receiver of the message holds those values. Similarly, in formal and accurate interpretation criticism, such critics seek to find references to values such as *truthfulness, objectivity, freedom, probability, unity,* and *believability* in a text. In fact, values must be examined by every critic. What then makes value analysis different?

First, the term *value* is generally used quite loosely. To be actively involved in value analysis requires a number of specific definitions so that analytical relationships can be observed and regularized. A value for the purposes of this chapter is "an enduring belief that a specific mode of conduct or end-state of existence is personally or socially preferable to alternate modes of conduct or end-state of existence" (Rokeach 1968, 160).

For our purposes in analyzing texts, a value must be differentiated from a belief: "any simple proposition, conscious or unconscious, inferred from what a person says or does and capable of being preceded by the phrase, 'I believe that' . . ." (Rokeach 1968, 113). Thus, all statements that express a belief about specific persons, places, things, or situations are belief statements. A value statement expresses a judgment about what is the preferred end state or means of actions: "Freedom is an ultimate goal of humans" or "Hard work will bring success." Belief statements may or may not include values: "Yellowstone is a beautiful natural wonder" or "Yellowstone is one of the last homes of the grizzly bear in the United States." However, even when a belief states no value, it implies one. In the case of the grizzly—preservation of nature.

Value analysis examines textual values to understand how those who use the text define the culture. For the deconstructive critic, values are human conceptions embodied in signs. The sender or the receiver of the message makes sense of these signs. The critic uses them to define the culture implied by the text.

When Ronald Reagan sought to identify his conception of the American experience with the words *family, work, neighborhood, peace,* and *freedom,* he made it an experience of relative autonomy for the individual. For him the family and neighborhood would be free of violence, and people would work to support themselves and theirs without much outside interference. Others might emphasize justice, equality, cooperation, peace, and freedom and imply a vision of a society united by laws and traditions to use government as part of a corporate effort to help the less fortunate.

Some value terms take on special meaning. When people use them to represent multiple values they become "ideographs" (McGee 1980a). Thus, the word *frontier,* for example, becomes an ideograph. It takes on a meaning in the culture that permits it to be used metaphorically in a wide variety of situations far beyond the original meaning imputed to it. Frederick Jackson Turner's (1947) time-bound and geographical definition of the frontier was as a "continually advancing . . . westward . . . meeting point between savagery and civilization" (2–3). Now there are "frontiers of science," "the New Frontier," "the frontier of space," "the frontier of the mind," and so forth.

The word *frontier*, taken in its original usage, was a belief about a specific place. However, in our culture it has acquired a much broader value orientation that implies progress and opportunity, values which are capable of application in situations never imagined by its original users.

These multiple value connotations may exist as powerful terms for people with different interpretations. Michael McGee (1980a) points out that the value terms *liberty, religion,* and *property* in Puritan England had meanings that united a culture even though "those who used the ideographs did not share meaning or intentions." He quotes Michael Polanyi, who shows that the value term *religion* could link Protestantism with patriotism, apply to the traditional fear for the safety of monastic lands, mean intense study of the scriptures, reinforce the Puritan orientation to spiritual equality, and imply greater freedom of speech (77). The critic using value analysis, then, looks at a text as a part of the process by which a society defines itself.

The critic looks for ideographs and for the beliefs and values that are stated and implied in the text. These are analyzed for their relationship to one another and for the definition of the culture they collectively identify. Such analysis requires a more careful look at values and beliefs, but before examining the actual process of analysis it is useful to remind ourselves of the assumptions which undergird value analysis. These are drawn from the assumptions of all deconstructive analysis.

THE ASSUMPTIONS OF VALUE ANALYSIS

Values may be discussed in any analysis. But to isolate values as a separate analytical subject strongly implies that the critic is interpreting a text in order to observe how it defines a culture. Thus, a situation comedy such as *Cheers* does not describe the reality of a Boston bar; rather it identifies, through the values inscribed in it, interpretations of certain subcultures of our society. The values can define the culture for people who have never been in a Boston (or any other) bar. The values may be read in different ways as well. They are signs that will produce different meanings depending on the cultural orientation of the viewer.

Value analysis, along with mythic, psychoanalytic, and ideological analyses, is, therefore, deconstructive and based on the semiotic assumptions discussed in Chapter 6. With those assumptions in mind, we will now examine four specific assumptions that underlie value analysis.

Humans Make Sense of the World by Identifying Values with It

Few would deny that valuing is a central part of our lives. We attach various degrees of importance to every person, thing, or idea with which we come in contact. This valuing process is built into our language. Our relationships with these value words tell us a lot about who we are. In American society there is no document that means more in the definition of our cultural values than the Declaration of Independence. It is "just words," but those words are vital. Consider, for instance, this important sentence:

> We hold these truths to be self-evident, that all men are created equal, that they are endowed by their Creator with certain unalienable Rights, that among these are Life, Liberty and the pursuit of Happiness (Commager 1949, 101).

This sentence, the warrant to the whole argument, is a collection of value concepts, including *truth, equality, creation, rights, life, liberty,* and *happiness.* Any one of these tells us something about how American society views itself. Together they tell us a great deal about what is important. Two of these values —"Equality" and "Liberty"—taken together have been the source of considerable controversy in this society. One point of view is that they are contradictory, that those people who put a high priority on liberty are less interested in equality and vice versa. Rokeach (1973), for instance, argues that the political-economic systems people identify with can be differentiated by the relative value they assign to liberty (or freedom) and equality. His claim is based on a content analysis of representative statements from spokespersons for each of four political views. His analysis is summarized by the following chart:

The Politics of Liberty and Equality

Politico-Economic System	Liberty	Equality
Fascism	Low	Low
Capitalism	High	Low
Socialism	High	High
Communism	Low	High

From Rokeach 1973, 170–172.

In addition to values (understood as general conceptions of the desirable) such as the words in the Declaration of Independence, there are also certain persons, places, texts, and institutions (icons) that serve as values. Chaim Perelman (1982) calls these *concrete* as opposed to *abstract* values (27). The Declaration of Independence itself, the Constitution, God, the flag, the Church, all, without reference to abstract verbal statements of values, have value characteristics of their own.

Whether abstract or concrete, whether stated openly or implied in belief statements, values are used by humans to define the world as they see it.

All Statements Can Be Interpreted for Values

The values in the Declaration of Independence seem obvious; they are clearly stated so as to serve as a warrant for the argument. Similarly, many icons such as the flag or the Constitution seem relatively clear in their value implications. But, where are the values in all those statements that we use to define our daily lives? Herbert Gans (1979), in his book *Deciding What's News*, says about journalism that "reality judgments are never altogether divorced from values":

> The values in the news are rarely explicit and must be found between the lines—in what actors and activities are reported or ignored, and in how they are described. If a news story deals with activities which are generally considered undesirable and whose descriptions contain negative connotations, then the story implicitly expresses a value about what is desirable. In the process, the news also assumes a consensus about values that may not exist, for it reminds the audience of values that are being violated and assumes that the audience shares these values. When a story reports that a politician has been charged with corruption, it suggests, *sotto voce*, that corruption is bad and that politicians should be honest (39–40).

Gans goes on to say that when news sources reported that black activist "Stokely Carmichael had 'turned up' somewhere, while the president had, on the same day 'arrived' somewhere else; or when another story pointed out that a city was 'plagued by labor problems' the appropriate values were not difficult to discern" (41).

In most communication there is a greater incidence of implied values than of specifically stated values. Patricia Ganer (1988) studied the campaign addresses and debates of John Anderson, Jimmy Carter, and Ronald Reagan in the 1980 presidential campaign. She examined them sentence by sentence. Even though her method permitted multiple explicit value terms and only one implicit value term per sentence, she found that the candidates used a greater number of implicit than explicit value terms in these public messages (213).

Values and Beliefs Are Linked Together in Cognitive Systems

Rarely do we see a text that is dominated by two or three salient values and it is virtually impossible to find one built upon only one value. Most often a critic will identify a system of values. The term *system* implies that values are linked to one another, influence each other's meanings, and provide the basis for a generalization characterizing the cognitive system. On that basis we hear certain texts identified as representing a "puritan," "enlightenment," or "collectivist" value system such as are discussed near the end of this chapter.

The identification of such systems is made possible because within a culture a rather limited number of values will be found. Rokeach (1968) says that "an adult probably has tens or hundreds of thousands of beliefs . . . but only dozens of values" (124). Indeed, Rokeach's (1973) research revealed that Americans identified 18 each of instrumental and terminal values (28). Rokeach obtained this list by asking people to identify what was of value to them. But to produce that number would require the analysis of a substantial text such as a political campaign. No shorter text has generated that many values.

Interestingly, the same is frequently true of a content analysis of beliefs in a text. An analysis of the 1896 campaign speeches of William Jennings Bryan, for instance, revealed a number of beliefs nearly equal to the number of values (Sillars and Ganer 1982, 187). If Rokeach is correct in saying that human beings have in their repertories tens of thousands more beliefs than values, then how is it that such a proportion is not reflected in texts? It is because no text reflects everything a person believes; rather, they are the specialized responses to a particular situation. A text treats only the beliefs that dominate that situation and only the values that reflect the subculture of the situation. *Car and Driver, Skiing,* and *Body Beautiful* are magazines that reflect a young, action-oriented culture, but the subject matter of and response to each is different. Each one represents a subculture of values.

Each text, therefore, will emphasize a limited number of articulated values and beliefs that all interact with one another to create a textual "web of signification" (Geertz 1973, 5). The result of this interaction is a cognitive system. The Code of the Society of Professional Journalists, discussed in Chapter 3, contains the value system of the journalism profession. Each principle—for example, being *truthful*, maintaining *objectivity*, treating others with *fairness*, supporting *freedom*, and accepting *responsibility*—embodies a value that is linked to and modified by each other value or belief, and can be characterized by a general understanding—in that case "accurate interpretation."

Value Systems Define the Individual and the Culture

Values and beliefs have both personal and social significance. Individuals live by them and as they adapt to new circumstances by adopting new language, they inject possibilities for change into the culture. And as cultures change they influence the language of the individuals in the culture. Such a process implies that values do not change very rapidly or easily. The values people were exposed to in childhood stay with them for most of their lives. Old values may be adapted to other values that are acquired later, but they are rarely abandoned. When the rare case happens, as when a person with strong religious views becomes an agnostic or when an agnostic is "saved," it usually means that the person has moved into a new subculture. The change has had a radical influence on all the values and beliefs previously held.

In 1970, Charles Reich wrote a popular book, *The Greening of America*, in which he claimed that the political unrest among young people in the late 1960s involving changes in their speech, dress, and social mores was a sign of a major value shift in American culture. In fact, he claimed that the transcendental values of this youth culture would be the dominant culture of America (326–353). Today that prediction has been long since proven false. Some elements of that subculture of the 1960s can still be found, but today's youth culture in its primary manifestations holds most of the traditional American middle-class values. As early as 1972, for instance, Richard Nixon received almost as many votes from voters aged 18 to 24 as George McGovern, even though Nixon was the open and avowed voice of the most traditional values ("The Landslide").

Cultures, as defined by the value systems they identify with, evolve slowly and can be identified in a variety of texts. The values and beliefs contained in the texts of a society can be used to define a culture. These four assumptions underlie value analysis and provide the rationale for the critic to use in articulating the culture discovered in the text.

METHODS OF VALUE ANALYSIS

The critic is a participant in his or her culture, hopefully a more perceptive participant than most. However, it must not appear that the critic has drawn an interpretation of a culture principally from his or her own mind. To do this requires specific methods for finding values. What do you look for when trying to reveal the richest understanding of the beliefs and values in a text?

What Words Are Used to Articulate Positive Values?

This chapter began with an example of the direct articulation of values: Ronald Reagan's "family, neighborhood, work, peace, and freedom."

David Paul Nord (1987) examined the coverage of the railroad strike of 1877 by the three major Chicago newspapers, the *Times, Tribune,* and *News.* He found that although they differed on specific sympathies during the strikes, "The editorials in these three newspapers during the 1877 strikes suggest some basic shared values." Among the values he identified were "public interest," "commercial order," and "social harmony." These were identified by direct statement. For instance, the *Chicago Times* said of social harmony, "The killing of some of the insurgents is not a matter which concerns society at all. If they stand in the way of *society's peaceful order*, the sooner they are killed the better" (268). Like Reagan, the values are clearly stated. These are examples of the most obvious form values take.

What Words Are Used to Articulate Negative Values?

The values that identify what is preferred also can be stated in the negative: life-death, freedom-slavery, saving-waste, peace-war, work-laziness, and so on. How a society defines its values negatively is as important as how they are stated positively.

In the depths of the Great Depression, Franklin D. Roosevelt (1946) delivered his First Inaugural Address. Much of the address is characterized by positive values of hope and action. Early in the speech, however, he tells the nation about negative values with this statement: "So, first of all, let me assert my firm belief that the only thing we have to fear is fear itself—nameless, unreasoning, unjustified terror which paralyzes needed efforts to convert retreat into advance" (26). Fear, namelessness, unreason, unjustified terror, paralysis, retreat—these are the negatives which need to be overcome.

Not only do both positive and negative terms help the critic to define a value system but the emphasis placed on one or another also helps. In F.D.R.'s speech negative values are limited while positive values predominate. Note how even the negative values are limited: "fear" is our only fear. It is defined by "unreasoning" and "unjustified" and it hinders "advance." The juxtaposition of positive and negative values helps the critic to define the value system seen in the text. In Roosevelt's case, it is a progress-oriented system which works through reason. Roosevelt can be placed, by this passage, at the forefront of the value system of Western liberalism and contrasted with an alternate, perhaps a collectivist, value system.

What Values Are Implied in Belief Statements Without Specific Value Terms?

Although all statements have valuative implications, not all state them directly. The critic must look beyond the belief statements to the values implied in them. Shortly after the negative value statements quoted above, Franklin D. Roosevelt (1946) stated his beliefs about the negative conditions in the land: "Values have shrunken to fantastic levels; taxes have risen; our ability to pay has fallen; government of all kinds is faced by serious curtailment of income; the means of exchange are frozen in the currents of trade; the withered leaves of industrial enterprise lie on every side; farmers find no markets for their produce; the savings of many years in thousands of families are gone" (27). Behind these simply stated beliefs are the implied negative values of economic stagnation and loss. To make such judgments about implied values, critics must find the silent or sub-texts in discourses.

What Values Are Implied by the Formal Elements Used?

Value systems are typically associated with rhetorical practices that identify, or at least confirm, the value system. Particular cultures have ways of talking that identify them. Extensive use of statistical and other mathematical evidence can suggest that science and formal reasoning are valued. Extensive use of quotations from figures such as Thomas Jefferson, Franklin D. Roosevelt, Karl Marx, or Gloria Steinem indicates identification with the value system based on authority and a particular tradition. A person wearing a swastika arm band clearly suggests sympathy for a fascist value system. Use of African American dialect or the metaphorical and repetitious language patterned after the African American sermon reinforces the overt statement of value systems typical of the African American church. Richard Weaver (1953) has even argued that one can identify value systems by the kinds of arguments used to support them. Conservatives, he says, typically use argument from principle while liberals tend to argue from circumstance (56–58).

Such evidence cannot be taken alone. Not everyone who speaks with the style of the African American church has the same values as Martin Luther King, Jr., or Jesse Jackson. Instead, a culture is defined by the total integration of language and visual elements although discordant elements will sometimes appear. They do not necessarily indicate that something is wrong with the critic's analysis; rather, they may indicate the complexity that is characteristic of cultures and subcultures as they vie for a place in the critic's consciousness.

The four methods just discussed for identifying values provide the critic with evidence from which to construct a value system. The following section will discuss the process of moving from individual values and beliefs to systems.

DEFINING VALUE SYSTEMS

Although the number of basic value systems in Western culture is limited, each has variations. Many people see themselves as living by their personal value system: "I'm my own person," "I live by what I think is right," "I don't follow the crowd." These statements imply that at least some individuals have a distinctive value system. But, when people are asked to explain more specifically what their values are, invariably they describe values similar to well-known value systems. For instance, all of the statements quoted above reflect the value of individualism, which is basic to the American application of the Enlightenment value system.

Nonetheless, there are variations from one subgroup in the society to another as well as differences based upon circumstances. Relation to God, for instance, while part of a person's value system, may have little impact on business practices. So, an employee's manual, even for a company managed by a devoutly religious person, will rarely say anything about reliance on God. But that same manager may give the value prominence in a letter of advice to a friend or in planning a speech to a church group.

Not all the values in a culture are operating at one time. Furthermore, there is no single established hierarchy of values. According to Milton Rokeach (1973), the number one terminal value during the Vietnam War was a world at peace (28). Today it is rarely ranked above the middle of the list (Sillars and Ganer 1982, 190). Clearly, situations have a part in defining the hierarchy.

Critics look for the value system hierarchy in the texts they are studying. Those texts are influenced by time and circumstance, and, therefore, established definitions of value systems are useful touchstones for analysis, but do not constitute a natural standard against which to "judge" a text. With that caution, let us now look at some of the established definitions of major value systems in the United States.

THE MAJOR AMERICAN VALUE SYSTEMS

Traditionally, the identification of major value systems of a culture comes through the examination of its political and philosophical literature. This method puts a great dependence on the intellectual understanding of values. Many such statements of American value systems have been defined by literary historians, intellectual historians, philosophers, rhetoricians, and sociologists (see for instance, Persons 1958; Ruesch 1951; Steele and Redding 1962; Weaver 1953; Williams 1970). Each of the six systems identified here is illustrated by some of the major positive and negative terms associated with it.

The Puritan-Pioneer Value System

This value system has been identified frequently as the Puritan morality or the Protestant ethic. However, it expands beyond the strong and perhaps too obvious religious implications of the terms *Puritan* and *Protestant*. This value system is what most Americans refer to when they speak of the "pioneer spirit," which was not necessarily religious. It also extends to a strain of values brought to this country by Southern and Eastern European Catholics, Greek Orthodox, and Jews who could hardly be held responsible for John Calvin's theology or even the term *Protestant ethic*. Despite the friction between these foreign-speaking immigrants from other religions and their native Protestant counterparts, they had many values in common.

The Puritan-Pioneer value system is rooted in the idea that persons have an obligation to themselves and those around them, and, in some cases, to their God, to work hard at whatever they do. In this system, people are limited in their abilities and must be prepared to fail. The great benefit is in the striving against an unknowable and frequently hostile universe. They have an obligation to others, must be selfless, and must not waste. Some believe this is the only way to gain happiness and success, others see it as a means to salvation. In all cases it takes on a moral orientation.

Obviously, one might work hard for a summer in order to buy a new car and not be labeled a "Puritan." Frequently, in this value system, the instrumental values of selflessness, thrift, and hard work become terminal values where the work, for instance, is valued beyond the other benefits it can bring.

Likewise, because work, selflessness, and thrift are positive value terms in this system, laziness, selfishness, and waste are negative value terms. One can see how some adherents to this value system object to smoking, drinking, dancing, or card playing. To them, these activities are frivolous; they take one's mind off more serious matters and waste time.

Some of the words that are associated with the Puritan-Pioneer value systems are:

Positive: *activity, dedication, dependability, dignity, duty, morality, righteousness, savings, selflessness, sobriety, temperance, thrift, virtue, work*

Negative: *dereliction, disgrace, dissipation, hunger, infidelity, immorality, poverty, theft, vandalism, vanity, waste*

Enlightenment Value System

America became a nation in the period of the Enlightenment. It happened when a new intellectual era based on the scientific and intellectual findings of people such as Sir Isaac Newton and John Locke were dominant. The Declaration of Independence is the epitome of an Enlightenment document. In many ways, America is an Enlightenment nation, and if Enlightenment is not the predominant value system, it is surely a first among equals.

The Enlightenment position stems from the belief that we live in an ordered world in which all activity is governed by laws similar to the laws of physics. Enlightenment persons theorize that people can discover these laws through the power of reason. The laws of nature are harmonious, and one can use reason to discover them all. They also can be used to provide for a better life.

Because humans are basically good and capable of finding answers, restraints on them must be limited. Occasionally, people do foolish things and must be restrained by society. However, a person should never be restrained in matters of the mind. Reason must be free. Thus, government is an agreement among individuals to assist the society to protect rights. That government is a democracy. Certain rights are unalienable, and they may not be abridged; "among these are life, liberty and the pursuit of happiness." Arguments for academic freedom, against wiretaps, and for scientific inquiry come from this value system.

Some of the words that are associated with the Enlightenment value system are:

Positive: *democracy, fact, freedom, individualism, intelligence, knowledge, liberty, natural laws, natural right, nature, progress, rationality, reason, science*

Negative: *bookburning, dictatorship, error, falsehood, fascism, ignorance, inattention, indecision, irrationality, regression, thoughtlessness*

Progressive Value System

Progress was a natural handmaiden of the Enlightenment. If these laws were available and if humans had the reason to discover them and use them to advantage, then progress would result. Life would continually get better. Although Progress is probably an historical spin-off of the Enlightenment, it has become so important on its own that it deserves to be seen quite separately from the Enlightenment.

In 1953, Richard Weaver found that "one would not go far wrong in naming progress" the "god term" of that age, the "expression about which all other expressions are ranked as subordinate. . . . Its force imparts to the others their lesser degrees of force, and fixes the scale by which degrees of comparison are understood" (212).

Today, the unmediated use of the Progressive value system is questioned, but progress is still a fundamental value in America. Most arguments against progress are usually arguments about the definition of progress. They are about what "true progress" is.

Some of the key words of the Progressive value system are:

Positive: *change, efficiency, evolution, future, improvement, modern, practicality, progress, science*

Negative: *backward, impossible, old-fashioned, regressive*

Transcendental Value System

Another historical spin-off of the Enlightenment system was the development of the transcendental movement of the early nineteenth century. It took from the Enlightenment all its optimism about people, freedom, and democracy, but rejected the emphasis on reason. It argued idealistically that another faculty, intuition, surpassed reason. Thus, for the transcendentalist, there is a way of knowing that *transcends* reason. Like the Enlightenment thinker, the transcendentalist believes in a unified universe governed by natural laws. Thus, all persons by following their intuition will discover these laws, and universal harmony will prevail. Of course, universal harmony implies social harmony, making government virtually unnecessary.

Transcendentalism usually has been more influential among younger people. James Truslow Adams (1949) once wrote that everyone should read Ralph Waldo Emerson at 16 because his writings were a marvel for the buoyantly optimistic person of that age but did not have the same luster at 21 (31). In the late 1960s and early 1970s, Henry David Thoreau's *Walden* and oriental mysticisms like Zen were among the popular readings of campus rebels. The rejection of contemporary mores, symbolized by what others considered "hippie behavior" with its emphasis on "doing your own thing," indicated the adoption of a Transcendental value system. In all Transcendental movements, emphasis is placed on humanitarian values, the centrality of love for others, and the preference for quiet contemplation over activity.

Although a full adherence to transcendentalism has been limited to small groups, particularly among intellectuals and youths, many of the ideas are not so limited. For instance, one can surely find strains of transcendentalism in the mysticism of some devout older Roman Catholics. And perhaps many Americans become transcendental on particular issues, about the value to be derived from hiking in the mountains, for example.

Here are some of the terms that are characteristic of the Transcendental value system:

Positive: *affection, brotherhood, compassion, emotion, equality, feeling, friendship, humanitarian, individualism, intuition, love, mysticism, personal kindness, respect, sensitivity, sympathetic, truth*

Negative: *anger, coldness, hate, insensitive, mechanical, reason, science, unemotional, war*

Personal Success Value System

The least social of the major American value systems moves people toward personal achievement and success. It can be related to the Enlightenment value system, but it is more than that because it involves a highly pragmatic concern for the material happiness of the individual. To call it selfish only would be to bias consideration against it, although there would be some from this value system who would say, "Yes, I'm selfish." "The Lord helps those who help themselves" has always been an acceptable adage by some of the most devout in our nation.

A 1982 Gallup poll revealed that American values are very heavily weighted toward personal values. The top-rated values include good physical health, self-respect, happiness, satisfaction, and freedom of choice. Even "good family life" rated as a top value can be seen as an item of personal success. This survey revealed only a few social values like "helping needy people" and "helping better America" and even those are phrased in personal terms; that is, the respondents were asked "how important do you feel each of these is to you." Americans are success-oriented in an individual way that would not be found in some other cultures.

Here are some of the terms that tend to be characteristic of the Personal Success value system:

Positive: *affection, career, consideration, dignity, economic security, enjoyment, fair play, family, friends, health, identity, individualism, personal, recreation, respect*

Negative: *coercion, disease, disgrace, dullness, hunger, poverty, routine*

Collectivist Value System

Although there are few socialists or communists in the United States, it is impossible to ignore the strong attachment among some people to collective action. In part, this is a product of social theories from Europe in the nineteenth century, from a perceived need to control the excesses of greed in a mass society, and a long-standing value on cooperative action. The same people today who condemn welfare payments to unwed mothers frequently praise their ancestors for taking care of the widow in a frontier community. Much discourse about our "pioneer ancestors" has to do with their cooperative action. And anticollectivist politicians and evangelists talk about "the team." At the same time, many fervent advocates of collective action argue vehemently for their freedom and independence. Certainly, the civil rights movement constituted a collective action for freedom. Remember the link in Martin Luther King, Jr.'s "I Have a Dream" speech between "freedom" and "brotherhood"?

But whether the Collectivist value system is used to defend socialist proposals or promote "law and order," there is no doubt that collectivism is a strong value system in the United States. Like transcendentalism, however, it is probably a value system that, at least in this day, cannot work alone.

Here are some of the terms that tend to characterize the Collectivist value system:

Positive: *brotherhood, cooperation, equality, humanitarian aid and comfort, joint action, order, social good, together, unity*
Negative: *disorganization, inequality, personal greed, selfishness*

These value systems do not stand as clear alternatives; combinations occur. Nor is a single word an indication of a value system. Note, for instance, that *nature* appears in both the Enlightenment and Transcendental value systems, though with quite different meanings because of the other values with which it is associated. Nor are these value systems equal in popularity. The Transcendental and Collectivist systems tend to be less frequently used to define American society. They usually appear as parts of another more dominant system or in a subculture's discourse. These values serve as broad classifications that others have observed as being fundamental to our culture. They are useful, therefore, as guideposts that will help to relate what a critic finds in the text of a culture to what others have found.

However, this method of defining cultural value systems is not universally approved. Some critics claim that the crucial flaw in this understanding of values is the kind of text from which it is most often drawn: intellectual writings. When you find the Puritan virtues in Cotton Mather, John Winthrop, Jonathan Edwards, and the like, the Enlightenment values in Thomas Jefferson or Benjamin Franklin, and transcendentalism in Ralph Waldo Emerson or Henry David Thoreau, you are using intellectual texts to define what the culture is. As a result, you are depending on systematic thinkers to define what much less systematic people think. In short, you are defining the particular culture of American intellectualism, but most people do not think that way.

Conal Furay (1977) argues that most people think in bits and pieces, not organized rational systems. Most people, Furay argues, "dance around their values" (19). People, he says, "will not substitute rational for emotionally vibrant [based on experience] models" (21). Popular culture such as television, popular novels, and films reinforces experience and, thus, reinforces the experiential "dance" around values.

However, even Furay, when he comes to defining American values in this context, discovers that individualism, the Puritan virtues, and optimism are central to the dance. They also are fundamental to the Puritan and Enlightenment value systems. Awareness of traditional classifications is useful to a critic as long as the text being analyzed leads to reasonable definitions of a culture and not to some preestablished classification.

DEFINING A CULTURE

Earlier, four kinds of markers for identifying values—positive terms, negative terms, values implied in beliefs, and formal indicators—were identified. Such values form into a system that is more than a collection of terms. The critic must identify their relationship to one another in order to understand the richness of the culture that the language represents. Asking five questions will help to reveal this culture.

What Is the Emphasis of the Value System?

Both number of references to a value and its placement at more or less strategic points in the message indicate its relative emphasis among the values of a system. We noted before Richard Weaver's 1953 claim that progress was the god term of the age ("that expression about which all other expressions are ranked as subordinate"). "It would be difficult to think of any type of person or of any institution," he said, "which could not be recommended to the public through the enhancing power of this word. A politician is urged upon the voters as a 'progressive leader'; a community is proud to style itself 'progressive'; technologies and methodologies claim to [be] 'progressive'; a peculiar kind of emphasis in modern education calls itself 'progressive' and so on without limit" (212–213). Linked to progress but lower on the hierarchy, Weaver placed "fact," "science," "modern," "efficient," and "American" (214–220). So, he defined a value system for America that was revealed in the relative emphasis on these words. He did not mean that these were the only words that represented values in 1953, but they were central to the period.

Progress, as Weaver uses it, becomes an ideograph that is associated with the other dominant value words in the society and that may be used by people who have conflicting visions. For one person, for example, progress might mean the exploitation of natural resources to provide a better material life for the citizen, while for another it might mean setting aside wilderness land. Weaver's ambitious claim (to name the god term of an age) may be more than anyone can hope to accomplish but it does illustrate how value systems have centers.

Critics cannot always find some defining value word around which a value system turns, but at least the critic must look for some way to characterize how the elements of the value system unite. A value system is itself a selection from available values reflected in a message. That message is a product of the persons and circumstances involved with the message. Another communication situation might make the emphasis in the value system different. Emphasis must be probed.

What Relationships Exist Among the Values?

To define a system, there must be some sense of how the values relate to one another. Each value takes on new meaning because of the other values with which it is associated. Perhaps the dominant values in the United States are composed of Puritan and Enlightenment value systems. In these values, activity, work, and morality combine with freedom, science, and rationality. People work hard and remain morally straight of their own choosing because it is the expected thing to do.

The Boy Scouts of America, says Conal Furay (1977), may be an important reflection of American values. As of 1988, it had a yearly membership approaching five million; the *Boy Scout Handbook* is second only to the Bible in all-time American sales (42). In its laws and oath are embodied the value system that makes this combination work. Boy Scouts pledge to keep themselves "physically strong, mentally awake, and morally straight." Its oath and laws are close to those of other organizations, male and female, young and old, indicating that its value system is more extensive than its own members.

The Boy Scout value system is so well-known that it seems almost natural to most Americans. But some systems provide different and even unusual combinations. The 1984 Chicago Cubs changed a long tradition for their diehard fans and won the National League Eastern Division only to fall in the play-offs. The rise and demise of the Cubs may have been the biggest sports story of 1984. Nicholas Trujillo and Leah Ekdom (1985) studied the sports stories about the Cubs and found six sets of value themes in the sportswriting over the season: "winning and losing," "traditions and change," "teamwork and individualism," "work and play," "youth and experience," and "logic and luck." "These themes," say Trujillo and Ekdom, "understood here as both a topic and a cluster of values through which that topic is organized and expressed, are discussed in pairs because they involve oppositional yet juxtaposed values and because over the course of the season each part of the theme pair was used as an interpretive frame for the other" (265). The value system portrayed in sportswriting about the Chicago Cubs is one in which seemingly contradictory values work together.

What Is the Relationship Between Implied and Stated Values?

More useful than the popular distinction between emotional and rational messages is a distinction between messages that are and are not value-intensive. Emotion, after all, is a human condition, lived subjectively, and in our society calling language "emotional" evokes a negative attitude. Popular wisdom portrays emotional messages as not rational. Looking at messages to see how value-intensive they are gives the critic a better way to differentiate.

Earlier we examined Franklin D. Roosevelt's (1946) Inaugural Address in 1933. Designed to reassure a frightened America at the depth of the Great Depression, it is value-intensive with statements such as these:

> I am certain that my fellow Americans expect that on my induction into the Presidency I will address them with a candor and a decision which the present situation of our Nation impels. This is preeminently the time to speak the truth, the whole truth, frankly and boldly. Nor need we shrink from honestly facing conditions in our country today. This great Nation will endure as it has endured, will revive and will prosper. So, first of all, let me assert my firm belief that the only thing we have to fear is fear itself— nameless, unreasoning, unjustified terror which paralyzes needed efforts to convert retreat into advance. In every dark hour of our national life a leadership of frankness and vigor has met with that understanding and support of the people themselves which is essential to victory. I am convinced that you will again give that support to leadership in these critical days (26–27).

Six days later he delivered his first "Fireside Chat" to explain to the people the actions he had taken in meeting the banking crisis:

> First of all, let me state the simple fact that when you deposit money in a bank the bank does not put the money into a safe deposit vault. It invests your money in many different forms of credit—bonds, commercial paper, mortgages and many other kinds of loans. In other words, the bank puts your money to work to keep the wheels of industry and of agriculture turning around. A comparatively small part of the money you put into the bank is kept in currency—an amount which in normal times is wholly sufficient to cover the cash needs of the average citizen. In other words, the total amount of all the currency in the country is only a small fraction of the total deposits in all of the banks (33).

The difference in these two passages is not that the crisis nor the circumstances have changed. What is different is the need in the First Inaugural Address to set a value agenda for the nation in the weeks and months ahead. In the banking crisis fireside chat, values are still there—values of reasonableness and understanding. But they are unstated; they are implied and as such a quite different tone is set.

What Is the Relationship Between Positive and Negative Values?

Some messages are positively oriented, others are negatively oriented. Such orientations throw light on the culture being defined. Frequently, these positive and negative values are found in a single speech. In his First Inaugural Address, President Woodrow Wilson (1956) called for reform of the nation's economy in the interest of the "New Freedom." In this passage you can see how he used both positive and negative values to define what he planned for the nation as opposed to what had been the case. It is a small example of a speaker defining two contrasting cultures. To illustrate, the terms identifying values Wilson considers *good* are italicized and those he considers **bad** are printed in boldface:

> But the **evil** has come with the *good*, and much *fine gold* has been **corroded**. With *riches* has come **inexcusable waste**. We have **squandered** a great part of what we might have *used*, and have not stopped to *conserve* the exceeding *bounty of nature*, without which our *genius for enterprise* would have been **worthless** and **impotent, scorning** to be careful, **shamefully prodigal** as well as *admirably efficient*. We have been *proud* of our industrial *achievements*, but we have not hitherto stopped *thoughtfully*, enough to count **human cost**, the **cost** of *lives* **snuffed out**, of *energies* **overtaxed** and **broken**, the **fearful** *physical* and *spiritual* **cost** to the men and women and children upon whom the **dead weight** and **burden** of it all has fallen **pitilessly** the years through (222).

Wilson sets this passage up in oppositional pairs: evil/good, gold/corrosion, riches/waste, squandered/used, etc. In the system to be abandoned, we see the negatives of the Puritan value system: waste, squandering, scorn, prodigal, human costs, spiritual costs, pitilessness. It is not surprising to learn that Wilson was raised a strict Calvinist. The positive view is not a radical one. There is no change in the basic value system of the society, no turn to Marxist ideology, for instance. We are "proud of our industrial achievements," our "riches" come from the "bounty of nature" and "our genius for enterprise." The need is not to alter the system radically but to be "thoughtful" of "lives" and "energies." These negative conditions are not the product of some flaw in the system but only that we did not follow one of our main values: reason.

What Values Are Not Present in the Text That Might Be Expected?

Looking for values in messages as a way of defining a culture is seldom a matter of examining a brief text like a single commercial, short speech, or editorial statement. Value analyses require a substantial textual base. The purpose of this analysis is to see some culture or subculture in its broader implications. Consequently, the critic will discover a value system embodying several values and a number of beliefs. Critics will understand the implications of that value system better by comparing it to similar systems that are not exhibited.

Such a practice is implied in every definition of a value system. Defining any system, therefore, not only brings to light values that are held by the culture but also discovers what values are not there. To observe that Ronald Reagan defined a culture based around "family, work, neighborhood, peace, and freedom" says that some values have been downplayed or dismissed from this value system. When these values so boldly stated at the beginning of Ronald Reagan's 1980 Acceptance Address are fleshed out with such specific beliefs as controlling inflation, reducing taxes, curbing spending, limiting federal power, permitting school prayer, and restricting access to abortion, the system begins to develop as a definite world view. Then it is easy enough to see values that are not in his system.

For instance, "family" does not mean women's equal rights; it does not mean civil rights for gays and lesbians. In a broader confrontation, Reagan had chosen one side of a classic controversy in our society: the clash between freedom and equality. What would it have meant if instead of "freedom,"applied mostly to economic freedom and protection against the Soviet Union, he had chosen "equality," or "equal justice," with the emphasis on women's and minority rights, greater economic support for poor people, or guaranteed income? In such a case, a quite different culture would have been implied.

A study by Mina Vaughn (1986) of the culture of nine high technology industries is based on her interviews with company officials and analysis of company publications. That study reveals a value system dominated by five values: "innovation, quality, teamwork, equality, and individualism." While some of these values ("quality" and "teamwork," for example) might be prominent in the language of most companies, others such as "equality" and "individualism" are unusual industrial values. High technology companies are different. For instance, one assigns parking spaces on the basis of seniority. A secretary is parked at the front door while a vice-president has to "walk in from the back lot." The differences omit and play down some traditional industrial values such as "administrative power" and "conforming."

Therefore, differences between one culture or subculture and another are significant. The values omitted from a particular system are, of course, important as well.

PROBLEMS WITH VALUE ANALYSIS

Some of the problems that make value analysis controversial are the same as those found in all deconstructive criticism; others are not. The first problem was discussed in Chapter 6: value analysis can only interpret a text; in itself it cannot judge. Ideological criticism (Chapter 10), because of its orientation to specific beliefs, can be judgmental. Value analysis is not judgmental because it deals in more general concepts of the good and the bad, while ideological criticism is oriented to specific beliefs—ideologies. Value analysis tends to be more "objective" and, in some ways, closer to common sense criticism. A critic could make judgments, but they would go beyond the values themselves. In the example of Reagan's values cited earlier, a critic would need to turn to an ideology to judge the usefulness of the value system expressed as opposed to the alternate suggested. But, its supporters would argue that value analysis provides the clearest basis for interpretation available.

A second problem with value analysis is its focus on intellectualized life. As noted earlier, value systems tend to come from examinations of established writers. These, as Furay and others argue, represent only a subculture of the nation while the vast majority of Americans would never recognize these value systems as their own. In response, one might observe that value analysis should use these systems only as touchstones to see where an analysis may be going. They are not hard categories for classifying value systems. For the deconstructive critic, the value systems must be interpreted from the text.

Furthermore, values are part of the culture and frequently the people who follow them do not realize that they follow them. Teens dress exactly like their peers in order to show their independence; they are enraged to be told that they are conforming. One strength of value analysis is its ability to explain a culture to members who do not understand their values.

The third problem with value analysis may be the most difficult to overcome. Value analysis is based on general statements about what is good or bad. This has a significant advantage over other sorts of analysis because, as noted, humans have considerably fewer values than beliefs. Therefore, values are more manageable in analysis. But beliefs are specific and can better pinpoint what the culture is about. Narratives (the subject of the following chapter) provide more and richer detail than do generalized statements of values.

Still, the proponents of value analysis can argue that in order to explain ideology or narratives, a critic must turn to values. Only values provide the means of generalizing, and generalization is essential in describing a culture.

CHAPTER EIGHT

Narrative Analysis
Reading Culture Through Stories

Folklorist Jan Brunvand (1987) tells of a story which had "shown up on the grapevine virtually everywhere," in 1987, "with only minor variation in detail." Here's one telling of it:

> A recently divorced man went to a singles bar, where he met a beautiful woman. They became friendly, and ended up going to his place, where they made love all night. The man woke up the next morning and she was gone. He went into the bathroom. Then he looked at the mirror. Scrawled there, in bright red lipstick was the message, "WELCOME TO THE WORLD OF AIDS."

The woman, so the story goes in most variations, had contracted AIDS from the man she loved. And so, furious at all men, she set out to give AIDS to as many men as possible. This story is what Brunvand calls an "urban legend." That is, there is no evidence for it, and no reason to believe that it happened. Of course, the woman cannot be found to verify it. A critic following the accurate interpretation approach could stop here.

Another way to examine the story is to see it as a reflection of the culture. AIDS is the most totally threatening disease in the United States today. Even though cancer and heart disease kill many more people per year, they are not as feared as AIDS. Usually transmitted sexually, AIDS evokes all the moral attachments that are associated with sexual practices. Although the major sources of AIDS at the time of the story were drug injection and male homosexual activity, there was a growing concern about its spread in the heterosexual community. Why is the woman the vindictive spreader of the disease? There is more evidence of men infecting women than the reverse. Could it be a reflection of our double standard that says only bad girls and fun-loving men get involved in such affairs? This story has a parallel with stories from the early 1900s about "Typhoid Mary." Today it is "AIDS Mary."

When deconstructed, this story tells much about our culture: our concern with AIDS, attitudes toward sex, and understanding of women's roles. One way to understand a culture is to examine the stories it propagates. Whether the stories are true is not the point. People define their world by telling stories about it and their place in it. The analysis of stories to learn about culture is the subject of this chapter.

Criticism that proceeds from analyzing stories comes under a variety of names. It has been associated variously with such terms as *mythic, narrative, narrative paradigm, dramaturgical, dramatistic, fantasy theme analysis, fictitious, archetypal,* and more. Narrative approaches are used by rhetorical critics, literary critics, historians, anthropologists, sociologists, professors of management and organizational communication, mass communication scholars, political scientists, and psychologists. Admittedly, there are significant differences among many of these but all study stories to reveal a culture. Narrative analysis's closest "common sense" approach is formal criticism. However, the major emphasis in formal criticism is on the form of the text while narrative analysis emphasizes the users of stories and the culture revealed in their understanding of symbols. Therefore, the same characteristics that the formal critic observes (such as theme, structure, character, and style) are used to reveal the cultural messages of the story.

THE ASSUMPTIONS OF NARRATIVE ANALYSIS

Like value analysis and other deconstructive approaches to criticism, narrative analysis is based on the semiotic assumptions discussed in Chapter 6. From that base we can identify four assumptions that are adapted to the analysis of stories.

Humans Make Sense of Their World by the Stories They Tell About It

When people attach such values as rationality, common sense, or truthfulness to behavior, they identify what actions "make sense." Their understanding of what "makes sense" originates in the stories that are told in a culture. While these stories make sense of the environment, they also reinforce the admired character traits of the culture. The mythology of ancient Greece, the Norsemen, or the American West, may not be factual in the usual sense of that word. Davy Crockett probably didn't "kill him a b'ar when he was only three," but that story tells you what was important in a culture that would create such a hero.

Two researchers studied a small-town police force and noted how the stories told constituted "tough talk" that helped to identify the police subculture. They observed: "For these policemen, talking 'tough' is an important social ritual—it's a time to swear, tell 'disgusting' jokes and brag about one's invincibility as a fighter and virility as a lover. . . . On one occasion

[Officer Hancock] claimed that when he gets to handle a traffic fatality, he's in 'fifth heaven,' though he matter-of-factly admits 'it does get bad, like when there's a little boy and his bones are all broke and every time his heart beats, blood rushes out of his head.'" Such talk, the researchers claim, is "an enjoyable social ritual and an important social test" (O'Donnell-Trujillo and Pacanowsky 1983, 226–228). Such talk establishes the officer's place in the culture and helps to define this culture for the critic.

Janice Hocker Rushing (1983) observes how western films reinterpret and reinforce part of the myth that originates in the paradox of the conflict of "individualism and community." In the paradox of the classic western film, the frontier individual needs to be a "rugged individualist" in order "to cope with the harshness and savagery of the frontier environment." "However, in order to settle and civilize the frontier, he must continually face the demands of the community for cooperation and conformity. The cattleman, one of the myth's most enduring heroes, was both a pioneer and a man of property" (16).

By the modern period, this paradox had shifted. Its community had grown into a city and we now have the "citified cowboy" of *The Electric Horseman* and *Urban Cowboy*. In *Urban Cowboy*, according to Rushing (1983), there is "too little room to roam":

> The Women's Movement, the Human Potential Movement, and the Sexual Revolution have stressed freedom and "space" in male-female relationships, resorting to "inner space" as the new last frontier. *Urban Cowboy* solves these problems by a pseudo-synthesis of individualism and community in scene, props, characters, and plot that implies an overall preference for appearance over reality.
>
> As in traditional Westerns, the saloon in this movie is the most important building because this is the only place where all the characters can be seen together repeatedly. . . . Here the saloon is Gilley's, three acres of bar and dance floor in Houston, Texas, where urban cowboys and cowgirls come to show off their stuff. As an indoor "frontier," this place is impressively huge. It is ridiculously minute, however, when compared to the long-gone real frontier. The appropriate dress is designer jeans, western shirts or tank tops, cowboy boots, and hats. The dance is the Twostep, Cotton-eyed Joe, or country swing. As one journalist describes the scene at Gilley's: "There seems to be a widely held belief that one can grow into an identity from the outside-in rather than developing from the inside-out. The external trappings get mistaken for the thing itself. Thus are city cowboys hatched" (28).

These stories built from words and scenes do not illustrate what people "are really like." Rather, in the words of anthropologist Clifford Geertz (1973), echoing Max Weber, "Humans are animals suspended in webs of significance they themselves have spun. I take culture to be these webs" (5). These "webs of significance" are spun from symbols for all deconstruction rests on the basic assumption that a human "is a symbol using animal" (Burke 1966, 16).

Thus, humans make sense of their world by the stories they tell about themselves, their experiences, and the other persons with whom they associate. With this understanding, then, a "critic," in the words of Ernest Bormann (1985), finds "visions, communities, consciousness" and from them "can make humanistic evaluations of the quality of the rhetoric and the social realities of the people who share the consciousness" (3–4).

Narrative Is a Pervasive and Vital Form of Interpretive Discourse

Traditionally, narrative has been considered one of the four parts of all discourse, the other three being exposition, description, and argument. But for those who deconstruct the stories people tell, narrative is much more than one of four equal parts of discourse. Let us begin with the observations of Roland Barthes:

> The narratives of the world are numberless. Narrative is first and foremost a prodigious variety of genres, themselves distributed amongst different substances—as though any material were fit to receive man's stories. Able to be carried by articulated language, spoken or written, fixed or moving images, gesture, and the ordered mixture of all these substances; narrative is present in myth, legend, fable, tale, novella, epic, history, tragedy, drama, comedy, mime, painting (think of Carpaccio's *Saint Ursula*), stained glass windows, cinema, comics, news items, conversation. Moreover, under this almost infinite diversity of forms, narrative is present in every age, in every place, in every society; it begins with the very history of mankind and there nowhere is nor has been a people without narrative. All classes, all human groups, have their narratives, enjoyment of which is very often shared by men with different, even opposing, cultural backgrounds. Caring nothing for the division between good and bad literature, narrative is international, transhistorical, transcultural: it is simply there, like life itself (Kaplan 1986, 556–557).

Barthes's description makes narrative pervasive while still leaving a place for the other three traditional forms of discourse (exposition, description, argument). But others go even further. Bormann (1985) argues that stories (which he calls "fantasy themes") are not "different in kind" from "argumentative discourse," for stories provide "the ground for the rational elements" of "persuasion" (16). Thus, for Bormann, stories support argumentative claims much as values support the same.

Walter Fisher (1987) has expressed the most comprehensive view of narrative to date. He sees narrative as a "paradigm," that is, as a means of explaining any discourse and he differentiates the "narrative paradigm" from the "rational world paradigm." According to Fisher, the "rational world paradigm" has dominated Western thought until now—in this book it is called "common sense." Fisher claims that we should add the term *Homo narrans* (narrative man) to the list of terms such as *Homo sapiens* and "rational man" that are used to define humans. All such terms, he says, are metaphors and "when narration is taken as the master metaphor, it subsumes the others"(62).

Few critics would go as far as Fisher in claiming that all discourse is narrative. However, many critics find narrative either a vital or a central element in human communication.

Stories Are Symbolic Actions That Create Social Reality

Culture, says Edward Sapir, is "never given" to the individual but is "gropingly discovered." Culture is not some monolithic social force that is imposed upon each individual. Instead, "far from being 'carried' by a community or group [cultures] are discoverable only as the particular properties of certain individuals, who cannot but give these cultural goods the impress of their own personality" (Turner 1981, 140). It is easy to think of culture as, in Sapir's words, a "closed system of behavior" where humans merely echo what is there in the culture. By such thinking, individuals "reflect" the culture. From the point of view of anthropologists like Victor Turner and Clifford Geertz, culture is the sum total of what people do and believe. As such, culture is dynamic and comprehended by understanding how its members symbolically define it.

The critic who examines stories in this manner must always be aware that the stories come from individuals. These individuals "carry" the culture. They learned it at their mother's knee and carry it in their own unique way. Stories are fiction, as Geertz (1973) says, but not false because they are true to what the individuals have experienced in their culture (20–21). However, a major problem occurs when a critic tries to derive a definition of the culture from individual stories.

Simply, it is too easy to identify the idiosyncratic story as the sign of the social reality for all members of a culture. This is the reason why many critics look for stories that are repeated by several tellers, why they take special notice of what tends to become recurring myths. In another sense, following the work of Carl Jung, some critics see in recurring myths a pattern of archetypes, a kind of biological memory that the human race shares. The critics of the deconstruction tradition, for example, Maud Bodkin (1963), who introduced Jung's psychology to literary criticism, find these stories in the culture. They have a "ritual genesis" and do not arise from some mystical biological memory (Hyman 1955, 157–158).

Kenneth Burke's (1978) term for such stories, *symbolic action,* has been used widely. "Dramatism" for Burke is no metaphor in the sense that "all the world's a stage" is a metaphor. Telling stories is as much a form of action as throwing a baseball, eating a sandwich, or shaking a hand. Language and thought are modes of action (16, 25, 27–30). They tell a critic as much about the culture and the individuals who are part of it as do any physical acts. Thus, stories are symbolic actions that draw upon and define social reality. They do not merely reflect a culture that has a given structure, nor do they represent some myths embedded in the blood of the race for all time and circumstances. They provide the means for a critic to learn what a culture is like from the people who live in it. They are the only sources that can communicate it.

THE NATURE OF STORIES

Before we examine the ways in which critics deconstruct stories, it will be useful to mention some of the relationships of stories to experience, to values, and to other stories.

Stories Are Linked to Experience

Even when stories are fiction, they are not false. Thus, even fantastic tales such as *Through the Looking Glass, The Lord of the Rings,* or *Star Wars* reflect the experience of their creators and receivers. "All great story tellers," says Walter Benjamin (1969), "have in common the freedom with which they move up and down the rungs of their experience as on a ladder" (102).

Ernest Bormann (1985) explains how small groups of people dramatize messages most significantly by creating or remembering stories that reflect their interpretation of experience. He says:

> The most important element of dramatizing messages . . . is a narrative or story about real or fictitious people in a dramatic situation or setting other than the here-and-now communication of the group. . . . As the members shared the fantasy [story], the tempo of the conversation increased. People grew excited, interrupted one another, laughed, showed emotion, and forgot their self-consciousness. The people who shared the fantasy did so with appropriate responses (4–5).

What Bormann says about small groups can be extended to all kinds of communication, from the solitary reading of a novel to watching the televised Olympics. Readers, writers, speakers, producers, and viewers share their stories and those stories that ring true to experience they repeat and in time make into cultural myths.

Stories Are Linked to Values

"Every historical narrative," says Hayden White (1981), "has as its latent or manifest purpose the desire to moralize the events which it treats. . . . Storytelling . . . is intimately related to, if not a function of, the impulse to moralize reality, that is, to identify it with the social system that is the source of any morality that we can imagine" (14). Louis O. Mink (1981) rejects White's use of "morality" and substitutes "human." Yet his explanation points clearly to value systems: "Any situation in which choice is possible, or by circumstances is rendered impossible, is a moral situation in the broadest sense" (237). Walter Benjamin (1969) says that in every case the storyteller "has counsel for . . . readers" (86). Whether one interprets the inherent nature of the story as "moral," "human," or "counsel," it is clearly rooted in value judgments.

Walter Fisher (1987) makes a case for linking storytelling and values. He turns to the concept of "good reasons," which Karl Wallace had called the "substance of rhetoric." "The term 'good reasons'," Fisher says, "does not imply that every element of a rhetorical transaction that warrants a belief, attitude, or action—that any 'good reason'—is as good as any other. It only signifies that whatever is taken as a basis for adopting a rhetorical message [story] is inextricably bound to a value—to a conception of the good" (107).

Types of Stories

Historians have long recognized three levels of stories that represent their craft: annals, chronicles, and narratives. For the historian, narrative is generally considered the most complete and preferred form but an understanding of the three and their relation to one another is useful.

Annal. A simple listing in chronological order of the events that the writer thought was important is called an annal. This form, most prevalent in the medieval period, is illustrated by an annal compiled by Louis O. Mink (1981) of his personal recollections in contemporary times:

1960. Kennedy elected President. First year of College of Social Studies.

1961.

1962.

1963. Carelton College, second semester. Family camping trip through West, Canada, Mexico. Kennedy shot.

1964.

1965. Family camping trip through Greece, Yugoslavia. For the first time came to see Vietnam as a national disaster.

1967.

1968. Semester sabbatical somewhere along here.

1968. Collingwood book finished.

etc.   (235).

Such a chronology represents the writer's memory. The gaps do not mean that nothing important happened in that year; they mean that the writer has no memory of it. Stories represent the memory of the storytellers and the culture implied in their experience. It is clear, however, that memory is only partial and personal. Nonetheless, all history, all stories, contain this characteristic. They are based on personal memory no matter how thorough the paper trail may be.

Chronicle.   The annal has memory but little else. The chronicle adds to memory greater comprehensiveness, organization of materials, a central subject, and coherence (White 1981, 20). In the words of Hayden White, it "often seems to wish to tell a story." If you have ever kept a diary, you have an idea of what the chronicle is. It tells what happened on a particular day or during a particular week. It more comprehensively tells about events and people. It is about you. It reveals your own interpretation of events. Because it centers around you, it has more coherence. In those ways it tells a story but it is not a complete narrative. It does not come to a conclusion.

Narrative.   The narrative has all the characteristics of the annal and the chronicle. It is based on experience, is a product of the memory, has a sense of chronology about it, is coherent, and defines a central subject. But the complete narrative has the additional characteristic of "narrative closure" (White 1981, 5). A complete story has a beginning and an end providing the listener or the reader with a completely developed point and a satisfying conclusion.

In one sense, the Vietnam War did not "end" with the withdrawal of American troops from that country. Many stories are told of how the Vietnam War is not over. Many television series and movies such as *Magnum P.I., China Beach, Platoon, Rambo,* and *Born on the Fourth of July* remind us that psychologically and culturally that war is not over. For those Americans concerned about prisoners of war (POWs) and those presumed still missing in action (MIAs) that war is not over.

As a result, the Vietnam War remains a continuing part of the American chronicle. People seek out narratives, however, to attain closure and explain their experiences and values. One story is of a war that was never declared but rather drifted into. It was a war of increasing American involvement and casualties, increasing open protests, and division at home. Slowly it was recognized as a war that could not be won, dramatized by the battle of Hue and television news. It was given closure by President Gerald Ford in a speech at Tulane University, April 25, 1975: "Today, America can regain the sense of pride that existed before Vietnam. But it cannot be achieved by refighting a war that is finished." Seven days later the Viet Cong and North Vietnamese captured Saigon. The war was over (Haines 1986, 1).

Another story, that of the combat veteran, required something more. The strong division in the country over the moral appropriateness of the war made these veterans unappreciated, even scorned, so there was an end only of the fighting—not of the Vietnam story in their lives. A new ending that would recognize the sacrifice of these veterans and reintegrate the nation was needed. The Vietnam Veterans Memorial in Washington, D.C., is found by many to satisfy that need. Said President Jimmy Carter as he signed the Memorial's construction authorization, "A long and painful process has brought us to this moment today. Our nation, as you all know, was divided by this war. For too long we tried to put that division behind us by forgetting the Vietnam war and, in the process, we ignored those who bravely answered this nation's call, adding to their pain the additional burden of our Nation's own inner conflict." Says Harry W. Haines (1986) in his analysis of the Vietnam Veterans Memorial, "Clearly, the Memorial is to be a sign signifying both a sense of loss for the dead and a sense of reincorporation of the survivors" (3–4). Another narrative is complete.

These two examples, then, illustrate how raw experience is divided up and put into stories that constitute a complete narrative so that sense can be made of it.

ANALYZING THE CHARACTERISTICS OF NARRATIVE

The purpose of narrative criticism is not to determine, as in formal criticism, whether the story is appropriately told, or as in accurate interpretation, whether it is "true" to known reality. Its purpose is to understand the culture that spawns narratives. It is necessary to remind ourselves of this distinction because many of its analytical principles have their roots in formal criticism. Indeed, although all the formal criteria are applicable, in this deconstructive mode their usefulness is for interpretative rather than for evaluative purposes. The narrative critic asks: What culture is reflected in the content and form of the story?

Looking at some of the prevailing formal characteristics of stories should help you to see how stories function in a society. Important among them are theme, structure, *peripeteia*, narrative voice, character, and style.

Theme

Culture is defined by the themes that are developed in the story. Such themes include those that are supported or rejected by the end of the story. Consider the children's story "Little Red Riding Hood." Little Red Riding Hood sets out to take some goodies through the forest to her ailing grandmother. She is warned by her mother to beware of the wicked wolf. In the forest she meets the wolf in disguise, who asks where she is going. She tells him she is going to her grandmother's house. The wolf takes a short cut through the forest, eats the grandmother, puts on her clothes, and lies down in the grandmother's bed. When Red Riding Hood arrives, after a brief conversation, he eats her and falls asleep. A hunter enters the house to investigate the snoring, kills the wolf, rescues the grandmother and Red Riding Hood from the wolf's stomach and everyone lives happily ever after.

What are children being told through this story? They are being told that there is evil in the world, that kindness and innocence are virtues, that things work out for the best in the long run because good triumphs over evil. All of these themes, and more, may be found here.

These themes, moreover, relate directly to social values that are fundamental links between the story and the culture. But the story is fanciful; it is a fairy tale based on impossibilities, such as a talking wolf and caesarean delivery of grandmother and granddaughter. How can it tell us about our society? What little girl walks through the woods these days to take goodies to her grandmother? Not many, but the story can relate to experience by metaphorical connection. Few Little Reds start out through the woods, and grandmother is probably in Florida or Las Vegas. Still, urban living has its notions of a "jungle" and the themes relate to experience even if the real experience of evil and good are found in quite different settings.

Analysis such as this can be quite foolish if restricted to single stories. Gilbert Ryle's term *thick description* becomes useful here (Geertz 1973, 3–30). To define a culture, this kind of thematic analysis must be based on an array of children's stories, not just one. Only when themes are repeated over and over do we come to see their importance to the culture. As themes change slightly from one story to the next, we begin to see their richness. Discovering society's belief that there is evil in the world is not much of a critical revelation. But discovering that from story to story the evil is so clearly defined as to be obvious (from the wolf to Darth Vader to the "Evil Empire") helps us to understand that our culture perceives evil as something to be easily identified.

What is left out of a story also helps the critic to understand a culture. If critics enter cultures or subcultures that are not their own, they make sense of them by comparing them to their own. Marilyn Robinson Waldman (1981), a historian of Islam, notes that the preference for narratives over annals is a modern Western idea. The use of the more incomplete annal in other societies is itself a reflection of the culture. Societies such as "medieval Europe and premodern non-western societies which tended to rely on indirection and esotericism" use story forms such as the annal to tell indirectly what the culture was like (242–243).

In contemporary America, a narrative analysis of the Republican and Democratic Conventions of 1984 revealed in Mario Cuomo's Democratic Keynote Address a story of the "Tale of Two Cities," while Ronald Reagan's Republican Acceptance Address was the story of "A City on the Hill." Cuomo's "Tale of Two Cities" is one of affluence and poverty reminiscent of the prelude to the French Revolution while Reagan's "City on the Hill" centers on a narrative of good fortune for everyone. "The problem [with Reagan's story] is the unquestioned acceptance of this vision of America, an America where everything is all right." "Our response," according to Paul Erickson, "to Reagan's rhetoric suggests that we are not an especially thoughtful or analytic nation of political readers, but a people seeking eagerly for answers rather than questions" (Sandmann 1989; Henry 1988). What Reagan leaves out of his story is for such critics as important as what is included.

Structure

Beginning, middle, and end comprise the most obvious structural form that a story can be expected to have. As elementary as this seems, its ramifications for cultural criticism are important. This is particularly true of beginnings and endings. Events do not naturally have beginnings and endings. The world is all of one piece and every event is related to every other. It is what people do with those events to make them into a coherent story that reveals the culture in which they live.

The concepts of beginning and ending are accepted in much of Western culture, but where a storyteller chooses to place the beginning and ending contains a message regarding cultural priorities. To illumine such priorities, communication critics and sociologists use the concept of the "movement": some collection of events and communication acts which taken together, constitute a unified social event. As a result, we can talk about the feminist movement, civil rights movement, consumer movement, antiwar movement, free-speech movement, and so on.

What differentiates one movement critic from another is what each considers the nature of a movement. Some critics believe it to be a phenomenon rooted in the natural condition of the society; to them, a movement is identified as having a beginning and end by the events that inaugurated it and ended it (Simons et al. 1984, 393). Such a view is in keeping with the critical perspectives of common sense. On the other hand, the deconstructive view sees movement as a story told by an individual or a culture wherein there is no "natural" beginning or end except as defined by the storyteller. Michael McGee (1983) has argued that a movement is defined by its supporters as a way of conveying a sense of "inevitable success" (75).

The following argument should serve to illustrate how movements come to be defined as movements:

> The [common sense] literature is explicit in claiming that a movement has an identifiable beginning and end. While for purposes of analysis a critic must put time limits on a movement to make it manageable, those limits are symbolic; they disclose a conceptual bias of the critic, not a definition of reality.
>
> For example, when did the Populist movement begin and end? Women's suffrage? Fundamentalism? Peace? Did the civil rights movement begin with the Montgomery bus boycott, the Emancipation Proclamation or when the first slave said "no" or slowed down in the work assigned? And did it end with the death of Martin Luther King, Jr.? It is clear that beginnings and endings are determined by the critic's perceptions and ability to get others to agree to those perceptions (Sillars 1980a, 21).

Therefore, where stories begin and end has considerable significance in defining their subject matter. Themes are derived from what is included in the story. It is not, however, just a matter of how much is included and left out. Beginnings and endings also are important because they tell us about the central themes and their significance to the culture. The civil rights movement is seen by many as a phenomenon of the 1960s and 1970s, beginning when Rosa Parks refused to give up her seat on a Montgomery, Alabama, bus and ending with the March on Washington or the death of Martin Luther King, Jr. Such a reading, of course, makes the civil rights movement seem shorter than in other possible readings, for example, seeing it begin with the first reluctant slave and still continuing today. But that would make it a chronicle and a different kind of movement. The shortened version makes it a temporary phenomenon, perhaps an unusual phenomenon when a few wrongs are redressed so that society can return to normal and its members live happily ever after. In the broader context, the movement is an ongoing struggle, involving many and varied questions, and has no end.

In addition to beginnings and endings, a story reveals culture by the order of themes it develops. Writers like Victor Turner (1981) claim that all stories have identical patterns of ordering. Turner says that stories go through steps of "breach," "crisis," "redress," and either "reintegration" or "recognition of schism" (145). To find stories useful, it is not necessary to accept Turner's claim. However, the pattern may frequently be useful in analyzing stories.

Important culture-defining questions, however, link such phases to the themes of the story: What is the nature of the events that establish the breach? What themes provide the conflict that produces the crisis? What values influence the redress and reintegration? What value conflicts maintain the schism? Whatever the order of the story, it will reveal tensions and conflicts. Such tensions and conflicts together with the means for resolving them should inform the critic of how the culture represented by the story views the world.

Characters

All stories have characters in them; for example, the innocent Little Red Riding Hood ("Oh, grandmother what big teeth you have,") and the Wicked Wolf ("All the better to eat you with, my dear!"). These and the other characters are *personae* with notions of what is and what is not acceptable behavior. Ernest Bormann (1985) shows how important characters are to a story:

> The unfolding of experience is often chaotic and confusing. Fantasy themes, in contrast with experience, are organized and artistic. When people dramatize an event, they must select certain characters to be the focus of the story and present them in a favorable light while selecting others to be portrayed in a more negative fashion. Without protagonists (heroes) and antagonists (villains) there is little drama. Shared fantasies are coherent accounts of experience in the past or envisioned in the future that simplify and form the social reality of the participants (9–10).

The names we give characters also tell us something about how we view our heroes and villains. The popular comic strip "Prince Valiant" tells us much about the hero in his name. Both Detective Belcher's name and his characterization of suspects on *Hill Street Blues* as "slimeballs" and "skuzzballs" tell us much about him and the suspects as well.

Martin Medhurst (1984a) shows how Ronald Reagan turned aside the "fairness issue" in the 1984 presidential campaign. While Democrats were arguing that his policies favored the rich and injured the poor, Reagan made an ethical appeal based on characters who defined his *personae*:

> Put simply, Reagan invited voters to identify with the *type* of person he was, a persona he had created in more than thirty years on the public stage. His was an ethical appeal. Voters were asked to cast their ballots not so much for Ronald Reagan, President of the United States who had a four year record that could be analyzed, debated, and defended, but rather they were asked to vote for George Gipp, Andy McLoud, Dan Crawford, Brass Bancroft, Jimmy Grant, John Hammond, Web Sloan and the values and qualities of character embodied in those roles (6).

The characters in the story help to organize the cultural meaning of an event. They reinforce themes that tell the critic a good deal about what is important in the communication situation.

Peripeteia

Peripeteia refers to the change of fortune, the reversal of circumstances that occurs in every drama. Events that seem to be flowing in one direction suddenly change. Television sports announcers like to talk about a shift in momentum. The Rams are leading but when the 49ers block a punt a shift in momentum occurs. Those sports announcers talk as if momentum were a natural phenomenon. Of course, momentum is a physical quality and not in human events until a story is told. Nonetheless, the sports announcers' story begins with the Rams dominating the game. They could have begun with the crowd, the weather, or the league standings. But they did not. They gave the momentum to the Rams, and as they give it they can take it away. However, it does make a good story.

In this story, the *peripeteia* is the blocked punt, the reversal of circumstances. As such, it has a special reason to be examined. Note how the announcers tell this part of the story. It is a matter of heightened drama. Before the *peripeteia*, the 49ers seemed "lethargic," they may have "given up," their offense was "frustrated," their defense was "down." Now they cheer, jump in the air. They seem to have "found new life and determination." The blocked punt is not just an act occurring on the field; it is a crucial turning point in the story being told. It is an indication, through the story, of how the American culture thinks of athletics and of itself.

Narrative Voice

Every story must have a storyteller. An important way of understanding the culture implied in the story is to ask: Who tells the story and by what authority? In biblical scholarship the words spoken by God are more important than those spoken by someone else about God. In the fourth chapter of Joshua there is a "narration of what God has done in Jewish history, put in the mouth of God himself and therefore given heightened authority." Following that, Joshua becomes the narrator. He gives his charge to the people. It has less authority because it is Joshua's interpretation of God's words (Kennedy 1980, 124).

For the critic interested in narrative, this authority is not given naturally but is constructed in the interaction of all the elements in the communication situation: the sources of the message, the message, the receivers of the message, and the environment. The narrative voice is thus constructed in the text and may be considered a point of view. As Susan Lanser (1981) states: "Human perception is always structured upon a relationship of perceiver to perceived—upon a *point of view*" (3–4). This point of view gives a text its authority:

> The term "author" designates not only the producer(s) of a message but a special kind of formalized power— *authority*—which the sender has

(presumably) received fron the relevant social community. Even messages like speed-limit signs on the highway are the product of such an author-(ity): if the sign has no author(ization), . . . it could simply be ignored. The verbal act, in other words, implies not only a sender, receiver, and message, but some potential for successful speech activity which depends for its realization on the sender's authority and the receiver's validation for this authority (82).

Lanser (1981) bases this textual authority on three factors: status, contact, and stance (86–94). Status is illustrated by the relationship implied above between God and Joshua. To Bible readers, God has higher status than Joshua.

Contact is established between the source and the receivers of a message by the form of the text itself. Does a text reveal itself in a one-on-one interpersonal communication, by television, by letter, or what?

> The display of words on a page, the size of paragraphs, the arrangement of text, the typography, even the stock of paper can affect the physical channel for communication between author and reader, just as in oral discourse the tone of voice, gesture, voice quality, [and] room arrangement can affect transmission. Small print densely packed on a page, for example, conventionally holds the aura of difficult, scholarly (boring?) material, while large print surrounded by ample "white space" suggests somewhat lighter and easier fare (Lanser 1981, 91).

The narrative voice also implies a stance, an attitude conveyed by the source implied in the text. Some writers and speakers imply by the language they choose that theirs is a reporting stance. They are merely telling others what happened. They have no ax to grind, no political objectives. They will tell you what happened and you may figure out its meaning for yourself. The accurate interpretation called for in Chapter 3 is just such a stance. Others make their stance known and hope to persuade the receivers of it. Still others take a stance of pure enjoyment that disavows any need for concern regarding information or persuasion. "Just lean back, relax, listen, and enjoy," says the disk jockey on an easy listening FM radio station.

Mary Strine and Michael Pacanowsky (1985) applied this concept of narrative voice to organizational communication. They examined the "stance, status and contact configurations" in four books about organizational life: Studs Terkel's *Working*, Rosabeth Moss Kanter's *Men and Women of the Corporation*, Tracy Kidder's *The Soul of a New Machine*, and Joseph Heller's *Something Happened* (289). They concluded:

> Terkel's *Working* and Kanter's *Men and Women of the Corporation* derive their authority principally from traditional sources: *Working* is grounded in the authority of generalization from numbers; *Men and Women of the Corpora-*

tion appeals to the authority of scientific method. Kidder's *The Soul of a New Machine* and Heller's *Something Happened,* on the other hand, develop their authority experientially: through the reader's progressive imaginative involvement in the dramatized interaction between researcher and subjects or in the dramatized representation of fictional characters (296).

The stance, status, and contact that define narrative voice are, of course, a product of the language and visual content of a text. It then becomes appropriate to look at another way that stories reflect a culture: style.

Style

Word choice, grammar, and figures of speech reflect a culture. Computer jargon, athletic talk, and literary language are special kinds of language that reflect an aspect of the culture of the people who use it. We are looking here at what Ernest Bormann (1985) calls "communication styles":

> The broad usage of a community of people engaged in a significant discourse for which they understand the rules, customs, and conventions. . . . Individual style and the style of the community are not unrelated. Individuals practice communication within the assumptions of a given rhetorical community. Joint social ventures such as dances, musical performances, games, and communication episodes have the common characteristics of allowing individual variations of style in performance, but these individual variations must always be according to the rules, norms, customs, and ideal models relating to the joint venture (19).

Style is not just a language phenomenon. There are visual styles. Characterizations of art as representational, abstract, and impressionistic are all ways of talking about visual style and like language, they represent the culture of a particular group or era. Television, too, has its special styles. A close-up shot, for example, is generally assigned a meaning of intimacy (Berger 1982, 38). A study of the television coverage of Reverend Jesse Jackson's speech to the 1984 Democratic National Convention contains an analysis of the ABC coverage of the last four minutes of the speech. The visual style tells a story of intimacy between Jackson and the women in the audience:

> Eleven reaction shots were used in the 4 minutes of Jackson's conclusion. All but one of these shots were of women, and all shots were close-ups or extreme close-ups. Five of the women were noticeably crying. One White woman was first presented in an extreme close-up framed between quivering lips and eyebrows. The camera zoomed back only to show her full face from chin to hairline as tears streamed down her cheeks. A Black woman

was crying and her mascara and eye shadow were smudged from wiping her eyes. The noncrying women also were animated, one shouted "go for it," another shouted encouragement and another clapped and cheered. The single shot of a Black man showed him listening intently. Only two of the ten women shown were White and both of them were crying. Bracketing the 11 emotional reaction shots, Jackson was always shown from the same camera angle—a full front close-up framed from his shoulder to the top of his head. The ABC audience members had a clear guide to help interpret the Jackson conclusion. Women, weeping and supportive, offered clues to meanings that were not available on the other news sources.

It was during these final minutes that ABC generated the evidence for commentator David Brinkley's remark that he had "never seen so many tears in a convention hall" (Tiemens et al. 1988, 13–14).

Newspapers use elements such as headlines, typeface, pictures, column size, and sidebars to create special styles. The comparison of any tabloid with the *New York Times* is not just a matter of different themes, or even of the style of the language. It is also the visual style of the way stories are arranged on the page that points to the culture being reflected.

The critic may use any combination of the six characteristics of stories (theme, structure, character, *peripeteia*, narrative voice, and style) to develop a critical claim. The way character and theme are related, for example, is perhaps more important to understanding the culture that generated the story than are the individual characteristics. Such a concern for relationships among characteristics and the way culture is thus identified is the beginning of the rhetorical analysis of narrative, the subject of the next section.

RHETORICAL ANALYSIS OF NARRATIVE

There are many ways of integrating the six characteristics into analysis that will explain how the message (the story) influences, and is influenced by, the culture. Such an explanation is rhetorical because it is concerned with influence, not just characteristics. Perhaps most useful here is the proposal of Kenneth Burke that the critic looks for the "principles" on which a story is organized and the ways in which these principles connect to one another. Burke called the principles "the pentad" and the relationship among the principles "ratios."

The Pentad

For Kenneth Burke (1954), there are five principles on which a story is organized: act, scene, agent, agency, and purpose. Inherent in Burke's pentad are the familiar questions of newswriting: what? when? where? who? how? and why?

But these principles are not the same as the traditional journalistic questions that come from the common sense orientation of accurate interpretation. The pentad is a guide to finding words that will represent the culture depicted in the story. Here is the pentad in Burke's (1954) own words:

ACT   [What?] "Names what took place in thought or deed."

SCENE   [When? Where?] "The background, the act, the situation in which it occurred."

AGENT   [Who?] "What person or kind of person performed the act."

AGENCY   [How?] "What means or instruments [were] used."

PURPOSE   [Why?] "The reason for the act" (x).

These five principles, says Burke, stand as key terms in a "grammar of motives." Together they permit the critic to understand the relationship of the elements in a story by highlighting the different interpretations that can be made.

In fact, this pentad is quite rich. When the critic moves past the common sense meaning of the terms and looks at them as principles to be applied to a story from a particular point of view, the interpretive horizon broadens. "For instance," Burke (1954) says, "we may examine the term Scene simply as a blanket term for the concept of background or setting *in general*, a name for any situation in which the acts or agents are placed. In our usage, this concern would be 'grammatical.' And we move into matters of 'philosophy' when we note that one thinker uses 'God' as his term for the ultimate ground or scene of human action, another uses 'nature,' a third uses 'environment,' or 'history,' or 'means of production,' etc." (xi).

Furthermore, each of these principles may need subdivision. For example, Burke (1954) shows that the agent of an act may have the "act modified . . . by friends (co-agents) or enemies (counter-agents). Also, an agent need not be a person, but may be a 'personal property' of a person such as 'ideas,' 'the will,' 'fear,' 'malice,' 'intuition,' 'the creative imagination' " (xiv).

Television news illustrates the expanison of the agent. The evening news usually has two anchors, frequently a weather reporter and a sports reporter. There are reporters who tell their stories from the field. One could even add those people who are interviewed or seen on news reports. The evening news, local or national, tells a story but it has multiple agents. It also has personal properties that are characteristic of these agents: *knowledge, objectivity, optimistic, friendly* are words that describe what these agents are like and are, therefore, an important basis for understanding the agent.

Martha Solomon's (1985) study of the Tuskegee Syphilis Project is an illustration of how pentadic analysis may be used to reveal more about a particular story than other kinds of analyses. Briefly, from 1932 until 1972, the United States Public Health Service conducted a study of 399 adults with syphilis to whom no treatment was administered so that the effects of the disease could be studied. During the period 1936 to 1973, 13 "progress reports" were published in major medical journals. Yet no one complained of the medical ethics of permitting human beings to die of a disease that could have been treated. It happened, says Solomon, because of the way the reports used scientific language to tell the story of the project.

The act was the project itself. The reports described it as a scientific study, in "pursuit of knowledge which may benefit mankind." The result was a horrible oversight—the "scientific" observation of humans dying, despite available cures, so as to fulfill the terms of the project. Solomon (1985) explains:

> [The project] . . . provided a unique opportunity "to compare the syphilitic process *uninfluenced* by modern treatment, with the results obtained when treatment has been given" (Vonderkehr et al., 260). A report . . . in 1954 pinpoints the values and purposes of the study. It notes that in 1930 "no accurate data relative to the effect of syphilis in shortening of life" and "no accurate history of the disease leading up to these complications" were available. "This *information* was necessary in order to *evaluate* the effectiveness of programs of public health control with a *reasonable* degree of *understanding* of the natural history of the disease." The italics, which are mine, highlight the directors' focus on acquiring knowledge (239).
>
> The agents or actors are the doctors whose credentials, affiliations with the Public Health Service, and usually prestigious titles are listed as author information in each article. Not only are their credentials explicitly listed, but they are depicted implicitly as members of a dedicated, self-sacrificing "team" (Rivers et al. 395). This view of the actors reveals itself in a 1955 report: "The contribution of time, thoughts, and energy of many individuals with the full knowledge that the fruits of their efforts would not mature until years later, and in other hands, has been vital. As in all such lifetime studies the devotion of these scientists and public health workers to the search for knowledge for the sake of knowledge and with selflessness must here be acknowledged" (Peters et al., 128).

The story has characters (agents) who carry out the project (act) for a noble purpose. There is a chronology to the story and an ending when scientific truth will be found. And where are the patients in all this? They are the agency and scene. As agency they "are the instruments or means through which the doctors achieve their [highly valued and socially beneficial] purpose." Solomon (1985) notes how the language of making human beings an agency tends to dehumanize them. She notes this as one example: " 'The shortening of life expectancy observed in man' has 'a counterpart in the white mouse, in which animal it has been shown by Rosahn that the syphilitic group has significantly lessened life expectancy' " (240).

What is revealed by this analysis is that the language of science permits a story to be told in which human beings are portrayed as scene and agency, thus making them inanimate and nonhuman factors while the Syphilis Project (act) is carried on by dedicated doctors (agents) for the pursuit of knowledge and the benefit of mankind (purpose). Obviously, another story could be told of how the patient was made victim (act) by the scientists (agents) for the purposes of science, but that is not the story told by the report. This example illustrates how the pentad can be used to deconstruct the language of a story, even a scientific report, to discover how that language communicates cultural meaning, even a meaning of extreme cruelty in scientific thinking.

Thus, the pentad provides a way of seeing the principles that make up a story. This combination of narrative elements also provides a basis for encompassing the complexity of the story because each of the principles in the pentad potentially has multiple meanings. Any full interpretation of a story will require that the critic consider all of these principles. But the most important point for analysis occurs when any two principles most clearly overlap. Here are points of greatest ambiguity that are, therefore, of greatest interest to the critic. Burke calls them "ratios."

Ratios

From the five parts of the pentad ten ratios can be formed: scene-act, scene-agent, scene-agency, scene-purpose, act-purpose, act-agent, act-agency, agent-purpose, agent-agency, and agency-purpose. Each of these pairs, these ratios, can be used to define the central relationship of any story. While it is possible to use the parts of the pentad to describe the parts of a story and perhaps even its structure, the identification of a central ratio will add an important unifying basis for understanding the story and, therefore, for shaping a critical claim in narrative analysis.

It also should be noted that each of these ratios can have one or the other of the pair of terms as its major term, the one that dominates the other. In this sense, there are potentially not ten ratios but 20. So, scene-act could be Scene-act or Act-scene (Burke 1954, 15 *passim*).

On October 23, 1983 a suicide bomber blew up the American Marine compound in Beirut, Lebanon, and more than 200 Marines were killed. Several hours later American forces invaded and quickly captured the Caribbean island of Grenada, according to government sources, to protect it from a Cuban takeover. In his speech to the nation four days later, President Reagan argued that "The events in Lebanon and Grenada, though oceans apart, are closely related."

David S. Birdsell (1987) points out that Reagan accomplished this unification by identifying a scene-agent ratio at the heart of the speech. All of his language identifies the Beirut bombing as a scene. His treatment, Bird-sell notes, is "both spatial and chronological":

> "Our marines are assigned to the south of the city of Beirut near the only airport operating in Lebanon. Just a mile or so to the north is the Italian contingent and not so far from them, the French and a company of British soldiers. This past Sunday, at twenty two minutes after six Beirut time. . . ." Much of the description centers on things: the troop encamp-ment, the trucks on the highway, and the road itself. The driver of the truck bomb is the only agent who enters the scene, and even his actions are distanced from the realm of the humanly explicable because it is "sui-cidal" or "insane." "Marine defenders" are portrayed as incapable of deal-ing with the scene, or even recognizing its dangers (268).

This use of scene to describe the events in Beirut is in sharp contrast with Grenada:

> The importance of the island arises not from its substance, but from its associations. The Cuban presence, invited by "Maurice Bishop, a protege of Fidel Castro," provides the challenge to the United States. The differ-ences between the malign agent of Grenada and the malign scene of Leba-non are apparent before any discussion of U.S. involvement in either situ-ation. In Lebanon, the principal feature of the situation is random danger and unreason. In Grenada, the principal feature of the situation is the calculated mischief of the communists.
>
> The importance of having the two evaluated in tandem cannot be over-stated. Troop deployment, a questionable policy on the evidence of Beirut, must be shown effective under at least some circumstances. The success in Grenada supports administration policy in the Middle East, just as the dangers of Lebanon justify American action in the Caribbean. In other words, the experience in Grenada rehabilitates the agent made suspect in Lebanon; the scene is proven malleable by proxy (270–271).

This use of ratios is not the only way to look at the story Reagan is telling, but it does provide a way by which the critic may interpret Reagan's point of view. It is not necessary (or even proper in this kind of criticism) to wonder what the president really intended, or whether his explanation was accurate or persuasive. The identification of the ratios re-vealed by the language provides a way to develop a rich understanding of how those seemingly ambiguous events of the tragic bombing and the invasion could be brought together in a unified theme.

The pentad and the ratios which grow from it serve as a means to pinpoint the overall meaning of a story. But they do not work alone. They utilize each of the six traditional methods, where appropriate, to tell them what elements of the pentad are emphasized. Solomon looks particularly at themes and style to define the language that is at the center of the scientific purpose. Birdsell uses those two and the narrative voice of Ronald Reagan to unite the two disparate events in the crucial ratio he developed. Indeed, all of the six traditional characteristics (theme, structure, characters, *peripeteia*, narrative voice, and style) are influential in both of these pentadic analyses.

PROBLEMS WITH NARRATIVE ANALYSIS

Let us return to the problems cited for semiotic criticism to see how they develop for narrative analysis. Looking for the culture revealed in stories provides a basis for interpreting a text but not for judging it. Even though categories of analysis in a narrative approach come from formal criticism, it does not use them as standards, only as tools in interpretation. When judgment is made in narrative analysis, other standards have to be applied. Here, then, at least, narrative analysis is less complete than ideological or common sense criticism.

Like ideological criticism, narrative analysis uses sufficient detail to avoid useless generalization. But the reverse is a possible problem for narrative analysis. Stories have to be converted to something else in order to say anything succinct. The ideologies or value systems in the narrative provide a much more manageable basis for describing a culture than does the narrative itself. A story will serve as evidence but it will not very well serve as a claim. Thus, in the story of Little Red Riding Hood the powerful characters (the wolf and the hunter) are male and the dependent figures (Little Red and grandmother) are female. Little Red Riding Hood is a story, yes, but it is better judged by seeing the story through value concepts, themes (the victory of innocence over evil), or the ideology of sexism.

Problems also are created for narrative analysis because some writers do not take a clearly deconstructive approach to criticism. The question that Bruce Gronbeck said haunted dramaturgy in 1980 applies as well to all narrative approaches: "Are we treating an analogy or a 'real' state of affairs?" (328). For instance, although Ernest Bormann's fantasy theme analysis is included with the deconstruction orientation of narrative analysis, and at times this seems to be his position, his statements about the process frequently portray it as a reflection of the natural condition. As such, it takes on the character of common sense criticism. Says Bormann (1985): "*Fantasy* is a technical term in the symbolic convergence theory and does not mean what it often does in ordinary usage, that is, something imaginary, not grounded in *reality*. The technical meaning for fantasy is the creative and imaginative interpretation of events that fulfills a psychological or rhetorical need" (5). With this statement a critic could use fantasy theme analysis for either common sense or deconstructive analysis. "Grounded in reality" can be taken to mean grounded in the world as it actually is. It could also be taken deconstructively as grounded in the experience of the participants "psychological or rhetorical needs."

Many critics have taken Bormann to claim that he has found the way things really happen (see Mohrmann 1982a, 1982b; Lucas 1986, 202). Yet at times Bormann (1983) clearly takes a deconstructive approach: "I define *communication* as referring to the human social processes by which people create, raise, and sustain group consciousness" (100).

As we have seen, narrative is an important function in common sense criticism. However, if critics wish to understand narrative within the scope of assumptions of deconstruction, they must be clear, at least in their own minds, that stories are particular means by which individuals and groups make sense of their experience. The result of such study will not tell people what *really* happens. But, says the exponent of narrative analysis, no one can know what really happens. The best we can know is how humans make sense of their experience through stories.

Narrative analysis has its proponents and detractors and considerable internal argument, as well, over what it is and should be. But no approach to criticism is as hotly debated as the two that follow. Psychoanalytic criticism and ideological criticism push hardest against the assumptions of both general and academic culture.

CHAPTER NINE

Psychoanalytic Criticism
The Interaction of the Conscious and the
Unconscious

Watching his grandson playing in his pram one day, Sigmund Freud observed the child throwing a toy out of the pram and exclaiming *fort!* (gone
away), then hauling it in again on a string to the cry of *da!* (here). This,
the famous *fort-da* game, Freud interpreted in *Beyond the Pleasure Principle*
(1920) as the infant's symbolic mastery of its mother's absence; but, it can
also be read as the first glimmerings of narrative. *Fort-da* is perhaps the
shortest story we can imagine: an object is lost, and then recovered. . . .
From this viewpoint, narrative is a source of consolation: lost objects are
a cause of anxiety to us, symbolizing certain deeper unconscious losses
(of birth, the feces, the mother), and it is always pleasurable to find them
put securely back in place (Eagleton 1983, 185).

Psychoanalysis is the viewpoint at the root of this interpretation. Since
its principles were introduced to the world by Freud at the turn of this
century, it has had a powerful influence on literary and film criticism.

In the example above, note also that psychoanalysis is closely linked
to narrative, the subject of the previous chapter. Stories are interpreted,
but from a special perspective. For many critics, psychoanalysis also provides a transition from story analysis to ideological criticism by recognizing
that a child learns to identify itself as an individual through a language-
learning process. The only language the child can learn is the language of
the culture and so the child is initiated through language into the ideology
of a particular culture (Flitterman-Lewis 1987, 177–178). For our purposes
here, however, the important thing to remember is that psychoanalytic
criticism is a special variety of narrative analysis that interprets the individual, the text, and the culture in stories to assess the state of the human
psyche.

THE ASSUMPTIONS OF PSYCHOANALYTIC CRITICISM

Psychoanalytic criticism developed from Freud's published works and
lectures during the early years of the twentieth century. His original con-

cerns, of course, were with the nature of mental illness and its treatment, which psychoanalysis revolutionized. Soon thereafter, the psychoanalytic method was adapted by a variety of critics to understand literature and film. Psychoanalytic criticism has also seen many adaptations of Freud's theories, principally in the work of Carl Jung, Alfred Adler, and Jacques Lacan. However, after a flourish of popularity as a critical approach in the 1920s and 1930s, Freudianism lost much of its influence and only today is undergoing a revival in an altered form.

Human Thought and Behavior Are Products of the Interaction of the Conscious and Unconscious

Human beings frequently do seemingly unexplainable things. Richard Nixon, who spent a lifetime in American politics as a cold war warrior attacking communism as a menace to this nation, became the president who normalized relations with China. Ronald Reagan, who referred to the Soviet Union as an "Evil Empire," signed a comprehensive disarmament accord with its leader, Mikhail Gorbachev. Television programs with totally improbable plots such as *Three's Company* and *Love Boat* maintained their popularity for years. Each of us, on more occasions than we like to recall, has been embarrassed by saying something in conversation we never intended to say.

These all have a rational explanation. Nixon recognized China as a potential counterbalance to the Soviet Union; Russia changed under Gorbachev so that for Reagan it was no longer an evil empire; or, Nixon and Reagan were naive and wished a secure place in history. There are reasons why they did these otherwise unexplainable things. People use television for frivolous and meaningless release from their everyday careers; *Three's Company* and *Love Boat* provide a romanticized version of human interpersonal relations which makes routine life more interesting. And, the time you said to an acquaintance of the opposite sex, "I'd like to spank you for the coffee," you were tired or rushed and "spank" and "thank" are close together linguistically.

These examples and explanations begin with the common sense notion that humans are rational and their behavior, even if bizarre, has a reasonable explanation. The most extreme unsocial acts like a mass murder can be explained by common sense reasons. Even the explanation that the mass murderer, Theodore Bundy, for instance, was "crazy" is a rational explanation. But Sigmund Freud, the father and primary theorist of psychoanalysis, offered explanations of a different sort. For Freud, humans have a rational conscious and seemingly irrational unconscious, and their interaction explains human behavior, thought, and language.

Freud's argument is built around four spheres of human existence: the id, the libido, the ego, and the superego. The id is an unconscious and substantially unexplainable repository of human needs and desires whose only function is to seek gratification. The libido is the desire for such gratification. If left alone without control, id and libido would savage the human being. The person would commit such antisocial acts as to destroy him or herself or society would intervene. Here, then, in very general terms is an explanation for mass murder. It is the act of a personality whose psyche is dominated by the unconscious forces of id and libido.

To counterbalance, Freud posits two controlling forces: the ego and the superego. The ego is that part of the conscious mind that reasons. Therefore, it understands that the extremes of behavior urged by the libido need to be restricted. The superego, a subconscious storehouse of the teachings, admonitions, and social values the person has learned, aids the ego here. Although the superego (or conscience) is a storehouse difficult to explain in rational terms (it is subconscious), we do recognize that indeed "something tells us an act is wrong." Thus, by reinforcing the ego, the superego aids in restraining the libido.

Through the interaction of the unconscious (the id and the superego) and the conscious mind (the ego), our behavior, thought, and language are defined. The so-called "Freudian slip" of saying "spank" for "thank" is a slip exactly because the ego let down its guard and permitted the libido to use a word that revealed or implied an unconscious, antisocial, and probably sexual desire. The *Love Boat* puts people's sexual desires into a romanticized and, therefore, acceptably veiled form. People "fall in love," "have an affair," "go to bed together," "make love," and so on. These are to varying degrees socially acceptable ways of using language (and actions) to reflect release of primitive sexual desires. The ego finds such phrases (and actions) acceptable but the ego and the superego of most prime-time viewers would not find the equivalent Anglo-Saxon words or explicit actions acceptable.

The unconscious libido continually probes for expression. The ego, reinforced by the superego, tries to control and adapt such drives to socially acceptable behavior. A caricature of this point of view is presented in a children's cartoon when a person trying to decide what to do has two figures —one of the devil (libido) and the other of an angel (ego)—giving alternate and antagonistic advice. In Freud's (1961) terms, this interaction is the struggle between the "pleasure principle" and the "reality principle" (312).

The Conscious and the Unconscious Are the Products of Childhood

What is the source of this interaction between the conscious and unconscious? It is a product of childhood. At birth the child is oriented to a pure pleasure principle, to the selfish fulfillment of desires for food, warmth, and comfort. The child develops beyond this by way of the Oedipus complex, named after Oedipus, a tragic hero in ancient Greek drama who fell in love with his mother. The child begins to associate its pleasure with the mother who holds, feeds, and comforts it. Associating its pleasure further with the mother, thus coming to love her, the child experiences three stages that constitute bases for explaining largely unconscious behavior. In the words of Sandy Flitterman-Lewis (1987):

> As the child grows, there is a gradual organization of the libidinal drives that, while still centered on the child's own body, channels sexuality toward various objects and aims. The first phase of sexual life is associated with the drive to incorporate objects (the oral stage); in the second, the anus becomes the erotogenic zone (the anal stage); and in the third, the child's libido is focused on the genitals (the phallic stage). What is important here is that the child, not yet having a centered self (an ego, an identity) nor being able to distinguish between itself and the outer world, is like a field across which the libidinal energy of the drives plays (174).

This close, loving relationship is disturbed later when the child finds that there is a rival, the father. The child then fears castration by the powerful father and so learns to repress the love of the mother. In fact, it is the father's authority that is the basis for the formation of the superego. The child learns in time what kind of behavior is acceptable, moral, and legal.

Humans have many complexes in their lives related to the struggle between the pleasure principle and the reality principle, between the unconscious and the conscious. However, the Oedipus complex is not just another complex. It is central to Freud's theory. According to Eagleton (1983),

> It is the structure of relations by which we come to be the men and women that we are. It is the point at which we are produced and constituted as subjects; and one problem for us is that it is always in some sense a partial, defective mechanism. It signals the transition from the pleasure principle to the reality principle; from the enclosure of the family to society at large, since we turn from incest to extra-familial relations; and from Nature to Culture, since we can see the infant's relation to the mother as somewhat "natural," and the post-Oedipal child as one who is in the process of assuming a position within the culture as a whole (156).

You may have noticed that much of this analysis is oriented toward males. Obviously, a female can have no fear of castration, so how could she develop repressions? Freud was probably responding to the male-dominated society of his day and, therefore, developed a theory which did not account as well for women. Feminist writers like Betty Friedan (1963) have pointed out this problem. She and others reject Freud because his theories, they say, reinforce society's subjugation of women. At the same time, there are advocates of feminist psychoanalytic criticism inspired by French psychoanalyst Jacques Lacan's interpretation of Freud.

Lacan (1982) rejects the physiological explanation of human maturation typical of American psychoanalysts. In his interpretation of Freud, such sexist concepts as "castration complex," "phallic stage," and "penis envy" are converted to quite different concepts. For Lacan, the contradictions in the human psyche are developed as a child learns about language. Language permits the child to express his or her desires as demands. But the child does not have the language to express the unconscious aspects of desire. So, language is the site of continual contradictions between the conscious and the unconscious. As Catherine Belsey (1980) explains it, "Entry into the symbolic order liberates the child in the possibility of social relationship; it also reduces its helplessness to the extent that it is now able to articulate its needs in the form of demands. But at the same time a division within the self is constructed" (65).

So, as Juliet Mitchell (1982) interprets Lacan, the unconscious or sexuality are not pregiven facts—they are constructions with histories (4). Some psychoanalysts see masculinity and femininity as natural biological facts given at birth, and, therefore, judge the principle of heterosexual attraction as natural. For the psychoanalytic feminist, however, humans are born without a sense of sexual identity. It is the ideology of the society that imposes sexual identity by way of what it (the society) considers natural concepts. A human, says Mitchell, is a "fragmented subject of shifting and uncertain sexual identity."

> To be human is to be subjected to a law which decentres and divides: sexuality is created in a division, the subject is split; but an ideological world conceals this from the conscious subject who is supposed to feel whole and certain of a sexual identity. Psychoanalysis should aim at a destruction of this concealment and at a reconstruction of the subject's construction in all its splits. This may be an accurate theory, it is certainly a precarious project. It is to this theory and project—the history of the fractured sexual subject—that Lacan dedicates himself (26).

As a result, argues Jacqueline Rose (1982), there is no feminine outside language. "First," according to Freud, "there is nothing in the unconscious which accords with the body" and secondly, "because the 'feminine' is constituted as a division in language, a division which produces the feminine as its negative term. If woman is defined as other it is because the definition produces her as other, and not because she has another essence" (55–56). In such a system of thought, "castration complex" and "penis envy" become not "natural realities" but concepts that have been forced on women as has the "natural" heterosexual relation between the sexes.

Taken from Lacan, the feminist explanation clearly provides the basis for an ideological psychoanalysis. As important, however, is the deconstructive criticism it implies. Psychoanalysis is not some complex common sense approach to the human psyche but one that deconstructs the symbol system of our culture as it is developed from childhood.

There Is a Central Force Behind the Unconscious

Freud believed that libidinous drives were sexual; indeed, the term *Freudian* is often popularly used to mean *sexual*. So, it is said, the central force behind the unconscious is sexual. Particularly in the United States, too many people took this to mean that any sexual practice was good because it released a person's repressions. Such lax reading of Freud opened the door to his being regarded as the "intellectual dirty old man."

Such a view has been countered by some of those who are most knowledgeable about Freud's writings. Bruno Bettelheim (1982) has argued, for instance, that English translations leave out Freud's desire to make us more human by "no longer being enslaved without knowing it to the dark forces that reside in us" (52). Freud's emphasis was on *eros* from the story of Eros and Psyche—a story of love and devotion. In order for sexual love to be an experience of true erotic pleasure, it must have beauty (Eros) and soul (Psyche) (54). Such a view does not remove or mask, in Bettelheim's words, "the dark forces that reside in us," but it does make the sexual force and its mediation with the social world something more than a powerful antisocial biological urge.

Nonetheless, in the prevailing interpretation of Freud, sex is the central force motivating human desire. Other psychoanalytic writers have attempted to redefine this centrality. For Carl Jung, it is a life force that is somewhat broader in its makeup than merely sexual, the sum total of all the urges (Horton and Edwards 1974, 357). For Alfred Adler (1956), the central force is an individual's "striving toward power, toward dominance, toward being above" (65). The id, and the libidinous drives originating in the id, seek power over others. Sex here is not the central force but, in its most uncontrolled state, an unconscious instrument of power. Thus, there exists the argument that rape is not a crime of sex but a crime of power. Rape is a means whereby one person demonstrates control over another.

Nonetheless, within the interaction of the conscious and unconscious, there is another alternative central force: the self. For Lacan, the infant self is an unconscious set of desires. At one stage the infant perceives itself as other and so recognizes a split between the "*I* which is perceived and the *I* which does the perceiving" (Belsey 1980, 64). The conscious ego defines the self through language ("I am a lawyer," "I am physically attractive," "I recycled more aluminum cans than anyone else in Kansas," "I am going to be famous"). Its relation to the unconscious self is one of tension.

However you interpret the psychoanalytic approach, there is a central force that dominates the unconscious and sets up a tension with the conscious, producing behavior that has both personal and social implications.

Human Behavior Is Both Personal and Social

From the discussion thus far, it is clear that psychoanalytic criticism applies to individuals and their understanding about self. Traditionally, much of the criticism of this approach, specifically its focus on the conscious-unconscious interaction, was of a source-message or message-source approach. Fawn Brodie (1974) examines Thomas Jefferson's writings for his unconscious "preoccupation" with, and confirmation of, his alleged long-standing relationship with Sally Hemmings, a slave. Her evidence is drawn from the text of his writings (message) and from it she draws conclusions about Jefferson's mental state (source).

Although a relatively new addition to the historians' critical approaches, psychoanalysis has been a popular approach for literary critics since the time Freud expressed his ideas in America with his 1909 lecture series at Clark University. By this formulation all art is neurotic, and one looks at *Hamlet*, or *Star Wars*, or the speeches of Jesse Jackson to discover the author's psychological makeup. During the 1988 presidential primary campaign, the media focused on the question "What does Jesse want?" Ironically enough, that question was more psychoanalytically rich than the questioners' thought.

Similarly, psychoanalytic criticism can be applied to characters in a text. Stanley Kowalski, in Tennessee Williams's (1947) *A Streetcar Named Desire*, can serve the critic as a dramatic representation of the libido; his only interest is the immediate gratification of his biological desires. As Blanche DuBois, his antagonist in the play, says,

> He's common . . . he acts like an animal, he has an animal's habits! Eats like one, moves like one, talks like one! There's even something subhuman—something not quite to the stage of humanity yet! Yes, something—ape-like about him. . . . Thousands and thousands of years have passed him right by and there he is—Stanley Kowalski—survivor of the stone age. Bearing the raw meat home from the kill in the jungle (80).

Such personal criticism of author or character has been the main thrust of the psychoanalytic approach. Terry Eagleton (1983), however, has found these approaches to source and content "the most limited and problematical." "Psychoanalyzing the author," he says, "is a speculative business, and runs into the same kinds of problems [as examining] the relevance of authorial 'intention'." Eagleton continues, "The psychoanalysis of 'content'—commenting on the unconscious motivations of characters, or on the psychoanalytic significance of objects or events in the text—has a limited value, but, in the manner of the notorious hunt for the phallic symbol, is too often reductive" (179). Most contemporary critics find such traditional analysis uninteresting. It is now a rather unimportant part of critical studies compared to interpretations that draw on the language and ideological explanation that comes from followers of Jacques Lacan.

The resurgence of interest in psychoanalytic criticism in recent years has come from critics who see it as a means to better understand the message as social. The interaction between the conscious and the unconscious is, after all, a social matter. The ego takes the desires of the id and attempts to adapt them to the outside world—the "reality principle." The superego is a repository of social knowledge. Therefore, psychoanalytic criticism may be applied to understanding the culture in which a message is received. Receivers—listeners, readers, and viewers—are part of the culture, and therefore find their own anxieties in the text (Eagleton 1983, 182).

Such culture-defining activities are further reinforced by the psychoanalytic theory of Carl Jung, who extended the idea that the superego was socially constructed—a repository of social laws and customs—to his idea of the "collective unconscious." To Jung, the unconscious is not just individual; it is a storehouse of the culture "which generated mythic heroes for the primitive and still generates similar individual fantasies for the civilized man, and which finds its chief expression in a relatively familiar and timeless symbolism endlessly recurring" (Hyman 1955, 133). The existence of this collective unconscious establishes certain "archetypes." Maud Bodkin (1963), the most important early literary critic to follow this lead, explained archetypes this way:

> The special emotional significance possessed by certain poems—a significance going beyond any definite meaning conveyed—he [Jung] attributes to the stirring in the reader's mind, within or beneath his conscious response, of unconscious forces which he terms "primordial images" or archetypes. These archetypes he describes as "psychic residua of numberless experiences of the same type," experiences which have happened not to the individual but to his ancestors, and of which the results are inherited in the structure of the brain, *a priori* determinants of individual experience (1).

Jung's original theory was questioned because it made archetypes biological ("in the structure of the brain"). Whether the wisdom of a culture is passed on from person to person or becomes embedded in the brain in some mystical biological way is not very important to the critic. Most, if not all, prefer to think of an archetype as Northrop Frye (1966) does: as a "symbol . . . a typical or recurring image which connects one [message] with another and thereby helps to unify and integrate our literary experience" (99). Individuals believe that they have found something for the first time only to discover that same idea and form in Aesop's fables, Shakespeare, Norse myths, or the Bible.

Literary theorists Murray M. Schwartz and David Willbern (1982) put the *"Fort-da"* game with which this chapter was introduced into the social matrix of criticism. "This behavior is not simply a symptomatic act of sublimated substitution [of the toy for the mother]. It is an adaptive and synthetic achievement that indicates the tractable exigencies of [the child's] environment" (210).

Thus, there are two thrusts to psychoanalytic criticism. One is personal, focusing on the psychological relation between source and message or between characters in a text (as source) and message. The second, and most popular orientation of late, is concerned about the relation of message to environment or, more narrowly, to reader, viewer, or listener.

Drawing extensively on the insights of Jacques Lacan, this second view includes those psychoanalytic feminists who see the earlier masculine-dominated physiological interpretation of Freud as an ideology used to maintain women as subjects of masculine power. But it is not limited to that approach. This deconstructive social orientation of psychoanalysis also can be applied by critics not particularly oriented to feminism. By understanding receivers of messages, a critic using psychoanalytic principles can better understand the culture that is formed, not only by conscious design, but by unconscious desires.

The Centrality of the Dream Metaphor

Because the psychoanalytic approach assumes an unconscious that influences meanings, the critic must be able to understand the unconscious. To have an unconscious constituting at least half of the communication process would seem to make psychoanalytic criticism impossible. How, then, does the critic applying the psychoanalytic approach understand the unconscious? Terry Eagleton (1983) answers this question:

> The "royal road" to the unconscious is dreams. Dreams allow us one of our few privileged glimpses of it at work. Dreams for Freud are essentially symbolic fulfillments of unconscious wishes; and they are cast in symbolic form because if this material were expressed directly then it might be shocking and disturbing enough to wake us up. In order that we should get some sleep, the unconscious charitably conceals, softens and distorts its meanings, so that our dreams become symbolic texts which need to be deciphered. The watchful ego is still at work even within our dreaming, censoring an image here or scrambling a message there; and the unconscious itself adds to this obscurity by its peculiar modes of functioning (157).

The phrase "dream metaphor" is used quite deliberately because there are waking phenomena which function in the same way as dreams even though the participant is physically awake. These are "what Freud called

'parapraxes,' unaccountable slips of the tongue, failures of memory, bun-
glings, misreadings, . . . mislayings [and jokes] which can be traced to
unconscious wishes and intentions" (Eagleton 1983, 158). The critic centers
attention on those points in the message where the symbolic representation reveals unconscious urges. However, moving from dreams and events
such as these to analytic judgments about an individual or the culture is a
very difficult process.

For contemporary psychoanalytic critical theorists, the dream is central. Schwartz and Willbern (1982) note that a dream is "a kind of poem—
a reciprocal analogy to Freud's notion of poetry as a kind of dreaming"
(208). This link of poetry with the dream can be extended to any message
and its receivers. However, poetry is particularly apropos. Poetry is the
most imaginative of the literary art forms, calling on the reader to interpret
meanings quite different from surface meanings. Poetic language is highly
symbolic.

Similar connections, although usually not so intensely symbolic, can
be made between the dream and the novel or the play. Newspaper reporting with its strong orientation to accuracy and observable fact is not as
likely to alert the critic to the imaginative component, and neither are messages of traditional persuasive intent such as speeches, editorials, or advertisements. But they too may be interpreted as a kind of dream. From a
psychoanalytic perspective, *objectivity* and *persuasion* are products of the
interaction of the conscious and unconscious just as much as are figures
of speech.

This assumption causes some crusaders for traditional public morality
to claim that the ice cubes in the highball glass of a whiskey advertisement
subliminally spell out "sex"; that rock music played backwards presents
arguments for satanic cults; and that pictures of a squeeze bottle of liquid
detergent in a feminine hand has deliberate phallic implications.

For the psychoanalytic critic, the dream metaphor can be seen to encompass all communication. Freud's (1961) explanation of the dream illustrates the metaphor's diversity of application:

> There are dreams as clear as [waking] experience, so clear that quite a time
> after waking we do not realize that they were dreams; and there are others
> which are indescribably dim, shadowy and blurred. Indeed in one and
> the same dream excessively definite portions may alternate with others of
> scarcely discernible vagueness. Dreams may be entirely sensible or at least
> coherent, witty even, or fantastically beautiful; others again are confused,
> feeble minded as it were, absurd, often positively crazy. There are dreams
> that leave us quite cold and others in which affects of all kinds are mani-
> fest—pain to the point of tears, anxiety to the point of waking us up,
> astonishment, delight, and so on. . . . In short, this fragment of mental
> activity during the night has an immense repertory at its disposal: it is
> capable, in fact, of all that the mind creates in daytime—yet it is never
> the same thing (91).

Thus, dreams reflect all kinds of human experience and come in all forms, from the most rationalistic argument to the most elaborate fantasy. And, the theory has it, the creative process by which language and visual symbols reveal ideas is like a dream—a merger of the human conscious and unconscious. Perhaps more important, the receiver of the message understands it in a similar way. The application of common sense standards for evaluating accuracy, formal worth, or persuasiveness can be interpreted as reflections of the interaction of id, ego, and superego.

Christian Metz (1976), who has explored the relationship between film and dream, argues this point. When we say a film is "dull," "boring," or "ordinary," we find the needs of the id "insufficiently nourished," and when we find films to be "in bad taste: (taste then becomes an excellent alibi), or extremist, or childish, or sentimental, or sado-pornographic . . . the satisfaction of the id has become too lively" (81).

Peter H. Wood (1982) has drawn a strong link between television viewing and dreams. He argues that there are six similarities between them:

1. Both TV and dreams have a highly visual quality.
2. Both TV and dreams are highly symbolic.
3. Both TV and dreams involve a high degree of wish fulfillment.
4. Both TV and dreams appear to contain much that is disjointed and trivial.
5. Both TV and dreams have an enormous and powerful content, most of which is readily and thoroughly forgotten.
6. Finally, both TV and dreams make consistent use—overt and disguised—of materials drawn from recent experience (514–516).

These similarities can be extended from television to all communication. As the earlier quotation from Freud indicated, some dreams are more visual, symbolic, disjointed, or disguised than others. So, communication messages differ in the extent to which the unconscious is active or the conscious disguises real intent, but all messages are made up of language and other symbol systems for which a meaning is ascribed by the individual and society and so is part of the psychoanalytic dream metaphor.

SCOPE OF PSYCHOANALYTIC CRITICISM

Earlier, we observed that psychoanalytic criticism can be both personal and social: used to understand the psyche of the author or of a character in a story; and used to understand the social system in a particular message and in those readers, viewers, or listeners who use it. Furthermore, the assumptions that apply to the source, message, and environment must also apply to the critic. The critic must participate in the interaction of the conscious and unconscious just as the source, message, and environment do.

Stanley Edgar Hyman (1955) notes that psychoanalytic critic Maud Bodkin,

> unlike the professional psychoanalysts, who rely as much as possible on case histories and clinical records, . . . relies chiefly on introspection, analyzing and reporting to the best of her ability her own psychological reaction. "'Our analysis is of the experience communicated to ourselves,'" she writes. She describes the sensations of her own mind on reading poetry, what images she becomes aware of, what significance or tension she feels, what associations are evoked, what reactions of empathy or projection arise, what transitions are made, even what dreams she dreams (140).

More recent literary critics such as Norman Holland, Harold Bloom, and Cary Nelson also acknowledge the critic's involvement. Holland (1975) says, "My interpretations must necessarily express my own identity theme," and Bloom acknowledges that his own theory is presented "in the context of his own anxieties" (Nelson 1978, 50). Nelson quotes Kenneth Burke as saying, "I worked out a way of getting along by dodges, the main one being a concern with tricks whereby I could translate my self-involvements into speculations about 'people' in general" (47).

Like all criticism, however, psychoanalytic criticism must be grounded in text and context while still openly acknowledging, even at times highlighting, the critic's subjective reactions to text and context. Thus, the psychoanalytic approach is potentially the richest of all the approaches because no limit is placed on what may be examined, what observations are possible, and what sources of observations are permitted.

In addition, the psychoanalytic approach permits a diversity of interpretations. As a matter of fact, because of the acceptance of the unconscious as a vital function of the human psyche, all interpretations are considered problematic and so lead to several interpretations of a communicated message. Tennessee Williams's classic play and movie *A Streetcar Named Desire* can illustrate this principle.

Blanche DuBois arrives in New Orleans to visit her sister, Stella, and comes into conflict with Stanley Kowalski, Stella's husband. We have already seen one interpretation of this story: Stanley is the representation of the id. He is an animal whose only concern is gratification. Stella acts as the agent for regulating Stanley's relation to the outside world (the ego), but while Stella is in the hospital having their baby, Stanley rapes Blanche, and she becomes insane and is taken to an asylum. Stella takes the baby and leaves Stanley.

Blanche is a study in and of herself. Although she plays the coquette fond of stories of southern gentility, she is haunted by the memory of a beau to whom she was married (or was she?) and who committed suicide (because of her?) (Was he homosexual?). It is not clear that there ever was such a beau except in her imagination. Stanley has information from a friend that indicates that Blanche has been a prostitute. Blanche, in this interpretation, becomes the center of the play, symbolizing the human psyche in which the pleasure and reality principles struggle.

Did Stanley actually rape her or is it, like so many other things, a part of Blanche's dream world as she moves through fantasy after fantasy toward insanity? And what of Stella, who balances her rationality with a need for Stanley? And what of Stanley, who seems moralistic about Blanche's past? In short, a number of interpretations are possible, all of them quite acceptable and informative. Stanley may be the personification of the id or he may be that only in Blanche's dream. There are conflicting elements about his personality that can lead to either or both interpretations.

Some critics would go beyond the characters in the play to Williams himself. They would see Williams's characters as extensions of his mind, struggling to reveal the interaction of the conscious and unconscious within him. Or are the events in his play a reflection of society, and not the author's internal state? The possibilities for psychoanalytic interpretation are virtually limitless.

One way to deal with this diversity is to see it as a primary strength, says Catherine Belsey (1980): "The object of the critic, then, is to seek not the unity of the work, but the multiplicity and diversity of its possible meanings, its incompleteness, the omissions which it displays but cannot describe, and above all its contradictions" (109). Thus, arguments critics make for others to accept or reject may be more diverse in psychoanalytic criticism than in other approaches.

THE TOOLS OF PSYCHOANALYTIC CRITICISM

Although unique in terms of possible depth and scope, psychoanalytic criticism starts with the examination of the same features of a text that formal criticism and narrative analysis do: principally theme, structure, character, and style. However, the interpretative tools used will be adapted to psychoanalytic assumptions, including: pleasure versus reality, coding mechanisms, identity themes, Oedipus complex, Eros and Thanatos, and symbolism.

Pleasure Versus Reality

The conflict of the conscious and unconscious is reflected in the pleasure-reality conflict of the gratification-seeking id and the rational ego. This struggle is frequently depicted as the juxtaposition of the primitive and the cultured, as in one interpretation of Stanley Kowalski and Blanche DuBois.

That is what Ronald Reagan stated quite openly when he portrayed the Soviet Union as an "evil empire."

Sometimes the conflict is portrayed in a single person who may be unaware of the contradiction. Catherine Belsey (1980) observes this in Shakespeare's *Julius Caesar* when Brutus, having led in the assassination of Caesar, "calls on the conspirators to present at once an image of violence and a cry for peace":

> Stoop, Romans, stoop,
> And let us bathe our hands in Caesar's blood
> Up to the elbows, and besmear our swords.
> Then walk we forth, even to the market-place,
> And waving our red weapons o'er our heads,
> Let's all cry "Peace, freedom and liberty!" (96).

The contradiction of violence and peace, primitive and cultured, pleasure and reality, passion and temperance, and a host of others may be found in a text. The conflict may be as obvious as in Brutus's speech or it may be hidden; a message may say one thing but with a second less obvious meaning, there to be found and deciphered. Finding these hidden meanings requires careful attention to the coded messages.

Coding Mechanisms

Freud identified four means by which "dream work" takes place. The "latent dream" is transformed into the "manifest dream" through coding mechanisms: condensation, displacement, inversion, and dramatization. The "work of interpretation" says Freud (1961), "aims at demolishing the dream work." So, the critic takes the manifest text and works backwards, looking for a latent message from which the manifest message was created. Peter H. Wood (1982) claims that these four characteristics of dream work "apply with uncanny directness to television" (519). Consider how each might be applied by a critic.

Condensation.   The "process of compressing, combining, fragmenting or omitting elements" from the original unconscious thoughts into the message as produced is called condensation (Wood 1982, 519). The *Cosby Show*, for example, is about an African American family. The father is an obstetrician and the mother, a lawyer. They have five children: four daughters and a son. This popular television situation comedy appeals to a wide spectrum of audiences. Whites frequently find it a show about "typical" family problems and their good-natured resolutions. However, the show is a highly stylized version of African American life. Both parents are highly paid and successful professionals. All the children go to college.

There are few whites in the show. One white boy is used as a source of contrast and humor to the youngest daughter and her African American female friends. The spouse, teenaged, and young adult opposite-sex companions of the children are all African American. Something is obviously omitted from the experience. The darker sides of racism including white fear of sexual inferiority are not present.

The *Cosby Show* is a family show, focusing on the traditional upper-middle-class, loving family relationship so central to our culture's understanding. It differs from *Leave It to Beaver, My Three Sons,* and *Ozzie and Harriett* only in that the characters are African American. Problem and solution are condensed into one half-hour. Dr. Huxtable seems to spend almost no time at his work. His office is conveniently in his home but, all the same, his life is clearly with his children, not miscarriages, people who can't pay for his services, sexual malfunction, or medical malpractice suits. Why is this show so popular? Because it condenses the African American family experience into pure entertainment of the happiest vision of reality imaginable. Ruled out is most of the conflict the pleasure principle enacts in our society.

Displacement.   Transferring the libidinous drive to another more socially acceptable form displaces it from its original meaning. Sometimes this will be called a "defense mechanism," or "transference." Wood (1982) illustrates it by an example from the *Mary Tyler Moore Show.*

> Mary finds herself serving dinner to Lou, her manly but insecure middle-aged "boss." (In condensed TV, as in condensed dream, one often "finds one-self" doing something with limited lead-in or prior explanation.) Much of MTM deals with displaced sexual wishes—the show is introduced by a song about "making it"—though this scene is more apparent than most. Among the things Mary wants to have at this Friday night rendezvous is a bottle of champagne, and the visual imagery and verbal dialogue of the scene, heavy with double meanings, focuses around how to open the bottle satisfactorily. Lou, uncertain but pretending to know how to do it, receives friendly encouragement and guidance from the more experienced and competent Mary. When he finally holds the large bottle erect in front of him and uncorks it, the prized white liquid comes bubbling out, giving Mary pleasure and transforming Lou's anxiety to satisfaction. The entire sequence, lasting only a few seconds, can be interpreted as wish fulfillment for both sexes around the prevalent concern of male impotence, all displaced in an acceptable but unmistakable way to a champagne bottle and the popping of its cork (521).

Inversion.   Sometimes messages are inverted. The meaning found in the common sense interpretation of the text is an inversion of its unconscious meaning. Therefore, the critic must find the unconscious meaning behind the common sense one. Of course, such complexity makes this analysis more difficult than any other. It must be seen repeatedly and in conjunction with other codings or it can appear as foolish. Saying that the text means the opposite of its common sense meaning could lead to a system where even the social meaning of language becomes idiosyncratic, as the critic picks and chooses at random what is and what is not inverted.

Sasha Torres (1989) illustrates this by examining the television show *thirtysomething*. "*Thirtysomething* is certainly engaged with traditional notions of home and family, and insistently puts women at the center of its domestic spaces." Yet "the unanswered and persistent question for the show is masculinity, not femininity." This condition of seeming to be centered on women while, actually, renegotiating the place of males is illustrated with "the final shot of the first season's credit sequence."

> As New Age guitar music twangs gently in the background, we see Hope holding Janey, her daughter, in the nursery. The camera backs out of the baby's room and pans to a view of Michael, looking at Hope and Janey through the banister rails. The camera's movement tells us that the initial view of Hope was from Michael's point of view, but disavows that knowledge by showing us Michael in the same shot, without an intervening cut. And in addition to appropriating Michael's point of view, the camera also contrasts his expression, an unreadable mix of emotions, with the simplicity of Hope's maternal contentment. It is impossible to tell what Michael is thinking or feeling. . . . The end of the credit sequence for the second season has a strikingly similar effect, . . . Both sequences end by asking the same question: in a world dominated by domesticity, where do men belong? (92).

Dramatization.   To say that people make their lives more dramatic than they are is virtually self-explanatory. Each person becomes the center of his or her own dreams—a version of the old adage "every man is the hero of his own stories." Louis Althusser has made the argument that society does not need the individual. The function that an individual performs is important to society but not necessary to society. "However," says Eagleton (1983), "I do not *feel* myself to be a mere function of the social structure which could get along without me . . . but as someone with a significant *relation* to society and the world at large" (172). So, all our messages say, contrary to what the unconscious knows, that we are important. Advertising sells us continually through dramatization of our own importance, as the beer drinker, car driver, toothpaste user are portrayed as dramatized visions of ourselves.

These four coding mechanisms—condensation, displacement, inversion, and dramatization—are ways by which humans convert unconscious desires to more socially acceptable forms. As a result, when viewing such forms, the critic must reverse them and, by using his or her understanding of the four coding mechanisms just discussed, reveal the latent content of what is expressed. Again, because of the complexity of this process, the

critic must carefully ground him or herself in the text and find reinforcement for any conclusion in more than one mechanism. We can now turn
to some more specific points of analysis.

Identity Themes

Each receiver of communication is said to have an "identity theme" by
which a particular message is read, a theme by which the person identifies
him or herself (Holland 1975, 56–64). Identity themes will differ from one
person or one social group to another, and provide a way for people to
say who they believe they are. The formal elements of a message (theme,
structure, character, and style) are interpreted by receivers of messages
according to their identity themes. Thus, when a text is perceived as
"beautiful," "explicit," or "disgusting," it is because the characterization
of the text has been filtered through identity themes developed from the
solutions provided by the ego as it responds to the needs of the id, the
superego, and the outer reality (Holland, 123).

Carol J. Clover (1987) analyzed the audiences and the texts of "the very
bottom, down in the cinematic underbrush [of horror films]. [There] lies—
horror of horrors—the slasher (or spatter or shocker) film: the immensely
generative story of a psycho-killer who slashes to death a string of mostly
female victims, one by one, until he is himself subdued or killed, usually
by the one girl who has survived" (187). These films (e.g., *Texas Chain Saw
Massacre, Psycho, Halloween, Friday the Thirteenth*) have audiences that are
"by all accounts largely young and largely male—most conspicuously
groups of boys who cheer the killer on as he assaults his victims, then
reverse their sympathies to cheer the survivor on as she assaults the killer"
(192).

Clover (1987) finds in these films, and in their young male viewers, an
identity theme of gender confusion. The male killer of the film is a feminine
male. " 'You got your choice, boy,' says the tyrannical father of Leatherface
in *Texas Chain Saw II*, 'sex or the saw; you never know about sex, but the
saw—the saw is the family' " (211). The "final girl" who disposes of the
psychopathic killer is a masculine female who "endures the deepest throes
of 'femininity'." Even during the final struggle, "She is now weak and now
strong, now flees the killer and now charges him, now stabs and is
stabbed, now cries out in fear and now shouts in anger. She is a physical
female and a characterological androgyne: like her name ["Stretch" in
Texas Chain Saw Massacre II], not masculine but either/or, both, ambiguous"
(221).

According to Clover (1987), the identity theme of young men, confused
about sex and gender roles, having grown up in an age of "The woman's
movement, the entry of women into the workplace, the rise of divorce and
woman-headed families," is one of "massive gender confusion" (220).

Oedipus Complex

Earlier we noted that the Oedipus complex is not just a complex; it is the dominant human complex. For psychoanalysis, the most important childhood experience is the early bonding between mother and child. Depending on how a person matures, humans will have various manifestations of the Oedipus complex—continued attachment to the mother. It may be as simple as a Freudian slip in which a man introduces his wife by saying to an acquaintance, "I want you to meet my mother." Or it may be as complex as being unable to form a relationship with someone of the opposite sex because a strong mother image makes every other companion unacceptable.

The psychoanalytic criticism of literature is replete with examples based on the Oedipus complex. The term comes, of course, from ancient Greek Drama, the story of *Oedipus Rex*, who unknowingly (unconsciously) killed his father and married his mother. Freud was the first to see the Oedipus complex at the root of Shakespeare's *Hamlet*. Hamlet returns home to discover that his father has been killed and his uncle has married his mother. In the course of the play, Hamlet talks to his father's ghost (dreams?), resolves to kill his uncle but cannot, and drives his fiancee to insanity and suicide, so a psychoanalytic interpretation has it, all because of his own attraction to his mother. The viewers of the play find satisfaction because they identify with Hamlet's confusion and indecision: Their unconscious has similar struggles.

Clover uses the Brian DePalma film *Body Double* (1984) to illustrate how the Oedipus complex functions on three levels:

> The plot—a man witnesses and after much struggle solves the mysterious murder of a woman with whom he has become voyeuristically involved—concerns us less than the three career levels through which the hero, an actor named Jake, first ascends and then descends. He aspires initially to legitimate roles (Shakespeare), but it becomes clear during the course of a method-acting class that his range of emotional expression is impaired by an unresolved childhood fear. For the moment he has taken a job as vampire in a "low-budget, independent horror film," but even that job is threatened when, during a scene in which he is to be closed in a coffin and buried, he suffers an attack of claustrophobia and must leave the set. A plot twist leads him to the underworld of pornography, where he takes on yet another role, this time in a skin flick. Here, in the realm of the flesh with a queen of porn, the sexual roots of Jake's paralysis—fear of the (female) cavern—are exposed and finally resolved. A new man, he returns to "A Vampire's Kiss" to master the burial scene, and we are to understand that Shakespeare is the next stop (188–189).

Clover also illustrates the Oedipus complex through these thumbnail sketches of three films from different genres.

Beneath the "legitimate" plot of *The Graduate* (in which Ben must give up his relationship with a *friend's* mother in order to marry and take his proper social place) lies the plot of *Psycho* (in which Norman's unnatural attachment to his *own* mother drives him to murder women to whom he is attracted); and beneath *that* plot lies the plot of the porn film *Taboo,* in which the son simply has sex with his mother ("Mom, am I better than Dad?") (189).

Eros and Thanatos

Probably secondary to the Oedipus complex but still quite powerful forces are Eros and Thanatos. In the film, *Shane,* two gunfighters oppose one another, one dressed in white buckskin (Alan Ladd) and the other all in black (Jack Palance). One acts out of love, the other for the pure pleasure of killing. They represent a conflict between life (eros) and death (thanatos). Peace and war, love and violence, health and sickness, and many similar opposing themes represent the continual struggle between life and death.

This struggle reveals ambiguities as well. General Douglas MacArthur (1988), at age 82 delivered his last address "Duty, Honor, Country" to the cadets at West Point. These words, he says, give the cadets "a freshness of the deep springs of life," and "the joy and inspiration of life," but the speech itself glorifies death.

> He gave all that mortality can give
>
> He has written his own history . . . in red on his enemy's breast
>
> He has drained deep the chalice of courage
>
> Driving home to . . . the judgment seat of God
>
> I do not know the dignity of their birth, but I do know the glory of their death (322).

The love/hate relationship between two arch sports rivals is another example. The Washington Redskins and the Dallas Cowboys are seen by football commentators to "hate" one another in a way which strangely bonds them together as a pair. The song "You Always Hurt the One You Love" illustrates another ambiguous situation where the life and death urge combine:

> You always hurt the one you love,
> The one you wouldn't hurt at all.
> You always take the sweetest rose
> And crush it till the petals fall.
>
> You always break the kindest heart,
> With a hasty word you can't recall.

So, if I broke your heart last night,
It's because I love you most of all (Fisher and Roberts 1944).

Symbolism

The tools discussed so far relate most closely to theme, character, and perhaps structure. The closest relation to the formal category of style is in the psychoanalytic examination of symbolism. Of course, language is symbolic and the words used may stand for meanings other than those of common sense. For instance, we noted in the *Love Boat* how people "fell in love," "had an affair," "went to bed together"; these are all symbolic of more physical acts. By now you are probably enough in tune with our language to recognize how the symbolic nature of language lends itself to almost continual psychoanalyzing. We all know how language can "say" one thing and "mean" another.

What has not been so carefully examined is visual symbolism. The comparison of television and dream (Wood), film and dream (Metz), and the traditional search for dream symbolism (a train entering a tunnel as intercourse, for instance) can lead the psychoanalytic critic to look more carefully at visual symbols.

The following excerpt, while actually a spoof on psychoanalysis, illustrates further the psychoanalytic base of visual symbolism. Here, football is portrayed as a religious rite related to the life urge and the Oedipus complex.

> Obviously, football is a syndrome of religious rites symbolizing the struggle to preserve the egg of life through the rigors of impending winter. The rites begin at the autumn equinox and culminate on the first day of the New Year with great festivals identified with bowls of plenty; the festivals are associated with flowers such as roses, fruits such as oranges, farm crops such as cotton, and even sun-worship and appeasement of great reptiles such as alligators.
>
> In these rites the egg of life is symbolized by what is called "the oval," an inflated bladder covered with hog skin. The convention of "the oval" is repeated in the architectural oval-shaped design of the vast outdoor churches in which the services are held every sabbath in every town and city, also every Sunday in the greater centers of population where an advanced priesthood performs. These enormous roofless churches dominate every college campus; no other edifice compares in size with them, and they bear witness to the high spiritual development of the culture that produced them.
>
> Literally millions of worshippers attend the sabbath services in these enormous open-air churches. Subconsciously, these hordes of worshippers are seeking an outlet from sex-frustration in anticipation of violent masochism and sadism about to be enacted by a highly trained priesthood of young men. Football obviously arises out of the Oedipus complex. Love

of mother dominates the entire ritual. The churches, without exception, are dedicated to Alma Mater, Dear Mother (Ferril and Ferril 1962, 1–2).

No examination of the television program *Miami Vice* would be complete without considering the visual and musical manifestations that set the fast pace and emphasize the confusion marking the identity themes of the show.

The program opens with an event identifying the scene and some of the characters, always including the two main characters, Crockett and Tubbs. There is always music and violence or threat of it and women set in a masculine-dominant situation. Then in one minute, 15 scenes are shown of fast-paced action (rushing through water, sailboarding, jai alai, dog races), bikini-clad women, affluence (Rolls Royce cars, speedboats, high-rise condos), and the exotic (palm trees, flamingos, parrots) accompanied by the theme music. These visuals and the music do as much for the psychoanalytic meaning of the show as the themes, characters, and words.

PROBLEMS WITH THE PSYCHOANALYTIC APPROACH

No approach to criticism is more controversial than the psychoanalytic. In fact, such criticism has been called a self-fulfilling prophesy. Such writers as James Joyce, D. H. Lawrence, Thomas Mann, Franz Kafka, Dylan Thomas, and Tennessee Williams clearly have such an orientation. Thomas Mann makes it clear in two essays on Freud that he consciously wrote themes susceptible of psychoanalysis into his novels. Says Stanley Edgar Hyman (1955), "The critic happily dredging up a psychoanalytic insight from [such] a work is somewhat in the position of a man finding buried treasure at Fort Knox" (159). How does a critic find the unconscious in authors who consciously introduce it in their writings?

Greater problems exist, however, when the critic offers psychoanalytic interpretations when they were not intentionally put there by the author. If critics are subject to the same forces as the author and the reader, how can the psychoanalytic critics know that their judgments are grounded on textual and contextual evidence, and not limited to the conflicts in their own minds?

True, all deconstructive criticism accepts the critic as a part of the interpretive process, but the unconscious application of that principle may be carried to the point where text is meaningless by any social standard. In such a case the critic is not interpreting a text but imposing a personal, unconscious interpretation on it.

This process of interpreting the unconscious aspects of a text is further complicated by the fact that unconscious ideas may be implied from specific statements at the same time that lack of specific statements also imply them. For example, there is Fawn Brodie's (1974) psychobiography of Thomas Jefferson. Brodie understands Jefferson's use of "mulatto" in his diaries as evidence of his preoccupation with an alleged affair with his slave, Sally Hemmings. Jefferson's exchange of letters with his daughter Martha, without using "mulatto" or any reference to Sally, is understood as evidence of the "elaborate fiction being maintained between Jefferson and Martha concerning his relationship with Sally Hemmings" (229–330, 295).

Of course, similar double standards or lack of standards for evidence can be laid at the doorstep of other critical systems, particularly those that turn to deconstruction. Whatever critics expect to see (reasons, values, stories, or ideologies), they are more likely to find than are critics using another approach. Critics are more likely to confirm than to deny their own points of view. But the psychoanalytic approach, with its acceptance of a nonrational unconscious, has a much greater problem of evidence than other approaches. Needless to say, all the earlier admonitions about looking for more than isolated evidence hold here.

A host of other problems also exits. First, there is the obvious masculine bias of psychoanalysis. The system based on a crucial fear of castration seems unable to account for women. Freud's argument that women are born castrated and, therefore, suffer from penis envy, a problem which is only satisfied by giving birth, is attacked by feminists (Friedan 1963, 106–107). Today, Freud's argument, as it has been described, is also considered demeaning as an explanation of women's powerful motivations. We try to talk this away by noting that Freud was responding to the social system and thought of his times and that times have changed. However, if we do this, we weaken the power of the approach to explain all human behavior. If the system is just a reflection of the times, it becomes a version of value analysis and not an approach of its own.

Some feminists have taken a psychoanalytic approach, however. They have turned to the language-based interpretation of Jacques Lacan for a critical system that seems to avoid a sexual bias by making it an ideological, not a biological, condition. But this position makes psychoanalysis useful and nonsexist only for those critics who accept a gendered ideology as fundamental to the culture. A critic might use Lacan's emphasis on language as the developmental human force without an ideological orientation. Such a critical application would emphasize the struggle between unconscious and conscious drives and bring one closer to Maud Bodkin's earlier ideas of psychoanalytic criticism.

The role of dreams is also problematic. Do humans really dream to a purpose, as psychoanalytic critics claim? Are dreams the reflection of a sexual or life urge? Does the psychoanalytic theory ignore the physiological causes for dreams (Horton and Edwards 1974, 353)? If dreams are not the "royal road" to the unconscious, then the critic has no way to understand the unconscious or, more powerfully, no way to know that there is an unconscious.

The unconscious is a serious source of problems for the critic. How did humans evolve a system of social living supposedly controlled by reason which must also rule the most fundamental and obscure impulses of human nature (Horton and Edwards 1974, 355–356)? Perhaps the idea that humans control (i.e., repress) the unconscious, as psychoanalysts describe it, is as unreasonable as the unconscious itself. And if there is no unconscious, then there is no psychoanalytic criticism.

These are just some of the problems with the psychoanalytic approach. Many of them go to its assumptions. If you buy these arguments, you reject the approach completely. However, while many critics would argue against terming their work psychoanalytic, they still find aspects of psychoanalysis valuable in their criticism. The idea of an inner conflict between a pleasure principle and a reality principle is, after all, fundamental to many of our stories, even our religious thought. The influence of childhood experiences and the significance of dreams have found niches in our thinking. Despite its problems, the psychoanalytic approach is a part of popular and academic thinking. We will not soon dispose of it completely. And, say its strongest proponents, utilized intelligently, it has considerable power to explain our communication.

CHAPTER TEN

Ideological Criticism
Conflict and Power in Language and Culture

In the preface to his book *Marxism and Literary Criticism,* Thomas Eagleton (1976) expressed concern that "no doubt we shall soon see Marxist criticism comfortably wedged between Freudian and mythological approaches to literature, as yet one more stimulating academic 'approach,' one more well-tilled field of inquiry for students to tramp" (vii). Ironically, that is exactly what we are about to do: position ideological criticism, a broader approach but none the less rooted in Marxist assumptions, "as yet one more approach" to communication criticism.

Ideological criticism is a reasonable consequence of moving from narrative analysis to psychoanalysis (Belsey 1980, 137). Narrative analysis is an approach that dissects the stories people tell; psychoanalysis examines the gaps, the silences, the unconscious elements of those stories; and ideological criticism digs out the politics that are hidden in the stories.

However, for the ideological critic, such politics are not just interesting points that explain the symbolic ways in which humans make sense of their culture. Ideology is the "pattern of ideas, belief systems, or interpretive schemes found in a society or among specific social groups" (Hall 1989, 307). Ideological critics examine the symbol systems of a society for the ideologies and the way ideologies, present or absent, are linked to the material conditions of the society. Just as in value or narrative analysis, ideological critics examine the symbols used by humans to interpret their culture but in a special and significant way. For them, the verbal and visual symbols that reveal the ideology of a culture cannot be divorced from the material conditions of the society. That is why Eagleton objects to considering Marxist ideological criticism as "yet one more stimulating academic 'approach,' " for within ideological criticism all other approaches to criticism can be explained.

Critics who follow this approach differ on several points, most particularly on what constitutes the material condition of society and how that material condition may be interpreted. Currently, the most significant difference lies between Marxist ideological critics and feminist ideological critics, between an economically based and a gender-based ideology. Even so, such critics share a conviction that material conditions interact with and influence the verbal and visual symbols by which groups make sense of their world. The complexity of this interaction is better understood by an examination of the assumptions of ideological criticism.

THE ASSUMPTIONS OF IDEOLOGICAL CRITICISM

Ideological criticism has strong connections to Marxist theory. Initially, this causes problems because for many people Marxism is a code word for world communism, revolution, the overthrow of capitalist society, atheism, dictatorship, the Stalinist purges, and so on. These associations have made many, if not most, contemporary manifestations of Marxism unacceptable to most Americans. Therefore, as you study the assumptions of ideological criticism, you must put aside its obvious Marxist political manifestations and view it as an intellectual system of criticism.

There is an irony in the suggestion that you "put aside its obvious political manifestations," because ideological criticism is the most political of all critical approaches. The fundamental political relationships in the society are what ideological criticism is all about. Yet, it need not be linked to specific past Soviet actions; it is best to begin with as few biases as possible and judge this system by the reasonableness of its assumptions.

There are strong disagreements among those ideological critics who see themselves as Marxists. Lawrence Grossberg (1984) has identified ten "strategies of Marxist Cultural interpretations" that, in terms of this book, are ten subcategories of the ideological approach to criticism. We will be simplifying a variety of technically separate positions in order to identify this ideological turn in criticism.

Material Conditions Determine Power Relationships Among People

Karl Marx developed the dialectic from Georg Hegel. Instead of basing the dialectic in idealist categories as Hegel had done before him, however, Marx rooted it in the material world. Simply put, the Hegelian dialectic posits a reasoning determined by its opposite; for every idea there is an opposing idea, for every thesis there is an antithesis. These two opposites produce a synthesis that serves as a thesis for another dialectic. The process continues until an ultimate form of truth is revealed. The following figures illustrate this process.

DIALECTIC

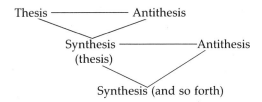

So, a dialectic about government might look something like this:

DIALECTIC OF GOVERNMENT

For Marx, the dialectic is based not on what people think or on their spiritual nature, but in the material conditions of society, conditions that create opposing classes of people. Marx observes that in each age there are fundamental clashes between opposing classes. So, there was a master–slave opposition, then a lord–serf opposition, and, in modern times, a capitalist–worker opposition. Thus, dialectical materialism means that the material economic conditions of the society, the means of production, determine its class structure. For Marx, the dialectical opposition of capitalist versus working class is the final dialectic that revolution will synthesize into a classless society where individuals are equal and exploitation unnecessary.

Equality is a powerful word in our society. Thomas Jefferson wrote it into the Declaration of Independence: "We hold these truths to be self-evident that all men are created equal and endowed by their creator with certain unalienable rights, that among these are life, liberty, and the pursuit of happiness." But the equality Jefferson discussed is not the Marxian equality of a classless society; "to each according to need, from each according to ability." Jefferson said that all citizens would have equal civil rights with which to pursue happiness including property and wealth. Because of Marxist economic interpretation, equality is a mixed value in our society. It is more likely to be negatively viewed than freedom. When equality means equal sharing of material wealth, the means of production, equality suffers as an American value compared to freedom.

For this reason, and because of Cold War antagonisms between the United States and the Soviet Union, Eastern Europe, and China, Marxist thinking has not been popular here. The same holds true for communication critics. For example, the critics of public address have proven almost immune to it (Pryor 1985, 1). In Europe, however, Marxist-based criticism has fared better and is far more popular and developed. Its sophistication is the result of the efforts of such influential groups as the Frankfurt School and the Center for Contemporary Studies in Birmingham, England.

The common American antagonism to Marxist approaches is weakening, however, and while most American critics do not use such approaches, interest is growing. In fact, there is a movement toward a more open interpretation of Marxist thinking.

For Marx, the material base of society was rooted in the organization of production—capitalism. From this emerges a superstructure of government and laws that establishes and protects the power of one social class. Furthermore, ideology, the communicated idea system of the society, also makes the power of the ruling class legitimate. "In the last analysis, the dominant ideas of a society [its ideology] are the ideas of its ruling class" (Eagleton 1976, 5). The key word for Marx, then, is *class*. The material conditions of society give power to one class, the capitalists, and denies it to the other, the workers. In contrast, for most Americans, money, education, or gender may be the root of power, not class. And power is shared; it is plural, not singular.

The first step in the liberalization of strict Marxist theory for critical purposes has to do with the source of power. Simply, the source of power need not be in economic class but in other material conditions. A useful example of this reinterpretation of Marxism is found in the gender-based dialectic expressed by feminists such as Adrienne Rich.

"The charisma of man," says Adrienne Rich (1979), about the work of two twentieth-century women poets, "seems to come purely from his power over her and his control of the world by force, not from anything fertile or life-giving in him" (36). Here we see the basis of power relations preserved in the dialectic but shifted from class to gender. Such a feminist position may differ little from the form of traditional Marxist thinking. Who controls the means of production, the government, the laws, the social system, and the ideology? Man. And "worker" seems to best fit a female description because women work at less powerful jobs (teacher, secretary, housewife, etc.), and are paid less for them.

In such an interpretation, male power in material conditions is preserved in the ideology of the language. From our earliest exposure to language, male and female positions are reinforced. "The artist, the banker, the president, the capitalist, *he*. . . ." But, "the housewife, the secretary, the grade school teacher, *she*. . . ." How strange it sounds to hear the word *househusband*. The new synthesis frequently proposed is one where men and women are no longer classes but participants in a new classless society. So both men and women have "spouses" when they marry. "The banker s/he," "the chair," not the "chairman," "the artists they," and "policemen" become "police officers." These are but a few examples, and you can add many more attempts to eliminate sexism from the language.

Nor need the shift in the Marxist dialectic be limited to feminist interpretation.

The Black Power movement of the late 1960s was clearly based on a division between white and black, and its very name indicates a desire to gain power that it is denied by the white control of the means of production, the government, the laws, and the language. The phrase "Black is beautiful" is a cultural succession to the Black Power movement. It contests the idea of white standards (blond hair, blue eyes, light skin, slim, pointed noses, etc.) for determining beauty.

The movement also publicized the lack of acceptable role models. In film and television, blacks were seen in subservient roles, even if whites considered those roles sympathetic—Rochester on the *Jack Benny Show*, *Amos and Andy*, the "mammy" in *Birth of a Nation* and *Gone with the Wind*, or more recently and more subtly, Diahann Carroll in *Mahogany*, Sidney Poitier in *Guess Who's Coming to Dinner*, and Morgan Freeman in *Driving Miss Daisy*. The material condition of the society, one may argue, is of white power and black opposition. The dialectical opposition manifests itself in the structure of the society and in the verbal and visual symbols of its ideology.

The dialectical opposition can be extended to include straight people versus gays and lesbians, and professors versus students. The key ingredient in any of these is the ability of a critic to see how in a particular culture or subculture a special power relationship exists that produces a conflict between the haves and have-nots.

In "British Cultural Studies and Television," John Fiske (1987) observes that division in society is the key that permits a much broader interpretation than capitalist-worker. He says:

> Also underlying this work [British Cultural Studies] is the assumption that capitalist societies are divided societies. The primary axis of division was originally thought to be class, though gender may now have replaced it as the most significant producer of social difference. Other axes of division are race, nation, age group, religion, occupation, education, political allegiance, and so on. Society, then, is not an organic whole but a complex network of groups, each with different interests and related to each other in terms of their power relationship with the dominant classes (255).

Thus, for some ideological critics a pluralism of ideological conflicts exists that reflects the material conditions, in effect the history, of the society. These interact with one another in the ideology of the communication. Always present here is the idea of dialectical opposition and conflict.

Does that mean that if there is no conflict the assumption does not hold? No, class opposition based on the material conditions of the society is a given and holds in all cases. Frequently, however, the subservient group accepts the situation. The housewife says that she is happy in her role and believes it is the way she gains her independence; the worker believes that he or she is just as important to building an automobile as is Lee Iaccoca; the secretary does not want to be a manager and prefers to work for a male supervisor. This willing acceptance by the subordinate classes of the social structure and language that keeps them in a subservient position is a product of a process called *hegemony*.

Ideology reinforces the powerful class but in order to preserve the power relationship, say some theorists, the consent of the subservient class

> must be constantly won and rewon, for people's material social experience constantly reminds them of the disadvantages of subordination and thus poses a constant threat to the dominant. So, . . . hegemony is not a static power relationship but a constant process of struggle in which the big guns are on the side of those with social power, but in which victory does not necessarily go to the big guns—or, at least, in which victory is not necessarily total (Fiske 1987, 259).

The critic, therefore, looks for ways in which the ideology preserves the acceptance of the power structure while granting concessions which seem to say that some new synthesis has emerged. Critic Mimi White (1987) has observed this process of maintaining power while seeming to share it in an extensive analysis of the *Cagney & Lacey* television program. Here are two women police officers with ideas of their own who are in frequent open conflict with the male power structure. Says White:

> The program . . . espouses a sympathetic liberal feminism. Individual episodes frequently foreground personal and professional issues that are perceived as being of particular concern to women—sexual harassment, problems of working mothers, child abuse, and so forth. Yet the visual and narrative strategies engaged in individual episodes may work to undercut or contradict the ostensible progressive orientation of the show, relying on conventional modes of plot structure and visual representation that have been seen as undermining the power and effectiveness of women. For example, framing and mise-en-scene are sometimes used in ways that imply that one or the other of the central characters is caged or trapped. This may produce an impression of weakness or helplessness on their part, even though as narrative characters they are supposed to be active, competent detectives (154).

By this analysis, the visual techniques of the program contradict the seeming gender equality. Cagney and Lacey illustrate that the material conditions of society determine the relationships among people through a dialectical opposition between the powerful and powerless class. Still, there is considerable variety in the way that assumption may be applied. In addition, the subservient class can fight back and the superior class constantly has to adapt through the process of hegemony to preserve its control. Therefore, ideological criticism has a rich and varied store of possible interpretations even though the text always bears the ideology of the dominant force (Fiske 1987, 284).

The Material Conditions and Communication Influence One Another

Although both institutions and ideology rest on material conditions, a simple cause and effect relationship does not prevail. Eagleton (1976) points out, "It would be a mistake to imply that Marxist criticism moves mechanically from 'text' to 'ideology' to 'social relations' to 'productive forces.' It is concerned rather, with the *unity* of these 'levels' of society. Literature may be part of the superstructure, but it is not merely the passive reflection of the economic base." Eagleton quotes Friedrich Engels, Karl Marx's collaborator, to support this position:

> According to the materialist conception of history, the determining element in history is *ultimately* the production and reproduction in real life. More than this neither Marx nor I have ever asserted. If therefore somebody twists this into the statement that the economic element is the *only* determining one, he transforms it into a meaningless, abstract and absurd phrase. The economic situation is the basis, but the various elements of the superstructure—political forms of the class struggle and its consequences, constitutions established by the victorious class after a successful battle, etc.—forms of law—and then even the reflexes of all these actual struggles in the brains of the combatants: political, legal, and philosophical theories, religious ideas and their further development into systems of dogma—also exercise their influence upon the course of the historical struggles and in many cases preponderate in determining their *form* (Eagleton, 9).

Thus, even from the beginning of Marxist thought the ideological element was considered significant, almost equal in the relationships that govern a culture. More recent theories developed from this base tend to interpret, even more openly than Engels, the relationship among the means of production, the institutions created, and the symbolic processes. As observed, conflict is considered natural and this conflict may be more than a simple capitalist versus worker confrontation; it may be extended to conflicts over sex, race, and more.

Such diversity of conflicts produces, as in the psychoanalytic approach, a diversity of interpretations. From one interaction, then, a number of meanings are possible. In this view, which is dependent on the theory of French Marxist Louis Althusser, the economic, political, and ideological practices produce meanings for individuals within the social formation (White 1987, 139–140). Thus, ideological analysis is concerned with the way that the ideology brings meaning to the individual or the group. And that means that equally valid though different interpretations of the culture may be developed from examining a particular text.

A television show such as *Kate and Allie* provides a useful example of this diversity of interpretation. The story of two divorced women (until recently unmarried) who live and raise their children together, Kate and Allie also run their own cottage industry, a catering service, from their home. One is very conservative about social relations, the other mildly radical. They run their business, raise their children, maintain contact with their ex-husbands, and have dates with other men.

One interpretation of the series emphasizes hegemony, for despite a number of problems, their adaptation to economic and personal hardships indicates that the system works. As women and workers, they are happy with their situations. No matter what happens the current situation is not bad even though Allie has few material possessions while her ex-husband (a physician) and his wife live a life of luxury. But the ex-husband is a jerk and his wife, mindless. So, Allie should be happy; she has health, friends, family, and, although she is a bit frazzled, happiness. Never mind the millions of women in similar situations who live desperately close to and below the poverty level. Never mind that they are not as attractive as Allie or Kate or do not have time to date. Their children do not have hard decisions to make on whether to go to Stanford or stay at home and attend N.Y.U. as do the children in this television series. *Kate and Allie* has glossed over the material conditions that prevail in society; it is an establishment show.

Viewed from another perspective, Mimi White (1987) speculates about a "'subcultural reading" of such shows as *Kate and Allie* that runs counter to the dominant ideology. She notes that while the characters are shown as heterosexual, "At the same time, they validate women's bonding as a form of social stability, a viable and attractive alternative to the traditional family, and even hint at the possibility of lesbian lifestyles—at least as far as possible within dominant ideology." In this interpretation, the womens' relations with one another are more important than their inadequate transient dealings with men. Such an interpretation explains *Kate and Allie's* appeal "for a particular segment of their audience" (162).

Thus, alternative interpretations of a message are possible, even welcome, and they may be quite different and still give insight into the nature of the culture. So long as the critic recognizes that the symbolic reflects and influences the material conditions of the society, and vice versa, ideological criticism encourages a wide variety of interpretations. Take the two interpretations of *Kate and Allie* indicated above. In a male-dominated capitalist society the conflicts quite reasonably can lead to diverse ideological meanings. But a message that tells divorced women that the current material arrangements of the society are just fine and natural and also hints at the need for a special kind of female bonding with possible lesbian overtones is not unreasonable. Both interpretations integrate the message with prevailing material conditions and help to define the culture without contradicting one another. If they did contradict one another, there is still no problem because the conflict that typifies the culture should be reflected in the ideology.

Conflict Is the Basis of the Society

It is necessary to discuss the idea of conflict briefly to emphasize the differences between a traditional Marxist understanding of ideology and its contemporary forms. In a traditional approach, ideology in a capitalist society is "false consciousness." That is, like government and laws, it serves to reinforce the existing material conditions of the society. Workers love their work and do not want to be owners. Capitalists organize the society for the benefit of everyone.

A traditional Marxist critic would easily see false consciousness in the following quotation from Ronald Reagan's (1981) first inaugural address:

> We hear much of special interest groups. Well our concern must be for a special interest group that has been too long neglected. It knows no sectional boundaries, or ethnic and racial divisions and it crosses political party lines. It is made up of men and women who raise our food, patrol our streets, man our mines and factories, teach our children, keep our homes and heal us when we're sick. Professionals, industrialist, shopkeepers, clerks, cabbies and truck drivers. They are, in short, "We the people." This breed called Americans.
>
> Well, this Administration's objective will be a healthy, vigorous, growing economy that provides equal opportunities for all Americans with no barriers born of bigotry or discrimination. . . .
>
> So, with all the creative energy at our command let us begin an era of national renewal. Let us renew our determination, our courage and our strength. And let us renew our faith and our hope. We have every right to dream heroic dreams.
>
> Those who say that we're in a time when there are no heroes—they just don't know where to look. You can see heroes every day going in and out of factory gates. Others, a handful in number, produce enough food to feed all of us and then the world beyond.
>
> You meet heroes across a counter—and they're on both sides of that counter. There are entrepreneurs with faith in themselves and faith in an idea who create new jobs, new wealth and opportunity (259).

Here Reagan has no sense of the class structure of society. Those who work at low-paying jobs are the same as the wealthy capitalists. Equality is implied even though economic equality is not in the system. This capitalistic system gives freedom and dignity to all and makes them heroes. Democracy and capitalism are one. Reagan's ideology is false consciousness.

A "false consciousness" interpretation is obviously limited. In fact, if ideology is only false consciousness, then critical interpretation is not necessary because Marxist theory predicts what a message will say. It is not even necessary to examine a text to know that it will reinforce the existing material condition—the only point to be observed is a somewhat formal interest in how this will be accomplished.

Traditional Marxist analysis also has some roots that are close to common sense criticism. To see ideology as false consciousness is to contrast it with a true or natural condition sometimes called "scientific socialism." Such Marxist criticism is also a kind of accurate interpretation criticism. It seeks to show the inaccuracy (false consciousness) of capitalist ideology and replace it with a correct system (scientific socialism).

Contemporary Marxist analysis is clearly deconstructive in its approach. It assumes that conflict is basic to the society and that the ideology of messages reflects this conflict. Thus, ideology reflects not only the "false consciousness" of the prevailing material condition but opposition to the economic system as well. Adrienne Rich (1979) has characterized this opposition in literature as the "subversive function of the imagination" (44).

Ideological Criticism Interprets Society as Other Approaches Cannot

The text, in ideological criticism, is examined for many of the same characteristics that other approaches to criticism use. Common sense approaches look at themes, forms, arguments, and statements of fact to see their relationship to some standard of human reality. Formal criticism claims not to be political at all, concerned as it is with aesthetic judgments. Neoclassical criticism, interested in the effects of arguments on audiences, is quite political but not in the same sense as ideological criticism.

Ideological criticism may be quite similar to accurate interpretation but, even then, it is openly political in its orientation, which makes politics and ideology the product of the material means of production. Similarly, although neoclassical criticism is political, its world view is that of Western liberalism. In its perspective, however, liberals and conservatives argue from essentially the same values to win the support of those in power to accept or reject their proposals. Neoclassical criticism is interested in ideologies but only insofar as they are persuasive devices available to all sides in a controversy, not as reflections of material conditions.

Formal criticism, with its concern for aesthetic principles and its rejec-

tion of political or historical interpretations, is the ultimate target of ideological critics. In Kenneth Burke's (1955) words, "Whenever you find a
doctrine of 'nonpolitical' aesthetics affirmed with fervor, look for its politics" (28). Even formal characteristics are ideological. Kathleen Jamieson
(1973) has pointed out how the form of a papal encyclical says much about
its political content and how it will be viewed.

> Expectations are created both in the rhetor and in the audience when the
> encyclical genre is employed. One expects a definite style, certain types
> of arguments, a given world view, and standard assumptions in the encyc-
> lical genre. Encyclicals are characteristically syntactically complex. They
> employ static, absolutistic vocabulary and are additionally constrained by
> the Latin language. Encyclicals rely on tradition for justification for their
> pronouncements. They tend to assert rather than argue. The world view
> imposed by encyclicals is essentially static rather than dynamic. Encycli-
> cals tend, moreover, to make the same assumptions. They assume, for
> example, the existence of natural law, and they also assume that the Pope
> has the right to interpret natural law for the Church (165–166).

Even essentially deconstructive approaches such as value analysis and
narrative analysis must be seen uniquely to be ideological. Bob Pryor (1985)
has observed that many critics get interested in

> the ideological domain, but some other concept has invariably been of-
> fered as an analytic substitute: values, ideas, symbolic systems readily
> come to mind. Unfortunately, these and other similar analytical concepts
> used to describe phenomena proper to the ideological domain do not carry
> the critical thrust associated with the concept of ideology. Something gets
> lost in the translation of ideology into myths, images, rituals, etc. . . . Lost
> in the translation is the critical perception of the forces of power and domi-
> nation and the means through which they are instituted in the social sys-
> tem (1–2).

So, while value and narrative analysis can interpret a culture through
its messages, only ideological criticism is openly and always judgmental
of the power relationship of the culture.

IDEOLOGICAL ANALYSIS

Critical methods can be repeated from one approach to another. Such
a truism is particularly applicable to ideological criticism. Here, the critical
assumptions are far more important than the specific methods used. In
fact, ideological critics can choose among all the tools discussed in earlier
chapters for their use.

The ideological, however, is not just another approach; to its proponents it is the only approach because all the others are reducable to it. One obligation of the competent ideological critic is to find the ideology in the criticism of others. Whether examining texts or the criticism of others, there are principles the ideological critic will want to follow.

Ideological Analysis Can Be Added to Any Other Critical Approach

We have just noted how, for the ideological critic, all approaches to criticism have an inherent ideology whether or not it is realized or acknowledged. Therefore, any approach can be made ideological by acknowledging its ideology. Ideological analysis exposes the hidden political elements in all criticism.

Thus, all other elements in other approaches, claims, evidence, themes, characters, forms, values, and stories, to name only a few, are sources of ideological judgments. Nonetheless, the ideological judgment based on an understanding of material conditions does differentiate it from other approaches.

Ideological criticism is judgmental because it has an inherent system by which judgments can be made. Narrative analysis can only describe what stories are and what they tell us about the culture; so too, value analysis. Formal criticism is judgmental only about form. Neoclassical criticism can only judge effect—there is no necessary relation of effect to the material conditions of society. Thus, as argued, only ideological criticism provides a true unity of form and content. Both form and content are ideological, and ideological criticism aims at a dialectical understanding of the material conditions of the society.

Ideological Critics Acknowledge a Political Point of View

This principle is obvious but worth repeating. Ideological critics do not merely survey the material conditions of the society in their criticism; they use it as a vital part of their analyses. Frequent references to capitalist or sexist societies and their manifestations clearly indicate that critics who offer ideological arguments are dissatisfied with the existing links between messages and power. They see themselves as critics of a special kind such as "radical" critics, "socialist" critics, "feminist" critics, or "African American" critics.

Philip Wander (1983) makes the argument for ideological criticism:

Criticism takes an ideological turn when it recognizes the existence of powerful vested interests benefiting from and consistently urging policies and technology that threaten life on this planet, when it realizes that we search for alternatives. The situation is being constructed; it will not be averted either by ignoring it or placing it beyond our province. An ideological turn in modern criticism reflects the existence of crisis, acknowledges the influence of established interests and the reality of alternative world-views, and commends rhetorical analyses not only of the actions implied but also of the interests represented. More than "informed talk about matters of importance," criticism carries us to the point of recognizing good reasons and engaging in right action. What an ideological view does is to situate "good" and "right" in an historical context, the efforts of real people to create a better world (18).

Clearly, critics following a consciously ideological approach see it as a part of the process of combating the "falseness" of the prevailing ideology. In a broader definition, the term *ideological critic* might very well include those who defend the existing system. There have, however, been only a few of these. Therefore, for most ideological critics, those who defend existing institutions do so largely by maintaining the sham of objectivity.

An ideological critic, nonetheless, may use the methods of a variety of approaches. He or she believes that society is divided and conflict is inevitable. But the ideological critic, unlike others, honestly recognizes a point of view and takes it in examining the relationship among messages, society, and power.

Ideological Criticism Requires Extensive Historical Analysis Outside the Immediate Text

All critical approaches in this book, except formal criticism, are concerned with some relationship between the message and the society with which it is identified. Therefore, to make critical arguments, each requires that the critic examine the context of the message. The adherents of each of the approaches discussed would object to the idea that ideological criticism requires greater study of the historical context. Yet, there is a way in which this is true. Neoclassical critics, for instance, are interested in context to better understand the text. But the ideological critic believes that the text is inevitably linked to the historical material conditions of the society.

Therefore, the ideological critic must look at the whole society, including the economic conditions under which media work. Michael McGee's (1980a) explanation of the way a critic relates the ideograph to history is instructive to the ideological critic. The ideograph that is used to characterize a particular text must be understood, according to McGee, "vertically" and "horizontally."

The history of an ideograph can be found in legal precedent, the *Oxford English Dictionary*, historical records, the writing of professional historians, and "the more significant record of vertical structures"—popular history (novels, films, plays, records, television, songs, etc.), and "grammar school history, [e.g.: Patrick Henry, 'Liberty or Death']." These are "the very first contact most have with their existence and experience as part of a community." From the examples gathered, the most usable ones are selected and organized to provide a *vertical* or chronological understanding of the ideograph (McGee 1980a, 11).

The *horizontal* development of ideographs from the vertical or historical development is seen "when people actually make use of them presently . . . as forces," says McGee (1980a, 12). Ideological critics must know how the ideology in the text developed over time and they must see how this ideology impacts today. History by itself provides a chronology of related material, but from it the critic must select what is relevant to the here and now of the struggle of dialectically opposed forces.

A. Susan Owen (1986), following up on earlier studies, sought to answer the question of "how (not whether or why) power manifests itself in social structures." Her particular case was that of millions of "Rosie the Riveters" who went to work in factories during World War II and then returned to traditional homemaking roles after the war. She studied the "advertisements, public service announcements, articles, and editorials" in ten major periodicals from *Time* to *Good Housekeeping* during 1942. But her study is more than a historical analysis; it sets up an ideological lesson for today.

Over and over again she found statements like "infiltration of women workers into war plants turns management's eyes forcibly from employee morale to morals," "women are 'invading the industrial domain of man,'" "DANGER-CURVES," "what kind of wife does *your* husband come home to?" (23–25). With this extensive and careful analysis of the text she was able to argue:

> By far the most disturbing aspects of the socially "positioned" female of 1942 are the things for which she is faulted: Women's bodies create distractions because the predatory male gaze is "normal." This social structure insists that women define themselves primarily through their bodies, and yet holds women, and *not* men, responsible for any of the negative consequences which come out of such a definition. This gives rise to a set of contradictions which position women as those who with their bodies comfort/seduce, support/distract, sustain/ interfere. These contradictions are successfully mobilized against working women in 1942 to create the illusion that women have no proper place in the male work space. Further, these contradictions set up a powerful set of constraints which neutralize potentially revolutionizing experiences by mobilizing discourses which argue convincingly for what is and is not "natural," "normal," as it should be. Thus are women abused and blamed for that abuse, victimized and blamed for that victimage, duped and blamed for naivete (28).

As a further example of how good ideological criticism looks for outside evidence to inform the critic about the text, we can look at John Fiske's

(1987b) study of the entertainer Madonna. Fiske found that hidden in Madonna's sex symbol image for men is a quite different liberated image for women.

> A study of the young girl fans of Madonna . . . showed that a major source of their pleasure was Madonna's control over her own image (or meaning) and the sense that this control could be devolved to them. They consistently saw Madonna as a woman who used the discourse of patriarchal sexuality to assert her control over that discourse and therefore over her own sexuality. Her sexuality was not represented in music video as a source of pleasure for men, but for herself and her girl fans. She used signs and images from a masculine discourse in order to assert her independence from men, from male approval, and therefore from that discourse (232).

Fiske not only looked at videos and song lyrics but also studied her fan letters. He argues that the critic must "study the meaning that the fans of Madonna actually *do* (or appear to) make of her. This involves listening to them, reading the letters they write to fan magazines, or observing their behavior at home or in public. The fans' words or behavior are not, of course, empirical facts that speak for themselves; they are, rather, texts that need 'reading' theoretically in just the same way as the 'texts of Madonna' do" (1987a, 272). Similarly, Janice Radway in *Reading the Romance* interviewed a group of avid readers of romance novels to understand what those texts mean to the women who read them.

Even the economic conditions of the media are important to an ideological understanding of a text. Although true of all communication, television is probably the most obvious example. "The viewer is positioned as a potential customer," demographic audiences are linked to time periods, "ratings are crucial to the television industry," and commercials are a part of the regular flow of programming (White 1987, 143–145). These links of the text to the capitalist system and the ideological interests of the critic make it a necessity that such a critic be concerned with media economics and the "bottom line."

So, the ideological critic has an almost unlimited source of information from which to support critical claims. And such a critic must make an extensive investigation into the historical use of ideology, and the practices of the current scene.

Ideological Criticism Involves All Four Variables of the Communication Situation

All four of Rosenfield's variables of criticism (Source-Message-Environment-Critic) are involved in ideological analysis. No question is exempt from analysis, including the competence of the critic. For instance, Thelma

McCormack (1983) closes her review of the studies which analyze the relationship of women to soap operas with this statement:

> Finally, the most difficult question, difficult and embarrassing, must be raised: Should men be doing research in this field at all? As we have noted, much of the professional literature in the research on female audiences has been by men, and their views have often been adopted by women in this field uncritically. While I believe men may do good research, I suggest that there is a deeper kind of flaw when men are studying female audiences, whether it is for soap operas, game shows or Harlequin romances: It is to see the female audience as they see women (282).

Even those ideological critics who accept some men as feminists or agree that some persons from the economic power structure can understand workers have to face serious issues. Feminists charge that women critics and readers have had to follow the male lead. In order to be praised by the establishment, first by teachers, then by editors, most critics have had to adopt a male orientation. Jonathan Culler (1982) summarizes an argument by Judith Fetterly in her book *The Resistant Reader* about the American classic, "The Legend of Sleepy Hollow":

> The figure of Rip Van Winkle, writes Leslie Fiedler, "presides over the birth of the American imagination; and it is fitting that our first successful homegrown legend should memorialize, however playfully, the flight of the dreamer from the shrew" (*Love and Death in the American Novel*, p. xx).
>   Confronting such plots, the woman reader, like other readers, is powerfully impelled by the structure of the novel to identify with a hero who makes woman the enemy. In "The Legend of Sleepy Hollow," where Dame Van Winkle represents everything one might wish to escape and Rip the success of a fantasy, Fetterly argues that "what is essentially a simple act of identification when the reader of the story is male becomes a tangle of contradictions when the reader is female" (*The Resisting Reader*, p. 9). "In such fictions the female reader is co-opted into participation in an experience from which she is explicitly excluded; she is asked to identify with a selfhood that defines itself in opposition to her; she is required to identify against herself (p. xii)" (51–52).

Because the material conditions of society are supported by the political system and the ideology constructed in messages, how can we expect a person who has never experienced being a woman, poor, or black—of being powerless—to explain how a powerless person would read a particular message? That would not be difficult in a common sense approach to criticism which accepts the notion of an objective or detached critic but, in the ideological approach, such a critic is an impossibility.

Still, there are men who claim to serve as feminist critics, whites who claim to understand African Americans, and, most prominently, economic establishment members who claim to speak for workers. Indeed, few

Marxist writers come from the working class. Names such as Fredric Jameson, Raymond Williams, Lawrence Grossberg, and Philip Wander should illustrate that point. And yet the controversy is quite real over who may serve as critic.

Controversy also surrounds the critical approach to be used. For instance, Jonathan Culler (1982) points out that feminist criticism, at one level, constitutes an attack on many of the traditional concepts of criticism as merely male orientations. "Men," he says, "have aligned the opposition male/female with rational/emotional, serious/frivolous, or reflective/spontaneous; and feminist criticism of the second movement works to prove itself more rational, serious and reflective than male readings that omit and distort" (58). Furthermore, a feminist critic may deny rationality as a standard because it is associated with the masculine bias. This does not imply a preference for the irrational but a rejection of the associations that male-defined rationality makes with it.

Jane Tompkins (1984) reverses the "rational" understanding that nineteenth-century sentimental novels (such as *Uncle Tom's Cabin*) written by women "traded in false stereotypes, dishing out weak-minded pap to nourish the prejudices of an ill-educated and underemployed female readership. Self-deluded and unable to face the harsh facts of a competitive society, they are portrayed as manipulators of a gullible public who kept their readers imprisoned in a dream world of self-justifying clichés."

Tompkins (1984) counters with the thesis that these novels represent "a monumental effort to reorganize culture from the woman's point of view; that this body of work is as remarkable for its intellectual complexity, ambition, and resourcefulness; and that, in certain cases, it offers a critique of American society far more devastating than any delivered by better known critics such as Hawthorne and Melville" (83).

Next time you watch the evening news on television make a list of the stories and what they are about. These are the "objective" reports of people who wish to be "accurate." Ask yourself such questions as which social classes, groups, and organizations are represented and which are represented positively or negatively? And ask what segments of the society are not there at all? This little exercise will identify what ideological critics have argued: that the messages of our society are supportive of the powerful and the existing system. From the ideological point of view, such an interpretation is not irrational. Rather it asks for an alternative reading wherein rationality is not cluttered with special conditions. The material conditions, and consequently the messages, must be freed from the dominant ideology of power.

This discussion of the controversy over who may be the critic and what constitutes criticism extends the boundaries of the critical experience. All economic and management issues become a subject for critical attention. So, in one sense, ideological criticism, with its demand for a thorough examination of history, is the most all-encompassing approach. However, what its proponents see as liberating, its opponents see as restricting; which brings us now to ideological criticism's opponents.

PROBLEMS WITH IDEOLOGICAL CRITICISM

There is really only one problem with ideological criticism. Although charges against it can be brought to bear on the credibility of its assumptions, the problem just mentioned is basic. Those who question ideological criticism see its assumptions as simplistic and limiting. It can appropriate any method available to other critics; in that sense, it would seem to be the most complex and pluralistic of all critical approaches. However, its detractors see it as simplistic because it assumes that there are basic material conditions that determine critical responses. Brenda Dervin's (1987) explanation of feminist scholarship illustrates this problem with ideological criticism well:

> It is not merely scholarship focusing on women. Marketing research focuses on women, but we would not call marketing research feminist scholarship. Much traditional social psychology includes gender as a variable, but we would not call it feminist scholarship either. In essence, these focus on gender and on women as women in comparison with men; they incorporate inherent stereotypes and power oppressions. A synthesis at a very abstract level of some recent definitions of feminist scholarship shows what feminist scholars are reaching for.
> Feminist scholarship sees gender as a (if not the) primary category of societal organization. It understands patriarchy as pervasive; it uses gender as a fundamental organizing category of human experience. In the same sense that Marxism uses class as a fundamental organizing category, gender is primary in feminist scholarship (109).

Although any critical methods may be used, they must be used in the service of what Dervin calls "a fundamental organizing category of human experience." To many other critics this seems quite limiting. Karlyn Kohrs Campbell (1983) has said, "I find the term 'ideology' a troublesome starting point for scholarly controversy because Marxian polemics have given it such intense connotations that whatever other meanings it might have had are overwhelmed by them" (126).

Campbell is an interesting adversary for ideological criticism because, in some senses, she has many of the inclinations of the ideological critics. In the same response in which she found ideology troublesome, she affirms that for her "criticism is subjective" (126). You will recall from Chapter 3 that Campbell's (1972b) analysis of Richard Nixon's Vietnamization speech served as an example of the ethical turn in accurate interpretation. Campbell (1980) also has sympathetically examined feminine rhetoric. But she did so in ways that would, by Dervin's definition, not be acceptable as feminist analysis. In short, Campbell is as close to being an ideological critic as one can find but her criticism does not reflect a "fundamental organizing category of human experience." Or perhaps her links are to Western democratic theory or humanism without its Marxist links.

Why do ideological critics insist on a materialist view? Why can't a critic use it at times where it seems appropriate and use something else on another occasion? Why can't a critic be a pluralist? Why must criticism be forever linked to a particular view of the world? Because dialectical power relationships are definitive of the material human condition, says the ideological critic. That answer chokes off many who might be inclined to the study of ideology.

Consequently, many turn to values, myths, stories, or ideographs as symbolic ways in which people define their world and believe these do an adequate job of definition without the narrowing traditional Marxist baggage.

Michael McGee (1980a) has argued what many believe, that the ideology of the cultural language is as powerful as the material conditions:

> Marx's thesis suggests that an ideology determines mass belief and thus restricts the free emergence of political opinion. By this logic, the "freest" members of a community are those who belong to the "power" elite; yet the image of hooded puppeteers twisting and turning the masses at will is unconvincing if only because the elite seems itself imprisoned by the same false consciousness communicated to the polity at large. When we consider the impact of ideology on freedom, and of power on consciousness, we must be clear that ideology is transcendent, as much an influence on the belief and behavior of the ruler as on the ruled (5).

That argument stands as a basis for rejecting the ideological position in its most traditional Marxist form. But, it also serves as a support for a more communication-oriented ideological criticism. For as we have seen, ideological criticism is complex, involving the integration of material, social, and ideological practices of the society. These interrelationships produce complex conflicts, leading to many alternative ideological interpretations. These interpretations become important for many ideological critics. Traditional Marxism and Professor Dervin's feminism miss that point. The defense of many ideological critics is not one of some iron law of class or gender power. Rather, these critics acknowledge the material conditions of the power struggles within society, but look for the subtle interactions of these conditions with the ideological symbolization of all parties. There is no iron law, but the material conditions (the history) are essential to their understanding of communication. Without an acknowledgment of this history, they argue, critics are left with a narrow formalism in which many alternative interpretations are ignored.

Bibliography

Adams, James T. "Emerson Re-read." *The Transcendental Revolt*. Edited by George F. Whicher. Boston: Heath, 1949, 31–39.

Adler, Alfred. *The Individual Psychology of Alfred Adler*. Edited by Heinz L. Ansbacher and Rowena R. Ansbacher. New York: Basic, 1956.

Allen, Robert C. ed. *Channels of Discourse*. Chapel Hill: University of North Carolina Press, 1987.

American Society of Newspaper Editors. "A Statement of Principles." (October 23, 1975).

Anderson, James A. *Communication Research: Issues and Methods*. New York: McGraw-Hill, 1987.

Anderson, James A., and Meyer, Timothy. *Mediated Communication: A Social Action Perspective*. Beverly Hills, CA: Sage, 1988.

Andrews, James R. *The Practice Of Rhetorical Criticism*. New York: Macmillan, 1983.

Ansen, David, Murr, Andrew, and Reese, Michael. "Wrestling With 'Temptation.' " *Newsweek* 15 August 1988, 56–57.

Aristotle. *Nicomachean Ethics*. Edited by Richard McKeon. *Works of Aristotle*. New York: Random House, 1941, 935–1112.

———. *The Rhetoric*. Translated by Lane Cooper. New York: Appleton-Century-Crofts, 1932.

———. *Theory of Poetry and Fine Arts*. Translated by S. H. Butcher. London: Macmillan, 1927.

Arlen, Michael. "Getting the Goods on President Monckton." *Television: The Critical View*. Edited by Horace Newcomb. New York: Oxford University Press, 1979, 160–169.

Arnold, Carroll C. *Criticism of Oral Rhetoric*. Columbus, OH: Merrill, 1974.

Associated Press Managing Editors Association. "Code of Ethics." (April 15, 1985).

Balthrop, V. William, and Long, Beverly W. " 'Yes, But'. . . . Voices in Current Literary Criticism." *Quarterly Journal of Speech* 66 (1980): 211–237.

Barker, David. "Television Production Techniques as Communication." *Critical Studies in Mass Communication* 2 (1985): 234–246.

Beasley, Maurine. "Eleanor Roosevelt's Press Conferences: Symbolic Importance of a Pseudo-Event." *Journalism Quarterly* 61 (1984): 274–279.

Becker, Carl. "Everyman His Own Historian." *American Historical Review* 37 (1932): 221–236.

Belsey, Catherine. *Critical Practice*. New York: Methuen, 1980.

Benjamin, Walter. "The Storyteller." *Illuminations*. Edited by Hannah Arendt. New York: Schocken, 1969, 83–109.

Benoit, William L. "Richard Nixon's Rhetorical Strategies in His Public Statements on Watergate." *Southern Speech Communication Journal* 47 (1982): 192–211.

Benson, Thomas W. "The Rhetorical Structure of Frederick Wiseman's *High School.*" *Communication Monographs* 47 (1980): 233–261.

———. "The Senses of Rhetoric: A Topical System for Critics." *Central States Speech Journal* 29 (1978): 237–250.

Berger, Arthur Asa. *Media Analysis Technique.* Beverly Hills, CA: Sage, 1982.

Bettelheim, Bruno. "Freud and the Soul." *New Yorker* 1 March 1982, 52–93.

"Better Living Through Public Relations." *Extra* 1 (1987): 6.

Birdsell, David S. "Ronald Reagan on Lebanon and Grenada: Flexibility and Interpretation in the Application of Kenneth Burke's Pentad." *Quarterly Journal of Speech* 73 (1987): 267–279.

Bitzer, Lloyd. "Aristotle's Enthymeme Revisited." *Quarterly Journal of Speech* 45 (1959): 399–408.

———. "The Rhetorical Situation." *Philosophy and Rhetoric* 1 (1968): 1–14.

Bitzer, Lloyd, and Black, Edwin, *The Prospect of Rhetoric.* Englewood Cliffs, NJ: Prentice-Hall, 1971.

Bjork, Rebecca S. "Reagan and the Nuclear Freeze: 'Star Wars' as Rhetorical Strategy." *Journal of the American Forensic Association* 24 (1988): 181–192.

Black, Edwin. "Ideological Justifications." *Quarterly Journal of Speech* 70 (1984): 144–150.

———. "A Note on Theory and Practice in Rhetorical Criticism." *Western Journal of Speech Communication* 44 (1980): 331–336.

———. "The Second Persona." *Quarterly Journal of Speech* 56 (1970): 109–119.

———. "Moral Values and Rhetorical Criticism." Lecture. University of Wisconsin, 12 July 1965a.

———. *Rhetorical Criticism: A Study in Method.* New York: Macmillan, 1965b.

Bodkin, Maud. *Archetypal Patterns in Poetry.* London: Oxford University Press, 1963.

Bormann, Ernest G. *The Force of Fantasy: Restoring the American Dream.* Carbondale: Southern Illinois University Press, 1985.

———. "Symbolic Convergence: Organizational Communication and Culture." *Communication and Organizations: An Interpretive Approach.* Edited by Linda L. Putnam and Michael E. Pacanowsky. Beverly Hills, CA: Sage, 1983, 99–123.

Bosmajian, Haig. "The Inaccuracies in the Reprinting of Martin Luther King, Jr.'s, 'I Have a Dream' Speech." *Communication Education* 31 (April 1982) 107–114.

Bowers, John W. "The Pre-Scientific Function of Rhetorical Criticism." *Essays on Rhetorical Criticism.* Edited by Thomas R. Nilsen. New York: Random House, 1968, 125–145.

Bradley, Bert E., and Tarver, Jerry L. "John C. Calhoun's Rhetorical Method in Defense of Slavery." *Oratory in the Old South.* Edited by Waldo W. Braden. Baton Rouge: Louisiana State University Press, 1970, 169–189.

Brazil. Directed by Terry Gilliam. Universal Studios, 1985.

Brock, Bernard L. "Rhetorical Criticism: A Burkian Perspective." *Methods of Rhetorical Criticism: A Twentieth Century Perspective.* Edited by Robert L. Scott and Bernard L. Brock. New York: Harper & Row, 1972, 315–326.

Brockriede, Wayne. "Rhetorical Criticism as Argument." *Quarterly Journal of Speech* 60 (1974): 165–174.

———. "Dimensions of the Concept of Rhetoric." *Quarterly Journal of Speech* 54 (1968): 1–12.

Brodie, Fawn M. *Thomas Jefferson: An Intimate History*. New York: Norton, 1974.

Brooks, Cleanth, and Warren, Robert Penn. *Understanding Poetry*. New York: Holt, Rinehart & Winston, 1960.

Brummett, Barry. "Consensus Criticism." *Southern Speech Communication Journal* 49 (1984): 111–124.

Brunvand, Jan Harold. "Watch Out for 'AIDS Mary'." United Feature Syndicate, 16 March 1987.

Bryant, Donald C. "Rhetoric: Its Function and Its Scope." *Quarterly Journal of Speech* 34 (1953): 401–424.

———. "Some Problems of Scope and Method in Rhetorical Scholarship." *Quarterly Journal of Speech* 23 (1937): 82–89.

Burgchardt, Carl R. "Two Faces of American Communism: Pamphlet Rhetoric of the Third Period and the Popular Front." *Quarterly Journal of Speech* 66 (1980): 375–391.

Burke, Kenneth. "Rhetoric, Poetics, and Philosophy." *Rhetoric, Philosophy, and Literature*. Edited by Don M. Burks. West Lafayette, IN: Purdue University Press, l978.

———. *Language as Symbolic Action: Essays on Life, Literature, and Method*. Berkeley: University of California Press, 1966.

———. *A Rhetoric of Motives*. New York: Braziller, 1955.

———. *Grammar of Motives*. New York: Prentice-Hall, 1954.

Campbell, Karlyn Kohrs. "Response to Forbes Hill." *Central States Speech Journal* 34 (1983): 126–127.

———. "Stanton's 'The Solitude of Self': A Rationale for Feminism." *Quarterly Journal of Speech* 66 (1980): 304–312.

———. "The Nature of Criticism in Rhetorical and Communicative Studies." *Central States Speech Journal* 30 (1979): 4–13.

———. " 'Conventional Wisdom—Traditional Form': A Rejoinder." *Quarterly Journal of Speech* 58 (1972a): 451–454.

———. *Critiques of Contemporary Rhetoric*. Belmont, CA: Wadsworth, 1972b.

Campbell, Karlyn Kohrs, and Jamieson, Kathleen Hall. *Form and Genre: Shaping Rhetorical Action*. Falls Church, VA: Speech Communication Association, 1977.

Campbell, Oscar J., and Quinn, Edward G. *The Reader's Encyclopedia of Shakespeare*. New York: Crowell, 1966.

Cantor, Muriel G., and Pingree, Suzanne. *The Soap Opera*. Beverly Hills, CA: Sage, 1983.

Carey, James W. "A Cultural Approach to Communication." *Communication* 2 (1975): 1–22.

Carpenter, Ronald. "The Historical Jeremaid as Rhetorical Genre." *Form and Genre: Shaping Rhetorical Action*. Edited by Karlyn Kohrs Campbell and Kathleen Hall Jamieson. Falls Church, VA: Speech Communication Association, 1977, 103–117.

Carter, Jimmy, and Ford, Gerald. "Presidential Debate." *The New York Times* 7 October 1976, 36–38.

Cater, Douglas, and Adler, Richard. *Television as a Social Force: New Approaches to TV Criticism*. New York: Praeger, 1976.

Cathcart, Robert. *Post Communication: Rhetorical Analyses and Evaluation*. Indianapolis: Bobbs-Merrill, 1981.

"Cheers 'N' Jeers." *TV Guide* 37 July 29, 1989, 31.

Clark, Donald L. *Rhetoric in Greco-Roman Education*. New York: Columbia University Press, 1957.

Clark, M. L. *Rhetoric at Rome: A Historical Survey*. New York: Barnes and Noble, 1953.

Clover, Carol J. "Her Body, Himself: Gender in the Slasher Film." *Representations* 20 (1987): 187–228.

Commager, Henry S. *Documents in American History*. New York: Appleton-Century-Crofts, 1949.

Conwell, Russell. "Acres of Diamonds." *Three Centuries of American Rhetorical Discourse*. Edited by Ronald F. Reid. Prospects Heights, IL: Waveland, 1988, 577–586.

Corliss, Richard. "Happy Days Are Here Again." *Television: The Critical View*. Edited by Horace Newcomb. New York: Oxford University Press, 1982, 64–76.

Crandall, S. Judson. "The Beginnings of a Methodology for Social Control Studies in Public Address." *Quarterly Journal of Speech* 33 (1947): 36–39.

Crane, R. S. *The Language of Criticism and the Structure of Poetry*. Toronto: Toronto University Press, 1953.

Crofts, Albert J. "The Functions of Rhetorical Criticism," *Quarterly Journal of Speech* 42 (1956): 283–291.

Culbert, David. "Television Archives." *Critical Studies in Mass Communication* 1 (1984): 88–92.

Culler, Jonathan. *Framing the Sign: Criticism and Its Institutions*. Norman: University of Oklahoma Press, 1988.

———. *On Deconstruction*. Ithaca, NY: Cornell University Press, 1982.

———. *Structuralist Poetics: Structuralism, Linguistics and the Study of Literature*. Ithaca, NY: Cornell University Press, 1976.

Daiches, David. *Critical Approaches to Literature*. Englewood Cliffs, NJ: Prentice-Hall, 1956.

Dervin, Brenda. "The Potential Contribution of Feminist Scholarship to the Field of Communication." *Journal of Communication* 37 (1987): 107–121.

Dickey, James. *Deliverance*. New York: Dell, 1970.

Eagleton, Terry. *Literary Theory: An Introduction*. Minneapolis: University of Minnesota Press, 1983.

———. *Marxism and Literary Criticism*. Berkeley: University of California Press, 1976.

Eason, David L. "On Journalistic Authority: The Janet Cooke Scandal." *Critical Studies in Mass Communication* 3 (1986): 429–447.

Ehninger, Douglas, Gronbeck, Bruce E., McKerrow, Ray E., and Monroe, Alan H. *Principles and Types of Speech Communication*. Glenview, IL: Scott, Foresman, 1982.

Elshtain, Jean Bethke. *Public Man, Private Woman: Women in Social and Political Thought*. Princeton, NJ: Princeton University Press, 1981.

Empson, William. *Seven Types of Ambiguity*. London: Chatto and Windus, 1970.

Estep, Rhoda, and Macdonald, Patrick. "How Prime Time Crime Evolved on TV, 1976–81." *Journalism Quarterly* 60 (1963): 293–300.

Faulkner, William. *The Sound and the Fury and As I Lay Dying*. New York: Modern Library, 1946.

Ferril, Thomas Hornsby, and Ferril, Helen. *The Rocky Mountain Herald Reader*. New York: William Morrow, 1962.

Feuer, Jane. "The MTM Style." *Television: The Critical View*. Edited by Horace Newcomb. New York: Oxford University Press, 1987, 52–84.

Fish, Stanley. *Is There a Text in This Class?* Cambridge, MA: Harvard University Press, 1980.

Fischer, David Hackett. *Historian's Fallacies: Toward a Logic of Historical Thought.* New York: Harper, 1970.

Fisher, Doris, and Roberts, Alan. "You Always Hurt the One You Love." New York: Sun Music, 1944.

Fisher, Walter R. *Human Communication as Narration: Toward a Philosophy of Reason, Value and Action.* Columbia: University of South Carolina Press, 1987.

Fiske, John B. "British Cultural Studies and Television." *Channels of Discourse.* Edited by Robert C. Allen. Chapel Hill: University of North Carolina Press, 1987a, 254–290.

———. *Television Culture.* New York: Methuen, 1987b.

———. *Introduction to Communication Studies.* New York: Methuen, 1982.

Flitterman-Lewis, Sandy. "Psychoanalysis, Film and Television." *Channels of Discourse.* Edited by Robert C. Allen. Chapel Hill: University of North Carolina Press, 1987, 172–210.

Fogarty, Daniel. *Roots for a New Rhetoric.* New York: Teachers College, Columbia University, 1959.

Foss, Sonja K. "Criteria for Adequacy in Rhetorical Criticism." *Southern Speech Communication Journal* 48 (1983): 283–295.

Foss, Sonja K., Foss, Karen A., and Trapp, Robert. *Contemporary Perspectives on Rhetoric.* Prospect Heights, IL: Waveland, 1985.

Freud, Sigmund. "Difficulties and First Approaches." *The Standard Edition of the Complete Psychological Works of Sigmund Freud.* Translated by James Strackey. London: Hogarth, 1961, 15, 83–99.

Friedan, Betty. *The Feminine Mystique.* New York: Dell, 1963.

Frost, Robert. *The Road Not Taken: An Introduction to Robert Frost.* Edited by Louis Untermeyer. New York: Holt, Rinehart & Winston, 1962.

Frye, Northrop. *Anatomy of Criticism.* New York: Atheneum, 1966.

Fulkerson, Richard P. "The Public Letter as a Rhetorical Form: Structure, Logic, and Style in King's 'Letter From Birmingham Jail'." *Quarterly Journal of Speech* 65 (1979): 121–136.

Furay, Conal. *The Grass-Roots Mind in America.* New York: New Viewpoints, 1977.

Gallup, George. "Americans Believe Personal Goals More Vital Than Material Gain." *Salt Lake Tribune* 28 January 1982, A3.

Ganer, Patricia. "An Analysis of the Role of Values in the Argumentation of the 1980 Presidential Campaign." Dissertation, University of Utah, 1988.

Gans, Herbert. *Deciding What's News.* New York: Pantheon, 1979.

Geertz, Clifford. *The Interpretation of Cultures.* New York: Basic, 1973.

Glasser, Theodore L., and Ettema, James S. "Investigative Journalism and the Legitimation of Moral Order." San Antonio, TX: Association for Education in Journalism and Mass Communication, 1987.

Godfrey, Donald G. *A Directory of Broadcast Archives.* Washington, DC: Broadcast Education Association, 1983.

Goodwin, H. Eugene. *Groping for Ethics in Journalism.* Ames: Iowa State University Press, 1983.

Gorbachev, Mikhail. "U.S.S.R. Arms Reduction." *Vital Speeches of the Day* 1 February 1989, 229–236.

Grimaldi, William M. A. *Studies in the Philosophy of Aristotle's Rhetoric.* Wiesbaden: Steiner, 1972.

Gronbeck, Bruce. "Dramaturgical Theory and Criticism: The State of the Art (or Science?)." *Western Journal of Speech Communication* 44 (1980): 315–330.

———. "Rhetorical History and Rhetorical Criticism: A Distinction." *Speech Teacher* 24 (1975): 309–320.

Grossberg, Lawrence. "Strategies of Marxist Cultural Interpretations." *Critical Studies in Mass Communication* 1 (1984): 392–421.

Grube, G. M. A. "Rhetoric and Literary Criticism." *Quarterly Journal of Speech* 62 (1956): 339–344.

Guest, Judith. *Ordinary People*. New York: Viking, 1976.

Hackett, Robert A. "Decline of a Paradigm? Bias and Objectivity in News Media Studies?" *Critical Studies in Mass Communication* 1 (1984): 229–259.

Haines, Harry W. "'What Kind of War?': An Analysis of the Vietnam Veterans Memorial." *Critical Studies in Mass Communication* 3 (1986): 1–20.

Hall, Stuart. "Ideology." *International Encyclopedia of Communications*. Edited by Erik Barnouw. New York: Oxford University Press, 1989, 307–311.

Hample, Judy. "The Textual and Cultural Authenticity of Patrick Henry's Liberty or Death Speech." *Quarterly Journal of Speech* 63 (1977): 298–310.

Hart, Roderick P. *Verbal Style and the Presidency: A Computer Based Analysis*. Orlando, FL: Academic, 1984.

———. *The Political Pulpit*. West Lafayette, IN: Purdue University Press, 1977.

———. "Absolutism and Situation: Prolegomena to a Rhetorical Biography of Richard M. Nixon." *Communication Monographs* 43 (1976): 204–228.

Hayakawa, S. I. *Language in Thought and Action*. New York: Harcourt Brace, 1949.

Heath, Robert L. "Dialectical Confrontation: A Strategy of Black Radicalism." *Central States Speech Journal* 24 (1973): 168–177.

Hemphill, Lex. "Cheaters Never Win? Don't Tell Sooners." *Salt Lake Tribune* 19 December 1988, D1.

Henry, David. "The Rhetorical Dynamics of Mario Cuomo's 1984 Keynote Address: Situation, Speaker, Metaphor." *Southern Speech Communication Journal* 53 (1988): 105–120.

Highet, Gilbert. *A Clerk at Oxenford*. New York: Oxford, 1954.

Hill, Forbes. "A Turn Against Ideology: Reply to Professor Wander." *Central States Speech Journal* 34 (Summer 1983): 121–126.

———. "Conventional Wisdom—Traditional Form—The President's Message of November, 1969." *Quarterly Journal of Speech* 58 (1972): 373–386.

Hirsch, E. D., Jr. "The Politics of Theories of Interpretation." *Critical Inquiry* 9 (1982): 235–248.

———. "Objective Interpretation" *PMLA* 75 (1960): 463–479.

Hoffer, Thomas W., and Nelson, Richard Alan. "Evolution of Docudrama on American Television Networks: A Content Analysis, 1966–1978." *Southern Speech Communication Journal* 45 (1980): 149–163.

Holland, Norman N. *5 Readers Reading*. New Haven, CT: Yale University Press, 1975.

Holsti, Ole R. *Content Analysis for the Social Sciences and Humanities*. Reading MA: Addison-Wesley, 1969.

Horton, Rod W., and Edwards, Herbert W. *Backgrounds of American Literary Thought*. Englewood Cliffs, NJ: Prentice-Hall, 1974.

Hyman, Stanley Edgar. *The Armed Vision*. New York: Vintage, 1955.

Ilkka, Richard J. "Rhetorical Dramatization in the Development of American Communism." *Quarterly Journal of Speech* 43 (1977): 413–427.

Ivie, Robert L. "Literalizing the Metaphor of Soviet Savagery: President Truman's Plain Style." *Southern Speech Communication Journal* 51 (1986): 91–105.

Jaggar, Alison M. *Feminist Politics and Human Nature*. Totowa, NJ: Rowman and Allanheld, 1983.

Jamieson, Kathleen H. "Generic Constraints and the Rhetorical Situation." *Philosophy and Rhetoric* 6 (1973): 163–170.

Jobes, Katherine T. "Introduction." *Twentieth Century Interpretations of The Old Man and The Sea*. Edited by Katherine T. Jobes. Englewood Cliffs, NJ: Prentice-Hall, 1968, 1–17.

Johnson, Julia, and McLeod, Scott. "The Burden of Being a Superstar." *Time* 135 25 June 1990, 20–21.

Johnson, Lyndon B. "The Great Society." *Voices of Crisis*. Edited by Floyd B. Matson. New York: Odyssey, 1967, 108–114.

Kaplan, Charles. *Criticism: The Major Statements*. New York: St. Martin's Press, 1986.

Kennedy, George. *Classical Rhetoric and Its Christian and Secular Tradition*. Chapel Hill: University of North Carolina Press, 1980.

Kerbel, Michael. "The Golden Age of TV Drama." *Television: The Critical View*. Edited by Horace Newcomb. New York: Oxford University Press, 1982, 47–63.

King, Martin Luther, Jr. "I Have a Dream." *Representative American Speeches: 1963–64*. Edited by Lester Thonssen. New York: Wilson, 1964, 43–48.

Kipper, Philip. "The Television News Report as Persuasive Message." Salt Lake City: Western Speech Communication Association, February 1987.

Kluckhohn, Clyde. "Values and Value-Orientations in the Theory of Action: An Exploration in Definition and Classification." *Toward a General Theory of Action*. Edited by Talcott Parsons and Edward A. Shils. New York: Harper & Row, 1951, 388–433.

Krippendorff, Klaus. *Content Analysis: An Introduction to Its Methodology*. Beverly Hills, CA: Sage, 1980.

Lacan, Jacques. *Feminine Sexuality*. Translated by Jacqueline Rose. New York: Pantheon, 1982.

La Capra, Dominick. "Rethinking Intellectual History and Reading Texts." *Modern European Intellectual History: Reappraisals and New Perspectives*. Edited by Dominick La Capra and Steven L. Kaplan. Ithaca, NY: Cornell University Press, 1982.

"Landslide, The: How and Why?" *Newsweek* 13 November 1972, 30.

Lanser, Susan S. *The Narrative Act: Point of View in Prose Fiction*. Princeton, NJ: Princeton University Press, 1981.

Lee, Irving J. "Four Ways of Looking at a Speech." *Quarterly Journal of Speech* 28 (1942): 148–155.

Leff, Michael C. "Interpretation and the Art of the Rhetorical Critic." *Western Journal of Speech Communication* 44 (1980): 337–349.

Leff, Michael C., and Mohrmann, Gerald P. "Lincoln at Cooper Union: A Rhetorical Analysis of the Text." *Quarterly Journal of Speech* 60 (1974): 346–358.

Lichty, Lawrence. "Video Versus Print." *The Wilson Quarterly* 6 (1982): 49–57.

Lincoln, Abraham. *The Collected Works of Abraham Lincoln*. Edited by Roy P. Basler. New Brunswick, NJ: Rutgers, 1953.

"Living Inside a Hero's Mantle." *U.S. News & World Report* 109 2 July 1990, 8–9.

Logue, Cal M., and Patton, John H. "From Ambiguity to Dogma: The Rhetorical Symbols of Lyndon B. Johnson on Vietnam." *Southern Speech Communication Journal* 47 (1982): 310–329.

Lomas, Charles. "Rhetorical Criticism and Historical Perspective." *Western Speech* 32 (1968): 191–203.

Lucas, Stephen E. Review of *The Force of Fantasy: Restoring the American Dream*, by Ernest Bormann. *Rhetoric Society Quarterly* 15 (1986): 199–205.

———. "The Schism in Rhetorical Scholarship," *Quarterly Journal of Speech* 67 (1981): 1–22.

MacArthur, Douglas. "Duty, Honor, Country." *Great Speeches for Criticism and Analysis*. Edited by Lloyd Rohler and Roger Cook. Greenwood: Alistair, 1988, 321–324.

McBurney, James H. "The Place of the Enthymeme in Rhetorical Theory." *Speech Monographs* 2 (1936): 49–74.

McCormack, Thelma. "Male Conceptions of Female Audiences: The Case of Soap Operas." *Mass Communication Review Yearbook* 4. Edited by Ellen Wartella and D. Charles Whitney. Beverly Hills, CA: Sage, 1983, 273–283.

McGee, Michael C. "Another Philippic: Notes on the Ideological Turn in Criticism." *Central States Speech Journal* 35 (1984a): 6, 14, 43–50.

———. "Secular Humanism: A Radical Reading of 'Culture Industry' Productions." *Critical Studies in Mass Communication* 1 (1984b): 1–33.

———. "Social Movements as Meaning." *Central States Speech Journal* 34 (1983): 74–77.

———. "The 'Ideograph': A Link Between Rhetoric and Ideology." *Quarterly Journal of Speech* 66 (1980a): 1–16.

———. "The 'Ideograph' as a Unit of Analysis in Political Argument." *Proceedings of the Summer Conference on Argumentation*. Edited by Jack Rhodes and Sara Newell. Annandale, MN: Speech Communication Association, 1980b, 68–87.

———. "In Search of the People." *Quarterly Journal of Speech* 61 (1975): 235–249.

Mailloux, Steven. "Rhetorical Hermeneutics." *Critical Inquiry* 11 (1985): 620–641.

Malcolm X. "The Ballot or the Bullet." *Malcolm X Speaks*. New York: Grove, 1965, 23–44.

Mander, Mary S. "The Public Debate About Broadcasting in the Twenties." *Journal of Broadcasting* 28 (1984): 167–185.

Maslow, Abraham. *Motivation and Personality*. New York: Harper & Row, 1987.

Medhurst, Martin J. "Reagan and the 'Fairness' Issue: A Rhetorical Vision That Failed to Chain." Chicago: Speech Communication Association, 1984a.

———. Review of *Verbal Style and the Presidency: A Computer Based Analysis*, by Roderick P. Hart. *Rhetoric Society Quarterly* 13 (1984b): 139–144.

Medhurst, Martin J., and Benson, Thomas W. *Rhetorical Dimensions in Media*. Dubuque, IA: Kendall/Hunt, 1984.

Medhurst, Martin J., and DeSousa, Michael A. "Political Cartoons as Rhetorical Form: A Taxonomy of Graphic Discourse." *Communication Monographs* 48 (1981): 199–236.

Megill, Allan. "Heidegger, Wander, and Ideology." *Central States Speech Journal* 34 (1983): 114–119.

Megill, Allan, and McCloskey, Donald N. "The Rhetoric of History." *The Rhetoric of the Human Sciences: Language and Argument in Scholarship and Public Affairs*. Edited by John S. Nelson, Allan Megill, and Donald M. McCloskey. Madison: University of Wisconsin Press, 1987.

Melville, Herman. *Moby-Dick*. Edited by Charles Feidelson, Jr. New York: Bobbs-Merrill, 1964.

Merrill, John. "A Semantic Analysis of the SPJ, SDX Code of Ethics." *Mass Communication Review* 9 (1981–82): 12–15.

Metz, Christian. "The Fiction Film and Its Spectator: A Metapsychological Study." *New Literary History* 8 (1976): 75–105.

Michaels, Marguerite, and Willwerth, James. "A Holy Fury." *Time* 15 August 1988, 34–36.

Mink, Louis O. "Everyman His or Her Own Annalist." *On Narrative*. Edited by W. J. T. Mitchell. Chicago: University of Chicago Press, 1981, 233–239.

Mitchell, Juliet. "Introduction—I." In Jaques Lacan, *Feminine Sexuality*. Translated by Jacqueline Rose. New York: Pantheon, 1982, 1–26.

———. *Women: The Longest Revolution*. New York: Pantheon, 1984.

Mitchell, W. J. T. *On Narrative*. Chicago: University of Chicago Press, 1981.

Mohrmann, G. P. "An Essay on Fantasy Theme Criticism." *Quarterly Journal of Speech* 68 (1982a): 109–132.

———. "Fantasy Theme Criticism: A Peroration." *Quarterly Journal of Speech* 68 (1982b): 306–313.

———. "Elegy in a Critical Grave-Yard." *Western Journal of Speech Communication* 44 (1980): 265–274.

Mohrmann, G. P., and Leff, Michael C. "Lincoln at Cooper Union: A Rationale for Neoclassical Criticism." *Quarterly Journal of Speech* 60 (1974): 459–467.

Monaco, James. *How to Read a Film*. New York: Oxford University Press, 1977.

Mudd, Charles. "The Enthymeme and Logical Validity." *Quarterly Journal of Speech* 45 (1959): 409–414.

Muir, Janette Kenner. "Flaming Figures of Speech: Form in Presidential Campaign Advertisements." New Orleans: Speech Communication Association, 1988.

Nelson, Cary. "The Psychology of Criticism, or What Can Be Said." *Psychoanalysis and the Question of the Text*. Edited by Geoffrey H. Hartman. Baltimore: Johns Hopkins University Press, 1978, 45–61.

Newcomb, Horace, ed. *Television: The Critical View*. New York: Oxford University Press, 1976, 1979, 1982, 1987.

Nixon, Richard M. "Apologia." *Representative American Speeches: 1952–53*. Edited by A. Craig Baird. New York: Wilson, 1953, 72–82.

Nord, David Paul. "The Business Values of American Newspapers: The 19th Century Watershed in Chicago." *Journalism Quarterly* 61 (1984): 265–273.

O'Donnell-Trujillo, Nick, and Pacanowsky, Michael E. "The Interpretation of Organizational Cultures." *Communications in Transition: Issues and Debates in Current Research*. Edited by Mary S. Mander. New York: Praeger, 1983, 225–241.

Oliver, Robert T. *The History of Public Speaking in America*. Boston: Allyn and Bacon, 1965.

Osborn, Michael. "The Abuses of Argument." *Southern Speech Communication Journal* 49 (1983): 1–11.

Owen, A. Susan. "Mobilizing Women for War: Politics of the Homefront in World War II." Chicago: Speech Communication Association, 1986.

Parker, Theodore. *Theodore Parker: An Anthology*. Edited by Henry Steele Commager. Boston: Beacon, 1960.

Parrish, Wayland Maxfield. "The Study of Speeches." *American Speeches*. Edited by Wayland Maxfield Parrish and Marie Hochmuth Nichols. New York: Longman, Green, 1954.

Parsigian, Elise Keoleian. "News Reporting: Method in the Midst of Chaos." *Journalism Quarterly* 64 (1987): 721–730.

Patterson, Oscar III. "An Analysis of Television Coverage of the Vietnam War." *Journal of Broadcasting* 28 (1984): 397–404.

Perelman, Chaim. *The Realm of Rhetoric.* Notre Dame: University of Notre Dame Press, 1982.

——. *The New Rhetoric and the Humanities.* Boston: Reidel, 1979.

Perelman, Chaim, and Olbrechts-Tyteca, L. *The New Rhetoric.* Notre Dame: University of Notre Dame Press, 1969.

Perrine, Laurence. *Sound and Sense: An Introduction to Poetry.* New York: Harcourt Brace Jovanovich, 1987.

Persons, Stow. *American Minds.* New York: Holt, Rinehart & Winston, 1958.

Plato. *Dialogues of Plato.* Vol II. Translated by B. Jowett. London: Oxford University Press, 1953.

"Principles and Practices for All Editorial Personnel of the Scripps-Howard Newspapers." *Editor and Publisher* 16 (1981): 7.

Pryor, Bob. "American Rhetorical Critics and the Concept of Ideology." Denver: Speech Communication Association, 1985.

Quadro, David F. "The *Congressional Record:* Another Look." *Western Journal of Speech Communication* 41 (1977): 253–259.

Radway, Janice A. *Reading the Romance.* Chapel Hill: University of North Carolina Press, 1984.

Reagan, Ronald. "Acceptance Address." *Vital Speeches of the Day.* 15 September 1984, 706–710.

——. "Speech to the Nation on G.O.P. Policy and the Economy." *Exetasis* 7 (1983): 3–17.

——. "Inaugural Address." *Vital Speeches of the Day.* 15 February 1981, 258–260.

——. "Acceptance Address." *Vital Speeches of the Day.* 15 August 1980, 642–647.

Redding, W. Charles. "Extrinsic and Intrinsic Criticism." *Western Speech* 21 (1957): 70–76.

Reich, Charles A. *The Greening of America.* New York: Random House, 1970.

Reid, Loren D. "The Perils of Rhetorical Criticism." *Quarterly Journal of Speech* 30 (1944): 416–422.

Renaud, Jean-Luc. "U.S. Government Assistance to AP's World-Wide Expansion." *Journalism Quarterly* 62 (1985): 10–16.

Rich, Adrienne. *On Lies, Secrets, and Silence.* New York: Norton, 1979.

Riches, Suzanne Volmer, and Sillars, Malcolm O. "The Status of Movement Criticism." *Western Journal of Speech Communication* 44 (1980): 175–187.

Rieke, Richard D., and Sillars, Malcolm O. *Argumentation and the Decision-Making Process.* Glenview, IL: Scott, Foresman, 1984.

Rogers, Richard A. "*1984* to *Brazil*: From the Pessimism of Reality to the Hope of Dreams." *Text and Performance Quarterly* 10 (1990): 34–46.

Roiphe, Anne. "Ma and Pa and John Boy in Mythic America: The Waltons." *Television: The Critical View.* Edited by Horace Newcomb. New York: Oxford University Press, 1976, 66–73.

Rokeach, Milton. *The Nature of Human Values.* New York: Free Press, 1973.

——. *Beliefs, Attitudes and Values.* San Francisco: Jossey-Bass, 1968.

Roosevelt, Franklin D. *Nothing to Fear.* Edited by Ben D. Zevin. New York: Popular Library, 1946.

Rose, Jacqueline. "Introduction—II." In Jacques Lacan, *Feminine Sexuality.* Translated by Jacqueline Rose. New York: Pantheon, 1982, 27–57.

Rosenfield, Lawrence W. "Ideological Miasma." *Central States Speech Journal* 34 (1983): 119–121.

———."The Experience of Criticism." *Quarterly Journal of Speech* 60 (1974): 489–496.

———. The Anatomy of Critical Discourse." *Speech Monographs* 35 (1968): 50–69.

Ruesch, Jurgen. "Communication and American Values: A Psychological Approach." *Communication: The Social Matrix of Psychiatry.* Edited by Jurgen Ruesch and Gregory Bateson. New York: Norton, 1951, 94–134.

Rushing, Janice Hocker. "The Rhetoric of the Western Myth." *Communication Monographs* 50 (1983): 14–32.

Ryan, Halford Ross. "Roosevelt's First Inaugural: A Study of Technique." *Quarterly Journal of Speech* 65 (1975): 137–149.

Sandeen, Cathy A., and Sillars, Malcolm O. "Stay the Course." *Exetasis* 7 (1983): 13–17.

Sandmann, Warren. "Tell Me a Story: Republicans and Democrats in 1984." Unpublished, 1989.

Schatz, Thomas. "Film Archive." *Critical Studies in Mass Communication* 1 (1984): 83–88.

Schiller, Dan. *Objectivity and the News: The Public and the Rise of Commercial Journalism.* Philadelphia: University of Pennsylvania Press, 1981.

Schoenfield, A. Clay. "The Environmental Movement as Reflected in the American Magazine." *Journalism Quarterly* 60 (1983): 470–475.

Schwartz, Murray M., and Willbern, David. "Literature and Psychology." *Interrelations of Literature.* Edited by Jean-Pierce Barricelli and Joseph Gibaldi. New York: Modern Language Association, 1982, 205–224.

Schwichtenberg, Cathy. "The Love Boat: The Packaging and Selling of Love, Heterosexual Romance, and Family." *Television: The Critical View.* Edited by Horace Newcomb. New York: Oxford University Press, 1987, 126–140.

Scott, Robert L., and Brock, Bernard L. *Methods of Rhetorical Criticism: A Twentieth Century Perspective.* New York: Harper & Row, 1972.

Sebeok, Thomas A. *A Profusion of Signs.* Bloomington: Indiana University Press, 1977.

Shakespeare, William. *The Complete Dramatic and Poetic Works of William Shakespeare.* Edited by Frederick D. Losey. Philadelphia: Winston, 1926.

Signorielli, Nancy. "Marital Status in Television Drama: A Case Of Reduced Options." *Journal of Broadcasting* 26 (1982): 585–597.

Sillars, Malcolm O. "Defining Movements Rhetorically: Casting the Widest Net." *Southern Speech Communication Journal* 46 (1980a): 17–32.

———. "The Rhetoric of the Petition in Boots." *The Rhetoric of Protest and Reform: 1878–1898.* Edited by Paul Boase. Athens: Ohio University Press, 1980b, 17–35.

———. "Persistent Problems in Rhetorical Criticism." *Rhetoric and Communication.* Edited by Jane Blankenship and Hermann G. Stelzner. Urbana: University of Illinois Press, 1976, 69–88.

———. "The Presidential Campaign of 1952." *Western Speech* 22 (1958): 94–99.

Sillars, Malcolm O., and Ganer, Patricia. "Values and Beliefs: A Systematic Basis for Argumentation." *Advances in Argumentation Theory and Research*. Edited by J. Robert Cox and Charles Arthur Willard. Carbondale: Southern Illinois University Press, 1982, 184–201.

Simons, Herbert W., Mechling, Elizabeth W., and Schreier, Howard N. "The Function of Human Communication in Mobilizing for Action From the Bottom Up: The Rhetoric of Social Movements." *Handbook of Rhetorical and Communication Theory*. Edited by Carroll C. Arnold and John Waite Bowers. Boston: Allyn and Bacon, 1984, 792–867.

Simonson, Harold P. *Strategies in Criticism*. New York: Holt, Rinehart & Winston, 1971.

Singleton, Loy A., and Cook, Stephanie L. "Television Network News Reporting by Female Correspondents: An Update." *Journal Of Broadcasting* 26 (1982): 487–492.

Sklar, Robert. "The Fonz, Laverne, Shirley and the Great American Class Struggle." *Television: The Critical View*. Edited by Horace Newcomb. New York: Oxford University Press, 1982, 77–88.

Smith, C. Zoe. "An Alternative View of The 30's: Hine's and Bourke-White's Industrial Photos." *Journalism Quarterly* 60 (1983): 305–310.

Smith, David H. "Communication Research and the Idea of Process." *Speech Monographs* 39 (1972): 174–182.

Smith, James Steele. "Visual Criticism: A New Medium for Critical Comment." *Criticism, A Quarterly for Literature and the Arts* 4 (1962): 241–255.

Smith, Michael L. "Selling the Moon." *Culture of Consumption*. Edited by Richard Fox and T. Jackson Lears. New York: Random House, 1983, 177–209.

Smith, Page. *The Historian and History*. New York: Knopf, 1966.

Smith, Robert R. *Beyond the Wasteland: The Criticism of Broadcasting*. Annandale, MN: Speech Communication Association, 1980.

Smythe, Ted Curtis. "The Reporter, 1880–1900: Working Conditions and Their Influence on the News." *Journalism History* 7 (1980): 1–10.

Society of Professional Journalists. "Code of Ethics." 1987.

Solomon, Martha. "The Rhetoric of Dehumanization: An Analysis of Medical Reports of the Tuskegee Syphilis Project." *Western Journal of Speech Communication* 49 (1985): 233–247.

Steele, Edward, and Redding, W. Charles. "The American Value System: Premises for Persuasion." *Western Speech* 26 (1962): 83–91.

Stelzner, Hermann G. "'War Message' December 8, 1941: An Approach to Language." *Communication Monographs* 33 (1966): 419–437.

Strine, Mary S. "*The Confessions of Nat Turner*: Styron's 'Meditations on History.'" *Quarterly Journal of Speech* 64 (1978): 246–266.

Strine, Mary S., and Pacanowsky, Michael E. "How to Read Interpretive Accounts of Organization Life: Narrative Basis of Textual Authority." *Southern Speech Communication Journal* 50 (1985): 283–297.

Sutton, Walter. *Modern American Criticism*. Englewood Cliffs, NJ: Prentice-Hall, 1963.

Thonssen, Lester, and Baird, A. Craig. *Speech Criticism*. New York: Ronald, 1948.

Tiemens, Robert K. "A Visual Analysis of the 1976 Presidential Debates." *Communication Monographs* 45 (November 1978): 362–370.

Tiemens, Robert K., Sillars, Malcolm O., Alexander, Dennis C., and Werling, David. "Television Coverage of Jesse Jackson's Speech to the 1984 Democratic

National Convention." *Journal of Broadcasting and Electronic Media* 32 (1988): 1–22.

Timber, Bernard. "The Rhetoric of the Camera in Television Soap Operas." *Television: The Critical Views.* Edited by Horace Newcomb. New York: Oxford University Press, 1987, 164–178.

Tompkins, Jane P. "*Uncle Tom's Cabin* and the Politics of Literary History." *The New Feminist Criticism.* Edited by Elaine Showalter. New York: Pantheon, 1984, 81–104.

Torres, Sasha. "Melodrama, Masculinity and the Family: *thirtysomething* as Therapy." *Camera Obscura* 19 (1989): 87–106.

Toulmin, Stephen. *The Uses of Argument.* Cambridge: Cambridge University Press, 1958.

Trujillo, Nick, and Ekdom, Leah R. "Sportswriting and American Cultural Values: The 1984 Chicago Cubs." *Critical Studies in Mass Communication* 1 (1985): 262–281.

Turner, Fredrick Jackson. *The Frontier in American History.* New York: Holt, Rinehart & Winston, 1947.

Turner, Victor. "Social Dramas and Stories About Them." *On Narrative.* Edited by W. J. T. Mitchell. Chicago: University of Chicago Press, 1981, 137–164.

Vaughn, Mina A. "Symbology Exhibited in Discourse Produced for the Formal Socialization Process in High Technology Industry." Fresno, CA: Western Speech Communication Association, 1986.

Vidmar, Neil, and Rokeach, Milton. "Archie Bunker's Bigotry: A Study of Selective Perception and Exposure." *Journal of Communication* 24 (1974): 36–47.

Waldman, Marilyn Robinson. "'The Otherwise Unnoteworthy Year 711': A Reply to Hayden White." *On Narrative.* Edited by W. J. T. Mitchell. Chicago: University of Chicago Press, 1981, 240–248.

Walker, Alice. *The Color Purple.* New York: Harcourt Brace Jovanovich, 1982.

Wallace, Karl R. "The Substance of Rhetoric: Good Reasons." *Quarterly Journal of Speech* 49 (1963): 239–249.

Wambaugh, Joseph. *The New Centurions.* Boston: Little, Brown, 1970.

Wander, Philip. "The Third Persona: An Ideological Turn in Rhetorical Theory." *Central States Speech Journal* 35 (1984): 197–216.

———. "The Ideological Turn in Rhetorical Criticism." *Central States Speech Journal* 34 (1983): 1–18.

Weaver, Richard M. *The Ethics of Rhetoric.* Chicago: Regnery, 1953.

Weber, Max. *On Charisma and Institution Building.* Chicago: University of Chicago Press, 1968.

Welleck, René, and Warren, Austin. *Theory of Literature.* New York: Harcourt, Brace & World, 1970.

Werling, David, Salvador, Michael, Sillars, Malcolm O., and Vaughn, Mina A. "Presidential Debates: Epideictic Merger of Issues and Images in Values." *Argument and Critical Practices.* Edited by Joseph W. Wenzel. Annandale, MN: Speech Communication Association, 1987, 229–238.

White, Hayden. "The Value of Narrativity in the Representation of Reality." *On Narrative.* Edited by W. J. T. Mitchell. Chicago: University of Chicago Press, 1981, 1–24.

White, Mimi. "Ideological Analysis and Television." *Channels of Discourse.* Edited by Robert C. Allen. Chapel Hill: University of North Carolina Press, 1987, 134–171.

Wichelns, Herbert A. "The Literary Criticism of Oratory." *The Rhetorical Idiom.* Edited by Donald C. Bryant. Ithaca, NY: Cornell University Press, 1958, 5–42.

Williams, Carol Traynor. "It's Not So Much, 'You've Come a Long Way Baby'— As 'You're Gonna Make It After All.' " *Television: The Critical View.* Edited by Horace Newcomb. New York: Oxford University Press, 1976, 43–53.

Williams, Robin M., Jr. *American Society.* New York: Knopf, 1970.

Williams, Tennessee. *A Streetcar Named Desire.* New York: New Directions, 1947.

Wilson, Woodrow. "First Inaugural Address." *American Public Address.* Edited by A. Craig Baird. New York: McGraw-Hill, 1956, 220–224.

Wimsatt, William K., Jr. *The Verbal Icon: Studies in the Meaning of Poetry.* Lexington: University of Kentucky Press, 1954.

Wines, Michael. "Reagan Juggled Statistics, Critics Charge." *Los Angeles Times* 25 August 1984, 4.

Wise, Gene. *American Historical Explanations.* Minneapolis: University of Minnesota, 1980.

Wood, Peter H. "Television as Dream." *Television: The Critical View.* Edited by Horace Newcomb. New York: Oxford University Press, 1982, 510–528.

Wrage, Ernest J. "Public Address: A Study in Social and Intellectual History." *Quarterly Journal of Speech* 33 (1947): 451–457.

Wright, Will. *Sixguns and Society: A Structural Study of the Western.* Berkeley: University of California Press, 1975.

Zarefsky, David. "Conspiracy Arguments in the Lincoln-Douglas Debates." *Journal of the American Forensic Association* 21 (1984): 63–75.

Zeidenberg, Leonard. "The Conservative Conscience of Reed Irvine." *Broadcasting* 27 April 1987, 40–45.

Zettl, Herbert. *Sight, Sound, Motion: Applied Media Aesthetics.* Belmont, CA: Wadsworth, 1973.

Credits

Index